Enemies of Civilization

SUNY Series in Chinese Philosophy and Culture
Roger T. Ames, editor

Enemies of Civilization

Attitudes toward Foreigners in
Ancient Mesopotamia, Egypt, and China

Mu-chou Poo

State University of New York Press

Published by
State University of New York Press, Albany

Printed in the United States of America

For information, address the State University of New York Press,
90 State Street, Suite 700, Albany, NY 12207

Production by Marilyn P. Semerad
Marketing by Susan M. Petrie

Library of Congress Cataloging-in-Publication Data

Poo, Mu-chou.
    Enemies of civilization : attitudes toward foreigners in ancient Mesopotamia, Egypt,
and China / Mu-chou Poo.
        p. cm. — (SUNY series in Chinese philosophy and culture)
    Includes bibliographical references and index.
    ISBN 0–7914–6363–X (hc : acid-free paper) — ISBN 0–7914–6364–8 (pbk : acid-free
paper)
        1. Iraq—Relations—Foreign countries.   2. Egypt—Relations—Foreign countries.
3. China—Relations—Foreign countries.   4. Aliens—Iraq—History—To 1500.
5. Aliens—Egypt—History—To 1500.   6. Aliens—China—History—To 1500.   7. Iraq—
Civilization—To 634.   8. Egypt—Civilization—To 332 B.C.   9. China—Civilization—
To 221 B.C.   10. China—Civilization—221 B.C.–960 A.D.   I. Title.   II. Series.

    DS71.P63 2005
    327.3'009—dc22

                                                        2004045401
                          10 9 8 7 6 5 4 3 2 1

To my daughters Cindy and Sheila
Who venture into foreign land bravely
And to my soul mate Ping-chen
Who travels with me lovingly

Contents

Illustrations

NOTE: All figures of ancient objects or images have been redrawn by Tze-hsuan Huang and Chia-yin Yao. Locations of published photos of the images are indicated below.

Preface

About ten years ago I was asked by my fellow graduate students at Johns Hopkins University to contribute an article in a Festschrift for my mentor, Hans Goedicke, a famous Egyptologist. After some thought, I decided to write something that is both Egyptological and Sinological, just to show my appreciation to my old professor for his generosity in helping a foreign student. He himself, by the way, was an immigrant from Vienna. The article, when it was published, was rather short, with the title "The Emergence of Cultural Consciousness in Ancient Egypt and China: A Comparative Perspective." I was not very satisfied with the result, however, and therefore began to conduct a more extensive study that will include not only Egypt and China but also Mesopotamia, one of my subfields when I was studying Egyptology at Johns Hopkins.

Looking back on the origin and process of this study, I recognized certain changes that occurred in my own understanding of the subject. My interest in the attitudes toward foreigners grew out of personal experience of being a foreign student in the United States. My subject of study, ancient Egypt, adds another layer of the feeling of foreignness: a foreigner in a foreign country studying a culture that was foreign to both. What is the relevance of my study to the contemporary society, a question that inevitably has to be asked for a student of humanity? The attitude toward foreigners, in light of Edward Said's powerful assail of the phenomenon of Orientalism, seems to stand out glaringly. If Orientalism describes a kind of Western attitude toward foreigners in the modern Orient, and the analysis of this attitude leads to a reflection of the nature of modern Western hegemonic order, what can one say about the ancient Orient? Here, of course, the problem becomes very complicated. Are we talking about our attitude toward the ancient Oriental civilizations, such as Egypt, Mesopotamia, and China, as also a form of reading "the other" according to our own preconceptions and implicit hegemonic or patronistic order? Are we talking about the ancient civilizations themselves, their attitude toward foreigners, and if or how they also espoused a form of Orientalism? Should we dig at the root of ancient studies—a form of intellectual, but also very political, pursuit of the "origin" of Western culture that could authenticate its hegemonic power—since the nineteenth century? Should I, a "Chinese" looking from the East with an eye trained in the West, take a look at the Chinese view of the West and talk about a form of Occidentalism? Being unable to solve all these issues at once, I took up perhaps the easiest one and decided to engage in the ancient attitudes toward foreigners, and, being unable to resolve my own identity—a Chinese trained in the West on the subject of Oriental studies—I decided to venture into a comparative study. Thus the present book.

When I began to investigate the issue of foreigners in the ancient world, I first adopted a positivist method in looking at the evidence. I examined textual and iconographic evidence and tried to detect the attitudes behind them. My intention was to investigate the nature of civilizations by looking at their attitudes toward others—as a reflection of the self. It seems straightforward enough, until I realized that, first, the concept of foreigner differs in each civilization, and that "foreign" is a relative and ambiguous term: one needs to delineate who are "we, the insiders," and who are "they, the outsiders," as the original meaning of "foreign" in Latin, *forās*, means "outside." The problem is, what if the "we" is not a homogeneous group? What if the "self" itself is an unstable thing that changes through time? How to capture this change? I find it very difficult to conduct research when facing the evidence that purports to express a certain attitude toward "the others" while it is uncertain whether the one who left the evidence is really so different from "the others." I then adopted a position that sees the construction of ethnic identity as a subjective choice, that the division between self and others was not necessarily based on any objective conditions such as race or culture, although these could have been the factors. From here I realized that the entire project of looking for foreigners might have been ill-conceived: as it was very much debated that the problem caused by modern nationalism was in part based on a conception that makes a forced distinction between "us" and "others, foreigners," to talk about the concept of foreigners in the ancient world seems to be perpetuating it by giving it a legitimating precursor. To avoid falling into this trap, I examined the various ways of looking at and treating the foreigners in ancient civilizations and discovered that the attitudes were not necessarily all negative. Moreover, if there were divisions between "we" and "they," the criteria were often cultural rather than racial or biological characteristics. I thus at least made a distinction between the ancient and modern attitudes.

As for the comparative aspect of this study, it is based on my personal conviction that knowledge is the result of comparison, and conscious and controlled comparative study in history can be very important for us to discover new aspects of human society that eluded conventional historical research. It should not be mere enumeration of similarities and differences, but an investigation into the reasons why there were the similarities and differences, and to shed some otherwise unavailable light on each of the parties involved.

This project received a substantial support from a grant from the CCK Foundation, 1995–97. During the process, I received continuous support and criticism from Drs. Hans Goedicke and Jerrold S. Cooper, two of my mentors at Johns Hopkins, as well as many other colleagues and friends. Parts of the chapters were delivered at Ann Arbor, Paris, Princeton, Berlin, and a number of international conferences. A fellowship from the British Academy in 2001 allowed me to use the libraries of London University and the British Library, which was essential for me to conclude this study. My colleague John Kieschnick read an early version of my manuscript and offered many useful suggestions. My students Tzu-hsuan Huang and Yi-chen Huang did the drawings and the chronological table and helped me in the final preparation of the manuscript, their efforts are very much appreciated. My wife Ping-chen has been the most important supporter and critical voice of my work, which I can never repay. I alone, however, should be responsible for all the shortcomings that still exist in this book.

Abbreviations

ANET	J. B. Pritchard, *Ancient Near Eastern Texts Relating to the Old Testament.* (Princeton: Princeton University Press, 1969).
ASAE	*Annales du Service des Antiquités de l'Égypte.* (Cairo)
HÄB	*Hildesheimer Ägyptologische Beiträge.* (Hildesheim)
JARCE	*Journal of American Research Center in Egypt.* (Boston)
JCS	*Journal of Cuneiform Studies.* (New Haven)
JEA	*Journal of Egyptian Archaeology.* (London)
JNES	*Journal of Near Eastern Studies.* (Chicago)
MÄ	*Münchener Ägyptologische Studien.* (Munich/Berlin)
MDAIK	*Mitteilungen des Deutschen Archaeologischen Instituts, Abteilung Kairo.* (Berlin)
SAK	*Studien zur Altägyptische Kultur.* (Hamburg)
Urkunden	G. Steindorff ed. *Urkunden des Ägyptischen Altertums,* 8 vols. (Leipzig: 1904–1961)
Wb	A. Erman & J. Grapow eds. *Wörterbuch der Ägyptischen Sprache* (Leipzig/Berlin, 1926–63)
WZKM	*Wiener Zeitschrift für die Kunde des Morgenlandes.* (Vienna)

Chronological Table

MESOPOTAMIA	EGYPT	CHINA
3100–3000 Jemdet-Nasr period	3100–2686 Early Dynastic period	
3000–2800 Early Dynastic I		
2800–2500 Early Dynastic II		
	2686–2200 Old Kingdom	
2500–2334 Early Dynastic III		
2334–2197 Sargonic (Old Akkadian)		
2197–2112 Guti	2200–2040 First Intermediate period	
2112–2004 Ur III		
2004–1595 Old Babylonian	2040–1786 Middle Kingdom	
	1786–1558 Second Inter- mediate period	1600–1066 Shang Dynasty
1595–1375 Dark Age		

MESOPOTAMIA	EGYPT	CHINA
1375–1155 Kassite (Middle Babylonian) (Middle Assyrian)	1558–1085 New Kingdom	
1155–626 Neo-Assyrian	1070–712 Third Inter- mediate period	1066–771 Western Zhou Dynasty
625–539 Neo-Babylonian	712–332 Late period	770–221 Eastern Zhou Dynasty *Spring and Autumn* *Warring States*
539–332 Persian		
332–143 Alexander and successors	332–30 Ptolemaic period	221–206 Qin Dynasty
143 BCE–240 CE Parthians		206 BCE–8 CE Western Han
240–636 Sassanians	30 BCE–395 CE Roman period	25–220 Eastern Han

1

Introduction

Now the other writers tell one about their (the Scythians) savagery, because they know that the terrible and the marvelous are
startling, but one should tell the opposite facts too and make them
patterns of conduct.

—Ephoros, c. 405–333 BCE

The Question about The Others

A genre of fantastic stories circulated Medieval Europe that recounted strange or monstrous peoples who inhabited faraway
countries—people with one foot, people with their face on their chests,
people with long lips that could be used as an umbrella, and so on.[1]
Not entirely created out of pure imagination, some of these stories
had their origins in the works of Greek authors of the fifth and fourth
centuries BCE. Travelers in late antiquity and the early Medieval period
brought them back to Europe as fabulous and amusing tales about the
never-never land outside the civilized world.[2] They were, however, more
than amusing stories, since geography—that is, information about the
natural and human environment in other places—was considered an
essential part of the knowledge of the universe and a key component
of "the truth" about the human condition.[3] This knowledge of the
monstrous races might be seen as a way to define one's own existence;
that is, by establishing a very different "other," sometimes exotic, often
grotesque and dangerous, one gains a positive and "normal" image for
oneself.[4] It was also a source that challenged people's conceptions of
what it means to be a human being, since there were so many incred-
ible "variations" of mankind.[5]

The monstrous races described in these stories remind us of the descriptions of foreign peoples found in the *Shan-hai-jing* (山海經), or *Classic of Mountains and Seas*, a Chinese text dated fourth century BCE. Comparable to the European stories, the *Classic of Mountains and Seas* presented the reader with fantastic foreign lands, one inhabited by people with holes in the chest, another inhabited by one-eyed people, yet another by people with one arm and one foot, and so on.[6]

While it is premature or unnecessary to suggest any connection between the Greek and the Chinese sources, these stories nevertheless show that similar modes of thinking regarding things foreign could have been developed in different cultures. When describing faraway places and peoples, although it was possible that in some cases the strange or monstrous figures might have originated from misunderstandings, exaggerations, or embellishment upon received traditions, it was also a natural tendency for the storytellers to let their imagination take the reins and create exotic stories. The medieval stories of monsters as well as those contained in the *Classic of Mountains and Seas*, though often relegated to the realm of folklore and sometimes used by modern scholars to reconstruct ancient geography or mythological traditions, are significant in another aspect: they hint at a deep-rooted cultural psychology that connects "the foreign" with "the monstrous and devil-ish," even "nonhuman" or "subhuman." It is most likely that the stories are no less the productions of cultural consciousness that betrays the self-images of the storytellers than descriptions of "reality." By cultural consciousness I mean conceptions of the characteristics of a culture commonly shared and employed by its people to distinguish themselves from people of other cultures. The importance of this sense of cultural identity in the formation and conflicts of peoples and countries cannot be overemphasized. The history of the modern world has provided ample evidence of the workings of cultural consciousness, such as the rise of nationalism.[7] In the ancient world, cultural consciousness was no less a forceful factor in the formation and development of individual civilizations.[8] The Greek attitude toward aliens and non-Greeks, for example, has been pointed to as the major factor in the formation of Christian civilization.[9] The entire history of the Jewish community can be described as a continuous effort to maintain its cultural iden-tity by stressing a specific Jewish cultural consciousness.[10] Christian civilization, under the Roman Catholic Church, distinguished the "they-Pagan" from the "we-Christian," and extended this distinction to the moral issue of good and evil, that is, what is different from "us" is necessarily "evil."[11]

The above observation seems to agree with a commonly held opinion, that in order to form a group identity and help preserve the prosperity of the community, it was natural and necessary for people to draw a line between a we-group and a they-group.[12] It was further taken for granted by many that prejudice against the "alien" or the "foreigner" was a natural reaction of any human society facing the "other." While not denying that there is a certain truth in this, one should not assume that it is always the case with every ancient culture. If we look closer at the evidence, we see the picture is not always black and white; that is, the "foreigners," for various reasons, as we shall explore in this study, were not always perceived or portrayed straightforwardly as evil.

Take for example the Greek writer Ephoros (c. 405–330 BCE), whose ethnography of the Scythians occupied an important position in the tradition of ancient geography writing.[13] In his account, Ephoros mentions that the Scythians were the most law-abiding people, with impeccable moral righteousness.[14] Here we find a highly praised foreign race that was to be envied by the Greeks. This praise of the foreign race was certainly a sort of "moralizing rhetoric," as Ephoros himself was quoted as saying: "Now the other writers tell one about their (the Scythians) savagery, because they know that the terrible and the marvelous are startling, but one should tell the opposite facts too and *make them patterns of conduct* (italics mine)."[15] Although the moralizing rhetoric might have reflected some truth about the nomadic life, the nomadic reality was probably not the main concern of the Greek authors, for they were mainly interested in using the "patterns of conduct" as a moralizing tool.[16] In other words, it is doubtful that one could confirm that Ephoros's actual concern was a sympathetic understanding of the nomadic people to the north. Rather, the idealized description of the Scythians was arguably part of the process of the construction of a Greek cultural identity that privileged and ennobled itself because it had risen to the height that could appreciate the "uncivilized" foreign race. Thus the act of exclusion, of division between "us" and "them" was subtly, even unconsciously, done by a "positive evaluation" of the foreigners. What was usually said about Greek prejudice against the "barbarians," therefore, needs to be qualified by admitting that the prejudice, while it indeed existed, could have been neither simpleminded xenophobia nor straightforward slandering, and that sources from different authors or social strata could have represented different perspectives.

The example of Ephoros indicates that ancient conceptions of foreigners or foreign lands are intimately related to the self-perceptions of the ancients themselves, and that descriptions or comments about the foreigners had more to do with the sociopolitical situations and moral-ethical values of the society that produced the comments than with the "true character" of the foreigners. In the words of one scholar, "between the (ancient) narrator and his addressee there exists, as a precondition for communication, a whole collection of semantic, encyclopedic, and symbolic knowledge common to both sides."[17] In this light, what the ancient writers noted down about "the others" is not static "facts" but is circumscribed by the relationship between the narrator and his presumed audience. The "others" are indeed the others, the "third party," of the discourse. The same argument applies to us as modern investigators. Our understanding and description of the ancients—in a sense a kind of foreigner to us—is also a reflection of our own self-perception, value system, and sociopolitical agendas, preferences, and prejudices that often have little to do with the ancients themselves.

Thus a revisit to the ancient evidence could not only produce some new understanding of the ancient mentality, but could also help us to reflect upon our own modern prejudice. For, in the case of an attitude toward foreigners, if we take it for granted that human societies are "naturally" xenophobic, this will only confirm and even perpetuate the situation. We will then discriminate against the ancients and will perhaps also show prejudice against our contemporaries, since we have subscribed to the predicament of inherent prejudice as part of human nature.

Before we proceed, it is necessary that we should further clarify the term "foreigner" in our discussion of the ancient world. Obviously, the modern idea of foreigner that refers to people from another sovereign state and with clear legal implications cannot suit the context of the ancient world. In the period under our consideration, a foreigner could be understood as someone who is from outside a certain geographical, cultural, or political sphere, or any combination of these elements. In addition, how an insider regarded other people as foreign often was based not only on these rational elements, but also on the workings of such irrational elements as prejudice and misunderstanding. All of these conditions that shaped the concept of foreigner might not be the same under different situations and in different cultures. In a word, the concept of foreigner in the ancient world is multifarious, and what constituted "foreignness" differs in each case. We need to assess in each case what the main emphasis was when a people encounter another people that could be described as foreign. It is nonetheless important to admit the fact that any evidence we have is likely to be atypical of the phenomenon that we might like it to represent, and hence a potential distortion of the reality. What we can do is to try to judge the extent to which certain evidence could reflect the possible attitude or mentality of some of the ancients.

On the other hand, once we use the term "foreigner," there is automatically a question as to from whose point of view this term is meaningful. Who are the "we" that are making the distinction between "we" and "they"? It would be problematic if the we is in fact a mixture that shared certain elements with they. As we shall discuss below, it has been persuasively argued that ethnic identity or the sense of us is largely a subjective construction. By the same token, the sense of they or foreigners is also a subjective construction that need not to accord with any objective reality such as physical features, lifestyles, or even cultural values. Our use of the term "foreign," therefore, must be understood in its earlier or original meaning in Latin, that is, *forās*, outside, and consequently foreigner as outsider, people outside of the "civilized" world, for which each ancient civilization has its own terms, whether as barbarians, enemies, or others.

As for the self-identity, the "we" of the ancient civilizations under discussion, it may in fact be questionable whether the concepts of "China," "Egypt" or "Mesopotamia" are useful or unambiguous enough in this context. In other words, we have to clarify what we mean by China, Egypt, and Mesopotamia. This involves complicated discussions of the origins of these concepts, their applicability in each case, as a term denoting a political and geographic area, a cultural sphere, or a state, throughout history. Without going into details, I will simply say that when I use the term "China" in this study, I use it as an equivalent of the term "Zhongguo" or "Central States" in its historical context, that is, it refers to, geographically, the area of the Central Plain, the present-day Henan, Shandong, southern Hebei, part of eastern Shanxi, and part of the Shaanxi Wei River basin, later also to include the lower Yangtze River Valley, and culturally, those states and vassals that were influenced by or subscribed to the Shang and Zhou cultural values and socioethical practices. In view of this evolving meaning of Zhongguo, when it is used in the documents in the pre-Imperial period (c. before third century BCE), it is both a geopolitical and a cultural term that refers to the political and cultural situation of the said area. Needless to say, this concept is the product of a specific cultural and political elite of the time that was interested in exerting a certain political and cultural agenda. It is often not easy to distinguish and define at each instance the precise meaning of this term, especially since China as a "nation state" is a modern concept that came about only since the nineteenth century. China, moreover, is still a state in existence. Whether or how should we trace the roots and identify the modern state of China with the ancient Zhongguo, of course, is a wasp's nest that I shall not poke in haste. For the moment, then, I will leave it just like that.

The use of the terms "Egypt" or "Mesopotamia," similarly, should be defined in their respective historical contexts—that is, Pharaonic Egypt and Pre-Persian Assyria and Babylonia. Unlike China, as both of them no longer exist in the modern world, they could be defined as the cultural areas of the Nile River Valley, and "Mesopotamia—the land between the two rivers of Tigris and Euphrates." My assumption is that the cultural developments of these areas are largely coherent, although not stagnant, despite millennia of political vicissitudes. More details are discussed in several chapters in this study.

With the above reference to the meaning of China, Egypt, and Mesopotamia, it seems that we are more or less taking a position that there were indeed these cultural entities out there that could be defined and recognized. Two qualifications, however, have to be spelled out. First is that we should recognize the ambiguity of the term "culture" and see it as a borderless conglomeration of ever changing value systems, religious beliefs, social ethics, and behavior patterns that are transmitted through human agency. It expands and moves when the agency moves and it changes and mutates when the agency absorbs new elements and abandons old, or even passing from one generation to the next. Secondly, because of its borderless state, a culture typically fades into its neighboring culture so that it would be difficult to draw a dividing line between one and the other. Archaeological cultures, often defined by pottery styles that gradually change from one area to the next but rarely with an abrupt division, typify this situation. Moreover, the fact that similar pottery styles could be used by quite different cultural groups further complicates the meaning of culture. Thus the idea of a foreigner, an agent who carries very different cultural values, and so on, in contrast to one's own, can only exist or be formulated when one takes a position from the "center," that is, if the cultural sphere is large enough geographically and/or strong enough psychologically. As a result the degree of "foreignness" of a foreigner is only felt for one who upholds a position in relation to the center of the main cultural values. One may say that it is largely a creation of positioned cultural consciousness. As such, the foreigner is a relative concept: it all depends on who is viewing whom from which position. This understanding is no doubt intimately related to theories on ethnicity.

Ethnic Theories and Ancient History

Greek writings about foreign people were often referred to as ancient "ethnography." It is often included in the modern discourses on race or ethnicity, a subject that has received intense attention from ethnologists, anthropologists, and sociologists as well as historians in the past few decades.[18] One of the theories that has received wide acceptance is that ethnic or national identities are subjective constructions that may not necessarily have anything to do with biological characteristics, and that race is a cultural construct with no fixed relationship to objective reality. This "subjective" view of the formation of ethnic identity, as expounded by F. Barth and others, has led many scholars to believe that what is most important in identifying an *ethnos* is not physical or material characteristics, but a shared value system and a commonly accepted descent or origin myth.[19] An ethnic group, according to this view, may be defined as a group of people who see themselves "as being alike by virtue of their common ancestry, real or fictitious, and who are so regarded by others."[20] This view implies that the "common ancestry" of an ethnic group could have been fabricated out of any number of practical or emotional reasons. On the other hand, some scholars still have reservations about an exclusively subjective view of ethnic identity, and believe that objective biological and cultural traits are also important in forming ethnic identity.[21]

When applied to the study of modern societies, the subjective view of ethnic identity has been used to deconstruct long-lasting racial prejudice, particularly the white prejudice against people of color. The argument consists of two elements. In terms of biology, scientists researching the composition of human genes have tentatively concluded that the usual distinctions of race based on physical features such as skin color and hair may be misleading; that is, similar physical features might belong to different lines of descent based on genetic traits, and vise versa. Seemingly different races, therefore, might be more intimately related genetically than those that look alike.[22] In terms of culture, moreover, it is doubtful if differences in the genetic traits could lead to cultural differences. Although people might be grouped together according to their genetic connectedness or physical features, this says nothing concerning their cultural affiliation. Since ethnicity is largely a subjective construction that has little or nothing to do with genes, no inherent or fixed ethnicity can be assumed.

Hence although the prejudice of the white against the coloreds is taken to the execution board, a number of scholars also took notice of racial prejudice among nonwhite peoples.[23] Most recently was Frank Dikötter, whose exposition of the discourse of race in modern China has excited considerable scholarly discussion.[24] Dikötter shows that racial prejudice was not a white people's privilege, that the Chinese had associated black skin color with racial types in a condescending way, and that they had imported black slaves long before the Europeans did.[25] To be fair, of course, one should point out that the use of black slaves in China is not comparable with the European situation either in the extent of the use of imported slave servants in society or in the degree of the use of slave labor in economic production. In any case, as far as we know, it was not an ancient phenomenon.

Not only the moderns are prone to racial prejudice, the ancient people were also capable of inflicting all sorts of prejudice upon foreigners. The use of the term βαρβαρος (barbarians) has often been cited as evidence of the condescending attitude of the Greeks toward foreigners, though perhaps not in the original sense of the word. According to recent scholarship, in most cases Greeks used the word βαρβαρος without a derogatory overtone but mainly as a reference to the cultural difference in the spoken language of the foreigners.[26] It was only after the Persian war that the Greek idea of barbarian changed from an earlier, more neutral sense of speakers of different languages, to represent a stereotypical and generalized image of an exotic, slavish, unintelligible, even morally corrupt barbarian. This has to do with the concomitant establishment of a "Greek identity" that did not really exist before the war. By defining the others—the barbarians, as the argument goes—"the Greeks" became a recognizable cultural entity.[27] As the example of Ephoros mentioned above shows, this process of constructing a cultural identity was a long and complicated process that should warn against any simplistic model of "ethnocentrism."

Similarly, the Egyptian term of "wretched Asiatics (^{c}3mw ḫsi),"[28] or the Chinese *man-yi* (barbarians) carry certain pejorative meanings about the foreigners that were used to distinguish the "civilized us" from the "uncivilized them." As noted above, however, one should be careful not to present a simple picture of any "group hostility" against foreigners without identifying the nature and intention of the sources and the cultural and sociopolitical background of the expressions that betray the so-called prejudice. People on the borderland or cultural periphery, for example, might have a very different view of the foreigners than those from the center of the social and political power structure. Since from their perspective the foreigners might actually be closer to them than the far away center of culture. Moreover, the drawing of boundaries between social and political groups was anything but the result of a unified conception of cultural identity of "us" versus "others." Rather, political and factional interests prompted by the ambitions and intrigues of the leaders and elites often lay behind the formation of an official or public ideology that depicted foreigners or aliens as culturally backward and morally corrupt. In Herodotus's report about his visit to Egypt, he noted that the Egyptians were unfriendly toward the Greeks. Was his report true? Or was he merely expressing his own prejudice? Was his praise of the wonders and wisdom of Egypt again mainly idealized accounts intended to reform his fellow countrymen who were his intended audience? It would be tremendously helpful if we could know the exact source of his information.[29] While all these could be interesting questions regarding the attitude of one Greek author toward a foreign country and its people, it would be equally interesting to learn what attitude the Egyptians had toward such foreigners as Herodotus. This falls into a larger framework that I intend to investigate. Since even the Greeks are latecomers compared to a number of ancient civilizations—for example, Mesopotamia, Egypt, and China—an inquiry into the problem of cultural or ethnic consciousness in these civilizations might produce some useful information for our understanding of the general phenomenon of cultural and racial prejudice.

Choice of Subjects

The aim of this study is to compare the attitudes toward foreigners and foreign cultures in ancient Mesopotamia, Egypt, and China. On a more general level, this is an investigation into the cultural consciousness of three ancient civilizations. In ancient studies, it is customary to focus on the achievements of a particular civilization in art, history, religion, philosophy, and the like. It is also customary for scholars to approach their subjects employing a positivistic, straightforward method. In the field of Egyptology, for example, if one is interested in religious beliefs, one studies such religious texts as the *Pyramid Texts* and the *Book of the Dead*; if one wishes to know about ethical values and moral principles, one studies biographical texts and wisdom literature. Our understanding of the characteristics of Egyptian civilization is largely the accumulation of such studies. This is a legitimate method, and important and irreplaceable results have already been achieved. Yet at least one aspect of Egyptian civilization, or any civilization for that matter, cannot be satisfactorily illuminated by this method. This is the cultural consciousness, the self-perception, of a given people. It is often said that one of the most difficult tasks for a person is to know oneself. One cannot know oneself and establish one's own identity, or self-perception, though, without somehow knowing the others. The character of a person, furthermore, often manifests itself in his attitude toward others. The same may be said of a culture, as its character constructed by the above-mentioned positivistic method tends to represent only one side of the picture. We cannot unconditionally accept the picture that a given culture has drawn of itself—or as reconstructed by modern scholars—without comparing this self-portrait with its portrayal of other cultures. From a people's portraits of other cultures, as manifested in their knowledge of, attitudes toward, and discourse about foreigners and foreign cultures, regardless of whether these could reveal the true character of the cultures depicted, one could learn much about the people who produced such portraits. The concept of foreigner is a kind of portrait that could reveal the value and prejudice of the painter. A number of questions could be posed in this regard. For example, how did people perceive the foreigners? Were the foreigners seen as human beings just like themselves, or were they viewed as less than human? How did such perceptions come about? What were the consequences of such perceptions, or, how did people treat foreigners? Moreover, did people in the ancient world distinguish different groups of people on racial, or "biophysiological," grounds, or on cultural grounds? Were the "foreigners" really different culturally and racially, or was the difference artificially constructed as the result of prejudice and misunderstanding? What was the nature and sociocultural context of the sources that bear information concerning foreigners? Were there different attitudes toward foreigners within a culture, in different times, and why? Was there any program or internal cultural mechanism that could somehow interact with foreigners and foreign culture in terms of acculturation or assimilation? By trying to answer these questions, this study purports to better understand how the ancient civilizations perceived other cultures. By comparing their attitudes toward other cultures, furthermore, we may begin to see the differences or similarities of the civilizations in question from a particular perspective, one that reveals their self-perceptions. Finally, when different perceptions of self are compared, certain fresh insight might be added to our understanding of each of these civilizations.

An obvious reason for our choice of China, Egypt, and Mesopotamia lies in a similarity shared by all three: each of them was the dominant culture, during their heyday, of their part of the world. As a result of their dominant positions, they had developed a mentality, each in their own way, that regarded themselves as culturally superior to their neighbors. To put it in a crude way, they all assumed a hegemonic role in relation to the "smaller" tribes or states around them. In ancient China, a clear cultural consciousness that regarded China as the center of the "civilized world" had gradually formed since the Western Zhou period from the eleventh century BCE onward. Previous studies on the formation of this cultural consciousness centered on problems such as the distinctions between Chinese and foreigners, the consolidation of the cultural identity of Zhongguo 中國 (the "middle kingdom" or "Central State"), or the origins of Zhongguo. Yet although many have discussed the origins of terms such as Zhongguo (middle kingdom, China) and Huaxia 華夏 (China), or the contrasting terms such as Rong 戎 and Di 狄, Man 蠻 and Yi 夷 (all "barbarian" tribes), the focus was primarily on the original meaning of the terms, the geographical area a certain term could have represented, or their ethnic associations.[30] What is missing in these studies is a comparative perspective that can provide insight into the "Chineseness" of this Chinese cultural consciousness. We need to know what was, if indeed there was, a particular trait in this cultural consciousness that was uniquely Chinese. On the other hand, scholars of Egypt and Mesopotamia have usually focused their attention on the explication and interpretation of the language, history, culture, art, and religion of these two civilizations. Among these studies the problems of ethnicity and interrelationship with surrounding areas have not gone unnoticed.[31] However, these works usually start from the assumption that comparison is meaningful only where there were direct and tangible contacts between different peoples, such as the circulation of goods or the borrowing of ideas or artistic motifs. Thematic comparison, although touched in passing in a few works, has not yet received enough serious attention by scholars from these disciplines until recently.[32]

The above realizations more or less prompted this investigation, this attempt to break new ground in comparative studies. The point of departure is not to establish whether there were any "relations" or "connections" between these ancient civilizations, although Egypt and Mesopotamia certainly had, but whether their responses and attitudes toward other peoples could reveal, through comparison, significant findings concerning the nature of civilization.[33] In the course of re-search, it should be noted, I decided to leave out the areas of ancient India and Greece, the former ranked with China, Egypt, and Meso-potamia as the four great civilizations of the ancient world, the latter the well of inspiration of European civilization. I leave out India due to a lack of proper training on my part. A preliminary survey shows that in the long and complicated history of India, linguistic distinction and, to a lesser degree, physical distinction, were the major factors that determined the concept and attitude toward foreigners. Later complications of identifying language difference with culture, ritual status, and geographic difference constituted a very involved story.[34] I only hope that qualified Indologists would be provoked by my study and join the discussion. As for Greece, there seems no immediate need to reexamine the Greek material since there already have appeared a number of excellent studies on this subject. Instead, to show that we cannot ignore the problem either created or faced by the Greeks, and finally, to entice experts in Greek studies to take a look outside their usual territory, I believe I have invoked enough evidence in this chapter to show the important implications of the Greek view of barbarians for this study. Before we proceed further, however, it is necessary to discuss some methodological issues related to the comparative study of history.

About The Comparative Study of History

Human knowledge is by and large the result of comparison. Through the comparative process one learns to distinguish and establish the nature and character of individual things. The study of history is no exception. We compare what comes before and what comes after a certain timeline and try to establish the causal relationships between the two, which is usually called the historical method. Historical study, in this perspective, is essentially a form of comparative study. As one scholar points out, "proper comparison is the foundation of historical judgment."[35] Yet often historians do not consider themselves as comparativists, nor do they pay particular attention to the extended meaning of comparison. They might have made comprehensive examination of their sources, which, consciously or not, must have involved certain comparative processes. As such, the comparison often operates within a self-contained cultural boundary, and all the references that are drawn upon are likely from a unified (ignoring the minor differences that inevitably exist in every culture) cultural milieu. The result of this is often a one-directional or one-dimensional understanding of history, either in the hows or in the whys that are offered as explanations of historical events. What is lacking is the effort to place the data in a comparative context that might generate different understandings and explanations. In other words, the idea of comparison in the study of history should not only be conducted within a certain historical tradition, but also in an intercultural context.

The comparative study of history, in a generally accepted sense, is to study different histories or cultural traditions and compare the course of these histories, in the hope that the comparison could help throw some light, otherwise less apparent, on the nature and evolution of individual societies. It can be useful as a way to elucidate the special features of the individual societies under scrutiny, because each may look different when compared with the other. It can also provide us with concrete material to establish social theories and generalizations. If, however, one accepts the necessity of comparative study, the logical next question would be: what to compare? The key, in my opinion, is to identify the relevant and significant issues that are common to more than one society. As Hodgson points out, "the process of comparison must be disciplined so that by choice of comparable units of comparison and by awareness of relevant context we can know what are the significant questions—what is and what is not a question."[36]

The emphasis on comparing different histories, then, originates from a concern with the tendency of scholars who are preoccupied with the study of one historical tradition, who explain everything within the reference framework of that particular tradition, and think that that is enough for the understanding of that tradition. What needs to be emphasized, without belittling the value of the former approach, is that in many cases human beings in different cultures face similar problems, and can come up with a variety of similar or different solutions. Through comparative studies, new ways of thinking about old problems could be suggested by calling attention to alternative approaches and solutions found in "other" traditions. As George M. Fredrickson, an eminent scholar of modern racism and nationalism, puts it, "historical comparison is not merely a method or procedure but also an antidote to the parochialism that may accompany a fixation on the history of one nation."[37] Fredrickson further distinguishes between "historicist" and "structuralist" approaches to comparative history. By "historicist" approach, he refers to a comparative approach that is aimed at better understanding of particular societies rather than the establishment or testing of universally applicable social theories. A "structuralist" approach, on the other hand, tends to be more congenial to historical sociologists, anthropologists, archaeologists, and political scientists in that it identifies a limited number of structural or institutional variables operating in a small number of historical situations and uses comparison to isolate the ones that account for similarities and differences.[38] These two approaches are different in their projected results: one focuses on the particularity of individual society, the other on arriving at a general theory of how societies function. Both are important for what they can achieve, although sometimes it might not be easy to make a clear-cut distinction between the two, for a deepened understanding of individual tradition is most likely going to affect the construction of a more comprehensive general theory. Thus an ideal comparative study is probably a study that combines elements of cultural contrast and structural analysis, as suggested by Fredrickson.

The historicist and structuralist approaches mentioned above may serve as the two ideal extremes of comparative studies. When conducting actual research, however, two practical modes of investigation could be suggested. A more usual way is the comparative perspective mode of study. This approach takes a certain cultural phenomenon in a particular historical tradition as its central concern. The understanding of this cultural phenomenon is based not only on the "native" material, but also on information gleaned from the manifestation of that particular cultural phenomenon in other societies or historical traditions. In this case, the researcher pursues one particular history or culture as his/her main object, but he/she utilizes more general or theoretical knowledge derived from a certain degree of familiarity with the manifestation of that particular phenomenon in other cultures or societies. It is clear, therefore, that both historicist and structuralist approaches are employed here.

Another mode of comparative study involves a more comprehensive investigation of all the histories or cultural traditions to be compared. The researcher is expected to have equal control of the original sources, and have done in-depth study of the problem in each tradition, before making comparisons. There is no one target tradition against which other traditions are compared. Instead, both or all traditions are compared against each other, and are illuminated simultaneously by each other in hopes that a new understanding of each of the traditions can be achieved. This is different from the comparative perspective mode, in which the problems or issues of a major, target tradition, are illuminated by other traditions, while the understanding of those other traditions are not necessarily elevated to a new level. Consequently this comprehensive mode of comparison is more satisfying than the comparative perspective mode of study. The need for the latter, however, is still very pressing in the present stage of historical scholarship, because without it the chances are lessened for new perspectives to take form. Needless to say, the difficulty involved in the comprehensive comparative study is considerably higher for the obvious reason that the researcher is expected to be equally competent in two or even more fields. This is indeed an obstacle in the present state of scholarship and historical training. Yet this should not be an excuse if we expect progress in the future.

If we look back at humanistic scholarship in the last century, we see that the comparative study of history and culture is not a novel idea. Arnold Toynbee's monumental work *A Study of History* was a most ambitious attempt at comparative history. His approach and the result of his study placed him firmly in the camp of the structuralist approach, in that he proposed a biological model for the growth and decline of civilizations, a model that treated every civilization as a living organism in itself, subjected to the laws of biology.[39] In the 1940s, American anthropologist A. Kroeber published his *Configurations of Culture Growth*,[40] which was another attempt at finding configurations or structures of the growth of culture. Calls for research in comparative history were issued from time to time, and with the appearance of the journal *Comparative Studies in Society and History* in 1959, a venue for the enterprise gained a foothold in the scholarly community. Undeniably, however, most of the works in this direction are concentrated on the modern to contemporary period. It is understandable that there is an obvious need for comparative studies in the modern period, because the different parts of the modern world since the sixteenth century are increasingly connected through the development of overseas traffic. The proliferation of interregional communications has made comparative studies between different regions not only relatively easier to formulate, but also more compelling. The models of comparison proposed by Hodgson, for example, are all based on interregional contacts of some sort.[41] On the other hand, it seems that ancient historians have been less enthusiastic about comparison between cultures or regions that had no physical contact. Since their subjects seem to be tucked in the remote past far away from each other, comparison seems at first thought to be a fruitless waste of time. Besides, there is the real doubt about the validity of comparative study, since, according to this line of thought, each culture is unique and can only be understood on its own terms. One recent attempt at breaking this mode of thinking is a most ambitious and exciting project of comparative study by Bruce Trigger, which aims at investigating seven ancient civilizations, with Egypt as the center against which other civilizations are measured.[42] Trigger's goal was to "learn more about the factors that constrain human behavior by examining the similarities and differences in the ways in which a significant number of civilizations that had evolved independently, or almost independently, in different parts of the world had been structured and how each of them had functioned."[43] In order to conduct a rigorous comparison, Trigger declared that he tried to collect detailed information on every aspect of each civilization, so as to have a comprehensive understanding of the way of life in individual civilizations.[44] It seems, nevertheless, that his method is rooted in the comparative perspective mode, as he obviously makes Egypt the center of attention. As it is only a preliminary report; the final result of this project is still in the waiting. The drive for comparative study, however, is expected to have more resonance in the future.

Another recent attempt at comparative study of ancient civilization, this time by a classicist, G. E. R. Lloyd, with the collaboration of a sinologist, N. Sivin, tackles a broad range of problems related to some common themes in science and medicine that are present in both Greece and China by comparing their origins and developments and investigating their social and institutional frameworks.[45] Lloyd's experience is valuable: he warned us not to make generalizations easily, nor to make direct comparisons between individual concepts across cultures as if they were addressed to the same issue, nor to assume that one concept could necessarily find its equivalent in another culture.[46] The context of the individual concepts and cultural phenomenon has to be established, and the nature of the evidence—the reason why it was preserved—has to be scrutinized before meaningful comparison can be conducted. Lloyd's approach to comparative study, obviously, does not assume that there was any contact between Greece and China. It was purely on the structural and conceptual aspects that comparison was conducted. Some recent studies in this direction are interestingly concentrating on the comparison of philosophical ideas.[47]

Lloyd's approach also differs from that of Toynbee's or Trigger's in an obvious and important aspect; that is, instead of comparing entire civilizations, he only concentrates on the theme of ancient science or scientific thought. This method implies that before the parts are clarified, the whole would not become clear. Just as to understand a great tradition one needs to have a clear idea of the individual parts of that tradition, a comparison between two cultures lacks firm foundation if comparisons between specific issues and phenomena have not been conducted.

A most recent study, somewhere between Trigger's and Lloyd's frameworks, is a comparative study of ancient civilizations focusing on the key concepts of order, legitimacy, and wealth,[48] initially posed by an article coauthored by John Baines and Norman Yoffee.[49] While this study is in essence a collection of essays by scholars studying different civilizations, their common focus on the concepts of order, legitimacy, and wealth as they manifested in different cultural contexts has to a certain extent revealed different patterns of interactions within each social structure. Although Baines and Yoffee's idea of a high culture as a dominant force that sustained the prosperity of civilization was not necessarily accepted by other scholars, the three analytical concepts proved to be useful tools for unlocking the dynamics of social discourse. As Baines and Yoffee states:

> We do not, then, compare the two civilizations to enumerate similar traits or to establish the core principles of an abstraction, the "archaic state." Rather, through this controlled comparison in time, place, and historical contact, we seek to identify major axes of variation and to advance an important anthropological principle: by knowing what is institutionally and structurally dissimilar in one society judiciously compared with another, we can begin fresh investigations of the principles of organization and change in either society, or in both.

Our larger intention is to contribute to the set of comparisons of
archaic states or early civilizations in general, to see what organiza-
tional principles are widely shared, what, if anything, is truly unique,
and what general societal and transactional models can address data
from a wide range of societies.[50]

While Trigger tries to compare the different civilizations in their
entirety, Baines and Yoffee's agenda focuses on certain key concepts
that point to a more universal principle concerning social organization and cultural interaction. The present study differs from both the
approach of Trigger and that of Baines and Yoffee. I am not trying, as
Trigger did, to conduct a comprehensive look at the entire civilization
to identify the underlying "factors that constrain human behavior," nor,
as Baines and Yoffee and others did, to discover the larger organiza-
tional principles that these ancient civilizations might have shared by
analyzing the interactions of different social strata, the elite and the
commoner. My only focus, somewhat similar to that of Llyod, is on
a particular aspect of the ancient civilizations, that is, their cultural
consciousness as manifested in their attitudes toward foreigners and
foreign cultures. I will try to discover, describe, and then compare the
attitudes toward foreigners and foreign cultures that each of the three
civilizations in question possessed.

Structure, Scope, and Sources

Having chosen the subject of cultural consciousness as the main concern, and having realized that the manifestation of cultural consciousness could at least partially be found in attitudes toward foreigners,
it is necessary that we should identify the specific themes that could
embody such manifestations. In chapter 2 I give some background
for the development of cultural identity in terms of geography and
language, so that the reader can, with the help of this background
and the comparative perspective it brings about, follow the main
themes developed in the later chapters. The comparative perspective
is this: each civilization is unique, yet within this uniqueness are some
common themes of development. The formation of cultural identity
was the result of the workings of various factors such as geographical
positions, linguistic affiliations, religious belief, socioeconomic developments, and lifestyles. On the other hand, race in a biological sense did
not come into the picture in any of the civilizations, or so it seems. By
exploring the common themes, one could gain a better appreciation of

the uniqueness and creativity of each of the civilizations in question, and of their commonality as part of the human experience.

Since cultural identity was to a large extent expressed through representations of self and others, it is necessary that we should look into the representations of foreigners in these ancient civilizations. In chapter 3, I discuss terminologies employed in these civilizations to designate self and others, and the graphic or textual representations of foreigners and foreign lands. The common tendency in all three civilizations seems to be an attitude that regarded the foreigners as culturally unsophisticated or even "barbaric" in contrast to their own culture. However, if one looks further into the sources, it is clear that beyond this basic attitude, foreigners could, under various circumstances, be perceived not only as either enemies or demons, but also as friends and allies, and sometimes even as subjects of appreciation. Chapter 4 outlines these different relations and attitudes toward the foreigners that are found in the three civilizations. It should be pointed out that the difference in attitudes might have been the reflection of the different sociopolitical background of the sources employed in our discussion. In particular, evidence for the appreciation of foreign culture seems to indicate the existence of a private and more balanced attitude, perhaps due to more experiences and contacts with the foreigners, that was often obscured by the official and consequently more belligerent and widely publicized attitude. To substantiate the above claim, it might be useful to investigate how the foreigners had actually been treated inside their host culture. In chapter 5, therefore, I discuss the social positions of foreigners, as well as the reception of foreign goods and languages. In Egyptian and Mesopotamian societies, as the evidence shows, the appearance of foreigners was not uncommon, although due to different causes. What can be suggested is that the necessity of daily life dictates that attitudes toward foreigners or resident aliens were much more practical and realistically benign when necessary, though perhaps never without certain prejudice. On the Chinese side, perhaps due to a different situation that involves an active attempt to assimilate foreigners, little evidence is preserved concerning the fate of foreigners in ancient China. To investigate this problem a step further, chapter 6 takes up the issue of cultural assimilation. As cultural assimilation usually occurs both ways when two different cultures encounter one another, this chapter not only discusses how the "barbarians" were transformed by our three "high" cultures, but also hints at how China, Egypt, and Mesopotamia were receptive to foreign influences. This, finally, provides a crucial understanding that touches upon the central issue of the entire study: the attitude toward foreigners can be characterized by the willingness to assimilate and to be assimilated. On this point, the three ancient civilizations reveal to us different pictures that, when compared and analyzed, should give us some very subtle, but nevertheless deeper, understanding of the characteristics of each of them.

The scope of this study, to state it briefly, comprises the entire periods of ancient Mesopotamian history (to the Persian period, c. sixth century BCE), Pharaonic Egypt (to the beginning of the Ptolemaic period, c. fourth century BCE), and Early Imperial (early Han c. third century BCE) China. The approximate timeline was not actually the major concern. Rather the choice of the cutoff line was dictated by their internal development. For Egypt and Mesopotamia the choice should be evident: both civilizations came to an end politically, and entered into a new period of cultural metamorphosis. China after the unification of the Qin-Han empire also changed greatly politically as well as culturally, particularly with regard to the establishment and consolidation of a Sino-centric worldview. For this I end my discussion in the early Imperial period, although at certain places, especially chapter 6, the discussions might be carried down the timeline a little further. Of course there is always the question of comparability whenever one has decided to take a position. My position is simply that the developmental stages of the three civilizations, in the periods I delineated above, are roughly comparable. Whether this is indeed a sound decision, remains to be seen in the following chapters.

A special feature of this study is the great variety and uneven distribution of the sources that are used. Graphic evidence regarding foreigners abounds in Egypt but is sparse in Mesopotamia and almost nonexistent in China. Written evidence varies with genre: in Mesopotamia there are epic poetry, royal chronicle, a few private letters, and abundant texts of an economic nature. In Egypt we have personal biographies, official inscriptions, and literary texts. In China, besides oracle bone inscriptions and bronze inscriptions, all of an official nature, there are historical works and philosophical treatises. The messages concerning attitudes toward foreigners contained in all these different sources are not of equal explanatory value and representative power, but they nonetheless should be treated with equal care.

A few words regarding the reading and interpretation of textual and iconographical evidence, moreover, are in order. As this study is interested in the attitudes toward foreigners, the sources, whether textual or archaeological, when used, will mainly be assessed by the intention that the source reveals, not whether the statement in the text was a representation of any historical fact, or whether the graphic representations were depictions of historical events. The historical fact, for our purpose, is the attitudes and intentions expressed in the texts or revealed in the archaeological records. In the case of Mesopotamia, therefore, when the Gutians are described as the arch enemy of the people, what is interesting for us is how and why the Gutians could have become the archetype of evil foreigners, not what exactly they had done to the Mesopotamian people. Or, when we examine the Narmer palette, we are not concerned with whether the scenes on the palette represent any historical event—the unification of Egypt for example—but the intention of the scenes and the attitude toward foreigners and enemies they reveal. Again, in the case of China, when we encounter a passage in *Zuozhuan* stating that the Rong people are the descendants of the ancient Chinese sage kings, we are not concerned with whether the statement is true, but try to understand why such a statement was made at that particular time and place, and what it can tell us about the conception of the Chinese toward foreign peoples and cultures.

Another concern is the source and agency of the sources. In particular, there is a question concerning the nature of the confrontations between the sedentary and the nomadic peoples that the ancients recorded. How could we be sure whether the "vile enemy" was indeed a threat to the party that made the statement, and not vice versa? One cannot exclude the possibility that the "invasions" of foreigners recounted by the invaded party turned out to be a one-sided report of what really happened. It has been suggested long ago by a prominent scholar that in the interactions between sedentary and nomadic peoples, the sedentary people often claimed to be the victim of the confrontation, even though they were the victors and aggressors.[51] The fact that it was usually those who possessed the art of writing, and thus could say what they deemed appropriate and necessary, contributed to the impression of them being the victims. Similar situations might have existed in other cases. It is consequently very important to make an effort, even though difficult because of the lack of opposite views, to assess the nature of the confrontations by examining the origin and the agency of the sources, as well as the explicit or implicit purposes of the records. For the researcher, there is always the problem of trying to decide whether to take the records about foreigners as faithful reflections of certain attitude, or casual and stereotypical reproductions of existing prejudice, or deliberate statements representing specific purpose.

Reflecting on the nature of the available evidence, one has to admit that all we have to use are only very limited in scope: we have the view of the elite, and that of the rulers. The story from the perspective of the great majority of people who might have direct encounter with the foreigners, if they did at all, has not been told. It is best to remember that at any given moment in history, our evidence can only serve as a very partial reminder of what might have been otherwise.

Last but not least is the methodological difficulty of comparative study. It is quite unsatisfactory when we can only reach the stage of describing "differences and similarities," not that this is unimportant. Comparative study, as I imagined and stated above, should allow us to have new understandings of the subjects that are otherwise difficult to obtain. Indeed, without this hope for new understandings, there is little incentive for one to engage in comparative study, given the inevitable and often insurmountable limitations of one person's knowledge and training, as Baines and Yoffee warned:

> [Few] Egyptologists and Assyriologists have the skills to assess all the periods in their particular culture, let alone two cultures. Moreover, few scholars of these civilizations are inclined to be comparativists, and many even regard the principle of comparison as violating the "conceptual autonomy" of their area of study—its unique developmental trajectory and historical character.[52]

My excuse in launching this study lies in the belief that, without trying, we would never know whether comparative study of history in its full sense is possible at all. How one could achieve new understanding through comparative study, on the other hand, seems to be more a matter of individual talent and insight than the mere fact that one is comparing. Obviously it will be impossible in this study to address all the questions raised above in a satisfactory fashion, but I hope what follows at least makes the point that comparative study can be useful, and that some new understandings of the three civilizations can be reached.

2

In Search of Cultural Identity

The soldier, when he goes up to Syria, has no staff and no sandals. He knows not whether he be dead or alive by reason of the (fierce?) lions. The foe lies hidden in the scrub, and the enemy stands ready for battle.
  —*Do Not Be a Soldier,* Egyptian text, c. 1300 BCE

Geography

When the Egyptian soldier went up to Syria, the journey on which he was about to embark was characterized as full of dangers, taking place in a foreign environment that was quite hostile. His identity as an Egyptian was keenly felt when encountering a very different terrain in a faraway place. Distance and terrain, therefore, are two important physical factors that influenced communication between different human groups in the ancient world. Lack of communication often led to hostility or other, curiosity-driven actions. The formation of a cultural identity among group(s) of people, on the other hand, rests upon the necessary condition of easy communication. Geographic factors, according to this line of thinking, bear important implications on the formation of cultural identity, and, by extension, attitudes toward foreigners.

Discussions of the origin of civilization in Mesopotamia often point out that the natural terrain of lower Mesopotamia was the major reason for the development of city-states.[1] From an ecological point of view, the southern part of the ancient alluvial plain—Sumer as it was called—was divided in ancient times by several branches of the Euphrates that formed some natural barriers that prevented territorial unity. The existence of strips of desert and marshes along the rivers also created obstacles for the formation of large communities or territorial states.[2] As a result, from very early on, the people of this area developed a sense of group identity built around the city. An indication of the existence of a group identity among the scattered city-states is the worshiping of a particular protecting deity.[3] Moreover, because of the close similarity of their living environment and therefore lifestyle, these city-states actually shared quite similar cultural characteristics. A telling sign of their common cultural background was the worshiping of the god Enlil at Nippur. During the third millennium BCE Nippur was a major religious center that was recognized by most other Sumerian cities and received offerings from them. Thus one could say that, despite their independent positions, the city-states shared a common religious and cultural heritage.[4] The intriguing thing is that this shared cultural heritage did not guarantee a peaceful relationship among the city-states. Plenty of evidence shows that conflicts often occurred between the Sumerian cities—for example, between the cities of Lagash and Umma, and between Uruk and Ur. These conflicts were mainly caused by disputes over water rights and borderlands. The leaders of the cities engaged in military confrontations with each other no less vehemently than when they faced invaders from outside Mesopotamia.[5] Toward the end of the Sumerian period, a number of rival political groups were formed, with Kish in the north, Lagash in the middle, and Ur-Urk-Umma in the south as the centers. From the use of the prestigious title of "King of Kish," it can be surmised that a hegemonic position must have been attained, at one time or another, by a number of these cities during this time, indicating a certain amount of intracity conflict.[6]

One kind of physical evidence for such conflict is the building of the city walls. In lower Mesopotamia, for example, walls were built for individual cities as early as 2700 BCE, indicating a need for protection against the constant threat of enemies and to keep off the foreigners, or outsiders.[7] These walls, therefore, are the material manifestations of the development of a group identity.

On the other hand, when one looks at the larger environment, the sharp division between the generally flat alluvial plain and the rugged mountains to the north and east, as well as climatic variations, entailed different lifestyles that in turn fostered different cultures and created different ethnic and political groups. There were, as a result, two kinds of lifestyles in and around ancient Mesopotamia that were competing with each other: the nomadic and the agricultural.[8] Nomadic peoples, notably the Gutians who caused the downfall of the Kingdom of Akkad, and the Amorites who contributed to the demise of the Third Dynasty of Ur (as we shall discuss later in chapter 3) caused some of the famous incidences of political and social disasters in Mesopotamia. Although it is tempting to see the conflicts between the sedentary and the nomadic peoples as the result of the conflicts of different lifestyles, recent studies of the interaction between the nomadic and the sedentary peoples suggest that their relationship should not be simplistically described as merely conflictual, but should rather be understood as existing in a state of symbiosis.[9] As we shall see in what follows, the relationships between the nomadic and the sedentary were sometimes hostile, sometimes friendly, and sometimes even cooperative. The conflicts between the nomads and farmers were no more common than those between nomads themselves, or between the sedentary city-states.

Thus, conflicts existed not only between the "Mesopotamian people" and the "invading nomads," but also among the Mesopotamians themselves. The city walls were meant for warding off any invasions, whether from nomads or from the neighboring city. The difference between nomad-sedentary opposition and conflict among the city-states is that while the former were often razzia-type operations, the latter were mostly disputes concerning water rights and land ownership.[10] Thus we can look at the problem of the cultural identity of Sumer from different geographical perspectives. On the one hand it was the divided terrain that forged the formation of independent city-states, yet on the other hand it was the similar lifestyle, itself a product of the environment, and the religious system that gave them a sense of cultural unity. This cultural unity, however, was not always strong enough to prevent the cities from having conflicts of interests among themselves. In later eras, when the kingdoms of Akkad and Babylon were formed, the force of localism under the umbrella of a unified "state" never really ceased to exert influence. The larger geographical environment, including Mesopotamia and the surrounding mountains and deserts, as well as the smaller environment of Sumer itself thus produced simultaneously similar and different results for the city-states: conflicts—whether between the mountain people and desert nomads and the Sumerian city-states, or among the city-states themselves—arose regardless of geographical difference. Taken as a whole area, cultural unity among the Sumerian city-states, in contrast to the nomadic and mountain folks, was formed because of a similar geographical environment; looking at them individually, each city-state tended to maintain an independent identity that was the source of conflict and competition with other city-states. Moreover, even the distinction between "nomadic" and "sedentary" lifestyle is not so clear in light of recent studies. For example, earlier studies of ancient Mesopotamian society stressed a nomad/sedentary dichotomy and were formulated according to an evolutionist sequence that demarcated transitions from hunting/gathering to nomadic to sedentary agricultural life. Recent discussions, however, have drastically changed this simplistic concept. In ancient Mesopotamia, it is said that

> irrigation agriculture, dry-farming, pastoralism, transhumance, and nomadism can be combined in a number of patterns by different segments of the same group or of different groups. In no case can it be said that a single named group exploits a section of the total environment.[11]

In sum, although geographic factors could influence lifestyle, which in turn could produce different cultural realities, it is doubtful whether these could be seen as decisive factors in defining and shaping group identity and attitudes toward outsiders. Cultural unity or identity, in the case of the Sumerian city-states, was a layered and relative concept: among themselves, each would claim its own independent identity; facing the outside world collectively, the need to stress similarities and cultural unity overran the differences.

Unlike the Mesopotamian city-states, Egypt took a very different route to statehood. It is generally agreed that the cultural development of the late Neolithic period in Egypt shows a strong continuity, as evinced by archaeological discoveries of the last few decades, which preclude theories of large-scale migrations or intrusions of "foreign" culture.[12] The formation of an Egyptian identity was understood as a gradual process from the prehistoric to the early dynastic period without obvious and major impacts from outside. The relatively isolated geographic position was often cited as the major factor responsible for this development.[13] Indeed, as we shall see in more detail in the next chapter, Egyptian self-identity was to a large extent based upon geographic characteristics. Thus Egypt was the "black land (*kmt*)" as opposed to the desert, "the red land (*dšrt*)," or Egypt was the "flat land (*t3*)," as opposed to the foreign, hilly country (*ḫ3swt*). In the absence of an open frontier environment easily susceptible to such foreign invasion as that which the people of Mesopotamia had to endure, the

Egyptians nonetheless developed a sentiment that in the majority of documents of official or public nature identified the foreign with the hostile. As will also be demonstrated in the following chapters, the opposition and hostility, real or imagined, between the people of the Nile and "those upon the sand (ḫyrw-š3)"—that is, people who lived on the edge of the desert, outside of the Egyptian cultural sphere, therefore foreigners, and many other "mountain peoples (ḫ3styw)"—had a constant representation in Egyptian sources. Why did the Egyptians express such lasting fascination or animosity toward the foreigners? One possible answer lies in the difference of livelihood between Egypt and the surrounding countries. The difference in lifestyles, as determined by geographical conditions, was one of the most important factors mentioned by the Egyptians when they made discriminatory remarks about the foreigners, as we shall see with the progress of this study. Another possibility was the difference in religious beliefs, which in itself could also be partially attributed to geographical difference. Exactly why difference in lifestyles and religious beliefs had to lead to conflicts and not mutual appreciation, and whether they in fact were the real or most important factors that caused the conflicts, and not more materialistic explanations such as resource competition and internal politics, however, remain to be discussed below. As for the more general question of the origin of violence and aggression in human society, it falls outside the scope of our present endeavor.[14]

It has to be pointed out that the officially pronounced or commonly held attitude toward foreigners, based upon geographical differences, needs to be placed in its historical and textual contexts. As we will see in the following chapters, the relatively isolated geographical position of Egypt did not really prevent it from having all manner of interaction with the outside world, be it peaceful or militant. Even attitudes toward foreigners assumed to have been based upon geographical factors were not based upon geographical factors alone.

In contrast to the flat and defenseless Mesopotamian plain and the relatively isolated Nile Valley, the Chinese situation presents another model. Recent archaeological investigations have demonstrated that the old view that Chinese civilization originated in the upper Yellow River Valley and expanded eastward is no longer tenable. Instead, it is now commonly recognized that there existed several distinct Neolithic cultural spheres that contributed to the rise of Chinese civilization.[15] A recent reassessment of archaeological discoveries suggests that as many as six major centers of Neolithic culture existed on the Chinese continent, which gives a rather complicated picture for the beginning of Chinese civilization.[16] The term "Chinese" itself, furthermore, is problematic if one uses it in a cultural sense in this period. Here we will have to settle for a general understanding: it designates the area of the eastern continent of Asia that later, say in the Han dynasty, was under the rule of a single government. Before the Qin-Han unification of the entire land in the third century BCE, the sphere of "Chinese culture" must be considered as a fluid one, leading from the Shang Dynasty onward, expanding and transforming during the Zhou Dynasty and the subsequent Spring and Autumn and Warring States periods. Before the Shang, as we are told, these cultural centers developed along several river valleys, which also served as conduits of cultural exchange. The actual interactions between these cultural centers could only be represented by the fusing and replacement of various styles in pottery manufacturing and decorative patterns.[17] From about 5000 BCE to 2000 BCE these cultural spheres expanded and interacted with each other, while a nucleus area was gradually formed in the "central plain"—that is, present-day Henan and Shanxi provinces—that was later the domain of the Shang state, the first historical dynasty in China. It is to be noticed, however, that archaeological evidence alone, as demonstrated by ethnoarchaeological studies elsewhere, cannot be viewed as representing cultural and ethnic activities in the proper sense of the terms.[18] They only indicate that a multiorigins explanation of early China is more viable than a monolithic one.

According to the Shang dynasty oracle bone inscriptions, the earliest script found in China, the Shang people engaged in various military conflicts with the surrounding tribes. Examples include records of military actions against tribes to the north and west of the Shang, as well as divinations that tried to determine whether there would be an invasion, or whether it would be auspicious for the Shang to launch an attack.[19] As far as documents are available, it seems that conflict between the Shang and the surrounding tribes was a common fact of life. The geographical features of these foreign tribes cannot be established with precision, although one suspects that both plain and mountainous tribes were possible sources of conflict.[20]

The nature of the "Shang Dynasty," moreover, if we accept what was suggested by the oracle bone inscriptions, was most likely an alliance built on unequal relationships between the Shang, the main state, and various tribes that had either submitted to Shang rule or had entered into alliance with the Shang.[21] While there is no doubt that, materially and culturally, the Shang was more developed compared to the surrounding tribes, the military power of these foreign tribes, who were probably the descendents of the ancient cultural centers, might have been not much smaller or inferior to the Shang. This is clearly shown by the fact that it was one of the vassal states to the west, the Zhou, which ultimately replaced the Shang.

In sum, the Shang state, as one, albeit the leading one, among many tribes that coexisted in China in mid-second millennium BCE, had sufficient opportunity to engage in all kinds of exchanges, militant or peaceful, with other tribes. This is obviously different from ancient Egypt, a geographically more unified area, in that the Nile Valley was the only area of intense cultural and agricultural development, which was the uncontested hegemonic power in the northeastern corner of Africa when the governing apparatus was formed. It is also different from Mesopotamia in that the cultural center of Mesopotamia consisted of a number of city-states, and that the alluvium was geographically unified in contrast to the mountainous area to the east and the north and the desert to the west. Not so in China. As has been pointed out above, in the development of cultural centers along the rivers—that is, the Yellow River, the Yangtze River, the River Huai, and the River Wei—each had its own momentum and formed enclaves of various degrees of cultural development. When the Central Plain states, that is, the Shang dynasty and its vassals, by absorbing other adjacent cultural areas along the way, gradually developed into a more or less unified cultural sphere, which later was recognized as Zhongguo or Central States, there were still a number of foreign tribes, mainly the so-called Rong-Di, that were dispersed among the Central Plain states, mostly positioned in mountainous areas. This, as we will discuss further in the following chapters, was the source of conflict in the eastern Zhou period, and was a significant factor in the development of the Chinese ethnocentric view.

Language

Linguistic evidence is usually treated as a very important criterion for the construction of cultural identity.[22] Whether this is true, of course, needs to be verified for individual cases. The linguistic situation in Mesopotamia was complicated from the beginning of recorded history. The Sumerians, whose language has been till now of unknown linguistic affiliation, may not have been the first to have lived in Mesopotamia, although no definite evidence has yet shown that they came from outside the area later known as Sumer.[23] Sumerian was used in Sumer during the first half of the third millennium BCE. It was a language shared by different city-states. Yet at the same time, people already were familiar with a Semitic language; some at least used it to write personal names. During the period of Sumerian cultural supremacy, between c. 3100 BCE and c. 2350 BCE, a Semitic-speaking people, the Akkadians, lived side by side with the Sumerians.[24] There was hardly any indication, however, that ethnolinguistic difference was the cause of conflict between the early city-states, since the sources of this period, written in Sumerian, do not mention the ethnolinguistic affiliation of either enemies or allies.[25]

In this period, the Sumerian writing system spread to the north, where most of the Akkadians lived.[26] In the process, the Sumerians showed a receptive attitude toward Akkadian culture. For example, in the city of Shuruppak, most of the residents were Sumerians, yet Semitic deities were worshiped there.[27] Moreover, the Sumerians also took a number of loan words from the Akkadians. Some of these loan words, such as "price," "arm," "mouth," "strong," and "pure," had strong cultural significance, either in their frequent use or in the ethical values that they implied.[28] This seems to suggest that the Sumerians in this period were to a certain extent receptive toward their Akkadian neighbors, and that they had little prejudice against the Akkadian language.

Following the end of the Sumerian period, the Akkadian Empire was established by Sargon of Akkad and lasted from c. 2334 BCE to 2197 BCE. In this period the land of Sumer was under Akkadian rule politically. The Akkadian rulers, however, continued to use both Sumerian and Akkadian in their official documents and religious texts. For nonofficial, economic, and private documents, Akkadian was used exclusively in the north, while Sumerian was regularly used in the south together with Akkadian. Thus the Akkadians had little prejudice against the Sumerian language and culture. This is only reasonable, since the Akkadians had by this time deeply absorbed Sumerian culture, especially those aspects represented by religion and literature.

Political measures could have served as transforming instruments for the spread of the dominant language. After conquering the south, Sargon replaced the Sumerian rulers with Akkadian officials and destroyed the walls of the Sumerian cities. Thus a strong policy of control was carried out by the Akkadians as part of their effort to establish political supremacy in the region. In consonance with this policy was a trend to standardize the written forms of the Akkadian language, obviously intended to facilitate communication and organization when the central government expanded and needed more control mechanism, which reminds us of the effort to standardize Chinese script when the Qin Dynasty unified China in 221 BCE.

When the Akkadian empire collapsed due to the Gutian invasion from the eastern mountains, the Sumerian language experienced a period of renaissance in the south for about 150 years. During this period, the Third Dynasty of Ur (Ur III) had managed to maintain unified rule over what formerly was the Akkadian empire. Yet this renaissance of Sumerian affected mainly the written language, while the trend to use Akkadian as a daily language continued in the country, as witnessed by the growing number of Akkadian personal and geographic names, and Akkadian loan words in Sumerian. The last three rulers of the Third Dynasty of Ur, moreover, bore Akkadian names, which symbolically shows the reality behind the curtain of the Sumerian Renaissance.[29] This could be seen as an indication of the final phase of the fusion of Akkadian and Sumerian culture. After the Third Dynasty of Ur, Sumerian became the real "classical language" of Mesopotamia, that is, a dead language only the learned scribes could read and write.[30]

In such a linguistically mixed environment, it has been pointed out that the Mesopotamians in general were free of prejudice based on ethnolinguistic difference.[31] If conflicts arose, they were more likely the results of the struggle for political and economic interests. However, such lack of ethnolinguistic prejudice does not necessarily imply that the Mesopotamians were free of any form of prejudice.

The Egyptian situation is quite different as far as language is concerned. As a unique branch of the Afroasiatic linguistic group, Egyptian had been the dominant language used in Egypt since the beginning of recorded history around 3000 BCE.[32] Throughout its history, Egyptian was never threatened by the intrusion of any foreign languages, except for the acceptance of individual foreign words, mostly during the New Kingdom.[33] The use of Egyptian language and script was therefore essential to Egypt's cultural identity. The most important trait of being an Egyptian, although there is no direct textual elaboration on this point, was probably the ability to speak like an Egyptian. This of course does not mean that the Egyptians ignored foreign languages. For people living on the "border," that is, the overlapping area between two cultural areas, bilingualism was always the norm. There is also ample evidence that shows that the Egyptians had no problem communicating with the foreigners, such as Nubians and the people from Palestine. The report of a Sixth Dynasty expedition leader, Harkhuf, indicates that he was able to communicate with the ruler of Wawat in Nubia:

> Then his majesty sent me a third time to Yam. I went up from the nome of this upon the Oasis road. I found that the ruler of Yam had gone off to Tjemeh-land, to smite the Tjemeh to the western corner of heaven. I went up after him to Tjemeh-land and satisfied him, so that he praised all the gods for the sovereign.[34]

We do not know how they communicated, yet it was not an obvious concern, therefore perhaps not a significant problem deserving mention. Interactions between peoples, moreover, need not involve complicated language when the content of communication is simple and direct.

It is of course true that there is a discrepancy between the written and the spoken language, and the user of a certain script does not necessarily speak—much less as a native speaker—the language that the script represents. The Hyksos during the Second Intermediate period no doubt adopted Egyptian writing, as evinced by the few traces of evidence of their existence in Egypt, although we cannot be certain whether they also spoke Egyptian. In any case, it is certain that a number of foreign-language groups existed in Egypt since the New Kingdom. One good example is the settlement of the foreigners mentioned on a stela of Amenophis III:

> Its (Theban temple) workhouse is filled with male and female slaves and with children of the princes of every foreign country that his majesty despoiled. . . . It is surrounded by Syrian settlements, inhabited by the children of the princes.[35]

No trace of the language spoken by these foreign slaves and royal children, presumably in their native tongue, was to be found. Most likely their written communications (if any) were all in Egyptian. Using Egyptian, therefore, was a way to achieve cultural assimilation with Egypt, as the Libyan dynasties had demonstrated by using only Egyptian as the means of written communication. The rulers of the Ethiopian Twenty-fifth Dynasty likewise used Egyptian in their monuments and left Egyptian style monuments. The rulers of the Twenty-sixth Dynasty, though of Libyan descent, even aspired to the old tradition of Egyptian art and literature and became more Egyptian than the people that they conquered.

The supremacy of Egyptian language ended with the coming of the Ptolemaic Dynasty. As Greek became the official language, Egyptian as a daily language retreated more and more to the private sphere. The intertwining process of the evolution of languages in Egypt during the Greco-Roman period and its relationship with the final disappearance of Egyptian culture is an enormous subject.[36] Suffice it to say that language was closely linked with cultural identity in Egypt. In contrast, the Mesopotamian cultural identity was less based on common language than the other elements of culture: custom, law, script, and above all religion. The Chinese situation, again, was quite different, since virtually no evidence of any "foreign" language that had ever been spoken in and around the Central Plain area was preserved.

Scholars have been pondering the possibility that the so-called pottery signs, dated to the pre-Shang Neolithic period, might be some kind of script. So far, however, it has not been proven beyond doubt as a form of written script.[37] The earliest evidence of the Chinese language is preserved in the Shang Dynasty oracle bone inscriptions, dated to the late fourteenth century BCE. From the continual use of this script, with its several phases of stylistic development, there is no doubt that the Shang people used a form of language that was the ancestor of present-day Chinese.[38] There is no evidence, however, for us to assess the linguistic associations of the peoples around the Shang state. Some linguists would like to see that, since Chinese belongs to the Sino-Tibetan language family, the non-Chinese peoples around Shang and Zhou were also peoples of the Sino-Tibetan family.[39] The "barbarian" peoples such as the Qiang had long had intensive interactions with the Shang state, and it seems that the Shang people had no problem communicating with them, or at least there was no indication that language was a barrier. This in itself, nevertheless, does not necessarily imply that they spoke similar languages. Judging from the modern situation—that is, there are still enclaves of minority people using non-Chinese languages inside, to the southwest, west, and northwest of China—there is good reason to assume that in the ancient period a similar situation existed. Chronologically closer to the Shang, evidence from the Eastern Zhou period indicates that people of the Rong tribe to the west of Zhou spoke a "non-Chinese" language, although this does not mean that they were linguistically unrelated.[40] The Zhou people themselves, according to their own tradition, came from the Rong-barbarian area to the west of Shang. In the *Book of Mencius*, King Wen, the founder of the Zhou Dynasty, was referred to as a "barbarian" from the west. The *Book of Documents* (*Shangshu*),

purportedly containing documents transmitted from as early as the
early Zhou period, records that when the Zhou was engaging in an
all-out confrontation with the Shang, it rallied the support of various
barbarian tribes. Although the text of the *Book of Documents* may have
been written much later then the event described, the story could have
been alluding to some historical circumstances concerning the origin
of the Zhou as one among the western barbarian tribes.[41] Whether or
not they originally spoke a non-Chinese language but later adopted
the Shang script and language, however, is difficult to fathom.

The use of Chinese script and language spread from the original
Shang and Zhou, the states of the Central Plain area, to the south and
southeast of China, the area known as the eastern Yi, which during
the eastern Zhou period was occupied by the states of Wu, Chu, and
Yue. It is significant that, although the Yi were probably Austroasiatic
in linguistic affiliation,[42] they lost almost all of their original cultural
characteristics after they adopted the Chinese language and script. A
typical case of cultural assimilation was that they assumed that their
ancestors were descendents from the ancient Chinese sage kings, so as
to establish their legitimate position as a member of the Hua-xia, that
is, Chinese states. The Chu state, in particular, developed a special style
of writing based on the Chinese script of the Shang-Zhou tradition.
The style is known as the Chu script, which has attracted scholarly attention in the past decades, as an abundance of newly excavated texts
has become available for study.[43] However difficult it is to decipher the
Chu script, there is no doubt that the script was a descendent of the
Shang and Zhou scripts, and the language it represented was "Chinese" in a linguistic sense. The Chinese language and script therefore
was a strong force in the integration of originally disparate tribes and
peoples, and created a unified cultural identity.[44]

Looking for Foreigners

Our discussion has shown that geographic and linguistic factors each
made its own contribution to the formation of cultural identity in the
three ancient civilizations. What meaningful observation can be drawn
from this concerning attitudes toward foreigners? In Mesopotamia,
relatively open frontiers of the alluvium made the area susceptible
to foreign invasions. When hostile attitudes toward foreigners were
formed as a result of the invasion, what was stressed as the difference between "we-civilized" and "they-barbarian" was not language

but lifestyle. This might have something to do with the fact that the Mesopotamians were accustomed to different languages, since the pluralistic linguistic situation had probably created a more open attitude for the people to accept foreign languages.

The Egyptians were relatively free from serious foreign invasions thanks to their rather well-protected borders. Their experience with foreign languages was relatively simple compared with that of the Mesopotamians, as there is little evidence of the wide and constant use of another language in Egypt. A term that they used to designate foreign language was 3^{cc}, which was probably an onomatopoetic term that indicated the incomprehensible foreign tongue, similar to the Greek use of βαρβαρόφωνος (barbarian tongue). This term could be interpreted as evidence for contempt toward the incommunicable foreigners, for they spoke incomprehensibly. In addition to this linguistic factor, geographic difference, and, by extension, different lifestyles between Egypt and foreign lands constituted a major factor affecting Egyptian attitudes toward foreign peoples. The physical difference between the fertile land of Egypt and the treacherous environment of the mountainous Syrio-Palestinian area, for example, was made proverbial by such texts as *Do Not Be a Soldier*: "The soldier, when he goes up to Syria, has no staff and no sandals. He knows not whether he be dead or alive by reason of the (fierce?) lions. The foe lies hidden in the scrub, and the enemy stands ready for battle."[45] Another text says: "Come, [let me relate] to you his journey to Khor (Syria) and his marching upon the hills. His rations and his water are upon his shoulder like the load of an ass, while his neck has been made a backbone like that of an ass. The vertebrae of his back are broken, while he drinks of foul water. He stops work (only) to keep watch. He reaches the battle, and he is like a plucked fowl."[46] Not that such hardship of being a soldier could not be experienced elsewhere, say, in Nubia. Nevertheless the Syrian terrain remained the epitome of an unfriendly foreign environment in Egyptian literature.

The Chinese of the Shang period had numerous encounters with neighboring tribes, and some of them must have spoken languages that were not "Chinese." Nonetheless, there is little on which we can base an assessment of the Shang attitude toward foreign languages. It was late in the eastern Zhou that a text mentioned that the Rong-barbarians spoke a different language.[47] In a famous remark, Mencius described the southern barbarians as "people who talk like birds."[48] Like the Egyptians, therefore, the Chinese had certain reservations about foreign languages. Although again it must be noted that this does not mean that they did not communicate with other peoples, and that some of them, people living on the borders of cultural spheres at least, could understand more than one language.

On the other hand, the extent to which geographic factors contributed to the formation of cultural identity in China is difficult to evaluate. Unless, of course, if we assume that the formation of cultural identity was concomitant with the formation of the territorial states of Shang and Zhou, the area which later was put under the rubric of the Central Plain, that is, the northern China plain of present-day Henan, part of Hebei and Shanxi. The term "central" implies automatically center-periphery relations, which also hints at a high-low/advanced-backward dichotomy. Thus identifying with the central plain states was tantamount to identifying with their superior culture. The term Central Plain becomes, therefore, a geographic designation that was infused with cultural implications.

Thus the interplay between geography and language forged the special character that each culture later displayed with regard to who was and who was not a foreigner. This forging process was of course long and imperceptible. The resulting attitudes however, could be felt or expressed by the ancients, and were sometimes employed by the ancients themselves to explain their conflicts or differences with other peoples. It should be pointed out here that these explanations reflect mainly the attitude of those ancient people who needed to find a logical and legitimate (in their sense of course) explanation for the conflicts and differences, because their attitudes were informed or influenced by their own geographic conditions and lifestyles. Their assessment of conflicts or difference between themselves and the "foreigners," in other words, need not necessarily reflect the reality, and we would likely be deceived if we were to mistake their attitudes for reality. To substantiate this assertion, we need to examine more closely evidence that purports to reflect their attitudes toward foreigners. Before engaging in the discussion of these attitudes, however, we need to know how the ancients represented the foreigners and foreign countries, both textually and graphically.

3

Representations

It is in these four [barbarian] regions that there are no rulers. Their
people are like the deer, wild birds, and the beasts, in that the young
order the old about, the old fear the able-bodied, the strong are
the "worthy," the violent and arrogant the "honored."
—*The Annals of Lü Buwei*, Chinese Text, third century BCE

For people ancient and modern, there are always foreigners outside
their political or cultural borders, since no identity could have been
established without the presence of at least the concept of "others." By
identifying the others, whether from a biological point of view or from
a cultural point of view (that is, language, religion, custom), people
could hold on to a line that defines what is "we" and what is "they."
This appears to be a basic cognitive mechanism of human thinking,
even though it may not be an entirely conscious act.

Considering the length of the history of human society over the
past ten thousand years, our knowledge of the activities of ancient
peoples is unquestionably confined to a very recent period. Even the
earliest extant written records of Mesopotamia and Egypt could only
reflect what may be said as the epilogue of a long story. It follows that
the formation of group consciousness and the establishment of cultural
boundaries happened long before the beginning of the historical period.
Seen from this perspective, what we tend to hold as the earliest evidence
concerning the attitudes toward foreigners are but the end of a long
history. We should, therefore, not expect what the earliest record has
shown us to be the beginning of an attitude. Thus the representations
of foreigners as expressed in iconographic and textual evidence that
we deal with are merely a more conscious, more mature or advanced
stage of representing the others.

When we touch on the issues concerning the image of foreigners in the ancient world, there is a further complication, that is, the modern researcher is in danger of applying his/her modern conception to the ancient situation. We need to be aware of our modern conceptions of "foreign" or "alien" and contemplate the possibility that, when we use these terms to translate such ancient terms as *nakru* or *ḫ3styw* or *man-yi*, we might have projected some of our modern conceptions onto the ancient terms. It is necessary that we make it clear that our modern conceptions may have contaminated the ancient reality, however much we may intend to approach that reality with caution. We recognize that ancient people employed certain terms to designate people outside their own "circle," whether political or cultural. What needs to be clarified is the criteria they used to make the distinction between "us" and "them" and whether the criteria changed through time, or under different circumstances.

Designations of Self and Others

In many ancient cultures names are considered part of the characteristics of the designated objects, persons, or group of people. To know the name of an object made it familiar to a person and consequently easier for him to locate the named object in the context of his mental world.[1] By giving a name to an "unknown" object or person, one projects his ideas and attitudes onto the named. Knowing the names may also be a way to have power over the named. In an Egyptian mythological tale, the crafty Isis sought after the true name of the Sun god Re, because knowing the name would amount to knowing the secret of the deity.[2] In the famous *Book of the Dead*, Chapter 125, to know the names of the forty-two gods who guarded the gates was prerequisite for the deceased who wished to enter the Western Land of Eternity.[3] It follows that names are important indications of attitudes toward the named persons or objects. As a first step in the study of attitudes toward foreigners, therefore, it is useful that we should examine the designations of the foreigners, to try to discern the attitudes implied by these names.

Some of the questions we intend to investigate in relation to the names of the foreigners are formulated around the way people named foreigners. Particular points of inquiry include whether foreigners were named by reference to their autonyms, their place of origin, their cultural characteristics and physical features, or some other criteria.

The Sumerian words used to express the sense of "foreign" or "foreigner" are related to the idea of "outside," "hostile," or "strange." Presumably it was often from the outside that hostile and strange people came. This is illustrated by the Sumerian word *bar* (Akkadian *ahu*), which means a foreigner, a stranger, an outsider, or an alien.[4] The term emphasizes what is strange and unusual, mostly in a neutral way, but could also carry some sense of hostility. Since hostility was often produced or provoked by enemies, and foreigners were seen as hostile, it is reasonable to assume that foreigners were often identified with enemies. Another Sumerian word that under different circumstances could represent foreigners or enemies is *kur* (Akkadian *nakru*).[5] The primary meaning of *kur* was probably "mountain" or "hill country," as the early pictograph of this word that consisted of three rocks suggests. As the mountainous region to the northeast of Mesopotamia was the home of the tribal peoples who were wont to invade the lowland area, it was perhaps natural for the Mesopotamian to make the connection between the ideas of enemy and people of the hill country.[6] The early Sumerian word for female slave, moreover, also includes the three "mountain rocks," which suggests that, when the Sumerian script was being created, the historical and social reference to the slaves was that they were prisoners or captives of the people from the hill country.

Yet another Sumerian word for foreign country is *ma.da*, which refers to the flat countryside extended between the Mesopotamian cities. Thus *ma.da* and *kur* form a pair of concepts that express the opposition between plain countryside and mountain area. Combined, however, they could designate the totality of foreign and hostile country, as opposed to *kalam*, the word for "Sumer" as a unified country or geographical area in a political sense.[7] From these basic vocabularies we can already sense that there was a feeling of uneasiness with regard to foreigners, for they could be hostile and might become enemies to the early Sumerians.

In the Ur III period, however, the term "foreigner" (*lu kur*) "did not seem to be used anywhere to qualify specific foreign persons in contrast with others who are considered natives."[8] The usual way of referring to foreigners in the Ur III period was "to state their provenance, ... with a gentilic adjective, or with an enitive clause of the type *lu* GN, 'man of a certain place.'"[9] This is an important indicator concerning the Sumerian attitude toward foreigners. Since the foreigners were referred to by their provenance, there is a sense of egalitarianism on the part of the Sumerians in treating all the "aliens," whether of the cultural sphere of Mesopotamia or not, as equally foreign. We should not assume, however, that this kind of designation implies that the Sumerians could not tell if these ethnic groups were non-Mesopotamian or just people from another city. Our discussion will largely focus on the "real foreigners" that originated outside of the Mesopotamian cultural sphere.

Who were the foreigners, and where did they come from? In ancient Mesopotamia, two foreign ethnic groups, the Gutian and the Amorite, were seen as the worst of the enemies.[10] The term *Martu* or *Kur Martu* (Sumerian) and *Amurru(m)* or *mât Amurri* (Akkadian) referred to a people or region to the west of Babylon, and appeared in the documents of the Akkadian Sargonic and Ur III dynasties. Wars against *mar.tu* were recorded.[11]

The origin of the name *mar.tu* is not certain, but recent scholarly consensus indicates that it was the name of a people who lived to the west of Mesopotamia. The term was later also used to mean the direction west.[12] The personal names that bore the *mar.tu* designation, moreover, show that the people using the names could be categorized into a branch of Semitic people.

Toward the end of the Ur III dynasty and the beginning of the Old Babylonian period, numerous Semitic names were found in Mesopotamia, and, as these names were identical with the earlier Semitic names that bore *mar.tu* designation, they testify to the fact that the Amorites were by now widely dispersed in Mesopotamia and were mingled with the natives. In fact, the Old Babylonian Dynasty was established by people of Amorite descent.[13] It has been pointed out that the ethnic phenomenon of "Amorites" was not a simple invasion of nomadic people into the sedentary and agricultural area, but that the Amorites themselves led a mixture of nomadic and agricultural life, and that they were in contact with the Mesopotamian people for quite a long time before the rise of the "Amorite Dynasty."[14] In other words, the idea that ethnic groups usually had a high degree of intragroup homogeneity and maintained infrequent or unimportant contacts with other groups was inadequate in explaining the behavior of ethnic groups.[15]

In the documents found at Sippar during the Old Babylonian period, foreigners were again designated with an emphasis on their place of origin.[16] Thus the Elamites were *elam.ki elam.ma* or *elam.ma.ki*, while the Kassites were often designated as *é.hi.a kaššû/î*. *É.hi.a* is a term for "encampment," so it probably referred to the nomadic origin of the Kassites, where their encampment was located. However, there is also a term *erin kaššû/î* that emphasizes the type of profession that the foreigners might have engaged in. *Erin* refers to a group of people in the context of civil or military labors, which implies that these foreigners were probably engaged in such work when they came into Mesopotamia. On the whole, foreigners could take up different professions in Old Babylonian society, including military and commercial trades, if they were not slaves.[17]

As for the word designating "Easterners," an Old Akkadian term was *sadium*. It was a general term for the inhabitants at the fringes of the northeastern mountains and beyond, and it did not become a popular term as its parallel term *mar.tu*, the "Westerner," had.[18] The Gutians, although from the eastern mountains, were not referred to by this designation.

Sometimes the name of a foreign people could become associated with degradation or evil intentions, presumably because the people in question was viewed as of lower moral standard compared with that of the Mesopotamians. Thus in Akkadian the term *nullû*, originally referring to the Lullû or Nullû, a mountainous people, was taken to mean "vile action."[19] In Chinese, similarly, the term "Man," a barbarian people to the south, later became a term that means "barbaric," or "brute."

In contrast, one should like to know how the Mesopotamians referred to themselves. It is unfortunate that we are still unsure of the etymology of the word for human being in Sumerian: *lu*. We have no indication as to its cultural, religious, or political significance that could illuminate the Sumerian self-perception in contrast to the foreigners. The Babylonian word *lullu* means human being, while the word *awilum* designates a citizen, a man with higher social status.[20] As for the land itself, the existence of terms that denominate the Mesopotamian region as a whole was indicative of a sense of cultural and political unity. Terms that denote the region of lower Mesopotamia, or Sumer, as a unified geographic area include: *kalama*; *ki-engi ki-uri* (Sumerian); or *mat Šumeri u Akkadi*; *mat Akkadi*; *mat Karduniaš* (Akkadian).[21] On the political and theological level, a sense of unity of the area can also be found in the Sumerian King List, in which kingship was said to have been given to successive cities by the gods, thus the entire known world was under the same divine government.[22] On the other hand, it is worth noting that the list was composed by the royal scribes whose main object was probably not discoursing on the political or cultural unity of Sumer, but primarily on the legitimacy of the reigning dynasty. Still, the fact that a single source of divine authority was used to justify one's political legitimacy itself says much about the ideological underpinning.

Following the lead of geographical thinking, one piece of interesting evidence that reveals the Mesopotamian cultural identity and self-consciousness is a Neo-Babylonian map of the world.[23] Carved on a clay tablet, this map shows the then known world with Mesopotamia in the middle, which indicates the self-centered mentality of the Mesopotamian versus the surrounding people. Comparable to this idea, but much earlier, is the royal epithet "king of four quarters," which came into use during the Akkadian period. It was a subjective imagination as well as literary embellishment of the idea that the "self" of the king, and, by extension, the kingdom, was the center of the entire world. As Piotr Michalowski puts it: "Geographical terms are not neutral, objective, descriptive indexes of natural landscape, but are subjective and emotionally loaded elements of a semantic subsystem."[24] This self-centered view of the world, however, was nothing unique or surprising from a comparative and psychological point of view, as we see from similar examples in the case of China.

The Egyptian terms for foreign countries and foreigners are formed in several ways. One is based upon the geographical characteristics of the named place and its people. For example, the term ḥryw-š3, "those upon the sand," that is, the Bedouins, is based on a description of the living environment of the nomadic people, the desert.[25] There is also a general term, Ḥ3styw, "people of the mountains, hill countries," which sometimes was used as a contrasting term with "the flat land," that is, Egypt.[26] Although Ḥ3styw could refer to people of the Syrio-Palestinian area, there are two other terms, ʿ3m and Styw, which usually refer exclusively to the Syrio-Palestinian area in general and are conventionally translated as "Asiatics" in Egyptological literature.[27] For the people of Syria, moreover, there are the designations Ḥ3rw and Rṯnw (Ṯnw). We do not know the etymologies of these terms, hence we do not know if they were originally geographic features. The term ḥ3st could also be used in a narrower sense that refers to the Palestinian hills, including "Syria" (Rṯnu), in contrast to the "Asiatics (ʿ3mw, Styw)." This is found in the Story of Sinuhe: "When Asiatics (Styw) conspired to attack the Rulers of Hill Countries (Ḥḳ3w-ḥ3swt), I opposed their movements. For this ruler of Retenu let me pass many years as commander of his troops."[28] During the Second Intermediate period, Ḥḳ3w-ḥ3swt was used to designate the foreign invaders, the Hyksos. In contrast to the Syrians, the term *Nḥsy* refers to Nubia, or people who lived to the south of Egypt,[29] and *Libu* refers to the Libyans.[30] They were never confused with *Ḫ3styw*, as the latter refers exclusively to people from the Syrio-Palestinian area.

The Egyptians also used cultural-specific names to designate foreigners. Most interesting is the *Pdwt psḏt*, the "Nine Bows." The "bow people" (*Pḏt*) is a term frequently employed to designate the southern Nubians, presumably because of their using bow and arrow as their main weapons. This association could be traced to the late prehistorical "hunters' palette" where a hunter (presumably a Nubian) is shown with a bow in hand.[31] The earliest attestation of this term occurs with a statue of Djoser, where figures of foreign captives with the designation of "Nine Bows" are pinned beneath the king's feet.[32] When the word nine was added after bow, however, the term takes on a general meaning of "foreigners," as the number nine is used metaphorically to express the meaning of totality, therefore the totality of the bow-using peoples, that is, all the foreigners.[33] This is similar to the situation that the word *psḏt* is also used to denote the totality of deities, that is, the "Ennead," of Egyptian pantheon.[34] The two terms actually appear together in the *Pyramid Texts*, as the king pleads to the Sun god: "Grant that I may rule the Nine (bows) and provide for the Ennead."[35] It is nonetheless clear that this term serves as a symbol of the world ruled by the king. On a stela of Montuhotep, the king is depicted in the act of smiting a Libyan, with the following words: "Binding the chiefs of the Two Lands, settling the Southern and the Northern lands, the foreign lands and the two (banks?), the Nine Bows and the Two Cities."[36] In view of the parallelism between "foreign lands—two banks" and "Nine Bows—Two Cities," it seems reasonable to assume that here the Nine Bows refers to foreign countries. In a temple relief of Amenhotep III, literally nine areas, each represented by a bounded prisoner with names written on an oval shield, are mentioned as corresponding to the "nine" bows. However, among these are mentioned Upper and Lower Egypt; thus the term "Nine Bows" must have connoted the meaning of "the entire world."[37] A large number of lists of foreign countries are found in the New Kingdom temples, and on monuments, although the areas mentioned may differ from one list to another.[38] It seems that by the New Kingdom the term Nine Bows is often used as a common designation for foreigners and enemies, although the meaning of "the world" did not really disappear completely. A stela of Thutmosis I has the following words: "He (the King) is one who turns back against all the Nine Bows together, like a young panther against a resting herd."[39] Thutmosis III similarly claimed that he had "made a slaughter among his enemies, even the Nine Bows."[40] In these last two examples, the Nine Bows clearly refers to the foreign enemies.

That the Nine Bows served as a stereotypical representation of foreign countries under Egyptian dominance was also emulated by the kings of the Nubian Dynasty. A statue of King Tarharqa of the Twenty-fifth Dyansty, found at Gibel Barkal, shows the king stepping on the Nine Bows signs.[41] He is also depicted in a typical Egyptian style in smiting the enemies.[42]

Another cultural-specific term denoting foreigners is the word 3^{cc}, "speakers of foreign language."[43] As mentioned in the last chapter, this term is comparable to the Greek *barbaros*, indicating that in the mind of the Egyptians the speakers of a foreign language could not talk in a civilized, Egyptian tongue.[44] Different from the Sumerian *kur* (Akkadian *nakru*), which may represent either "foreigner" or "enemy," the term for enemy in Egyptian is either *ḫfty* or *ḫrw*, both words followed by a "fallen enemy" determinative. In this light the Egyptians did not automatically assume foreigners to be enemies, despite the fact that foreigners often appear in a hostile context.

The Egyptians referred to themselves as (*rmṯw*), which is translated as "human beings" in modern Egyptological literature.[45] The etymology of this word is unfortunately obscure. The word first came into use in the *Pyramid Texts* in the late Old Kingdom. Before this, there seems to have existed no particular term for "human being." A word for "man" is *s* (*st* for woman), but it is in general used to indicate a person, and there is no specific stress on the human nature of the person. In the Middle Kingdom period, *rmṯ* can still be used to express the meaning of man, whether a free person or a servant. Even a slave could be referred to as *rmṯ*, as a text has it: "I bought oxen, I bought men (*rmṯw*), I bought field, I bought copper."[46] Another text gives a similar example: "The men (*rmṯw*) (i.e., slaves) at the service of my father, Mentuhotep, were born at home, the property of my father and mother. My men also come from the property of my father and mother, and apart from those who belong to me, there are others I have bought with my own means."[47] The term *rmṯw*, however, could sometimes be used in contrast to the foreigners, and thus could be translated as "Egyptians."[48] Positive evidence comes from the decorations in the tombs of Seti I and Ramesses III, where four kinds of people—Asiatics (ᶜ3mw), Nubians (Nḥsyw), Libyans (Tḥnw), and Egyptians (rmtw)— are shown.[49]

As for the terms designating Egypt, there is the "Black Land" (Kmt), the fertile land, as opposed to the "Red Land" (Dšrt), or the barren desert. Although the Black Land is originally a geophysical term that is nonpolitical in nature, it later became synonymous with Egypt as a state. Another term for the country of Egypt is T3-mri, the "chosen land" or "land under Egyptian rule."[50] This term emphasizes the legal aspect of the rulership of the Pharaoh.[51] During the New Kingdom, Kmt and T3-mri seem to be used interchangeably denoting Egypt in contrast to the foreigners, the Nine Bows. In the inscription relating the first Libyan war of Ramesses III, for example, Kmt and T3-mri are used interchangeably in opposition to Libya (Tḥnw), and the Nine Bows (Pḏt psḏt).[52]

The situation in China is somewhat different. The oracle bone inscriptions mention Shang as the name of the first state that preserved historical records in China. The term, originally refering to the capital city, later became the name of the state.[53] It has to be stressed that at that time Shang was only one of the numerous states or polities in existence. The Shang people referred to the foreign tribes or states with various names such as Guifang, Gongfang, Tufang, and Qiangfang.[54] Most of the fangs (i.e., regions) were inhabited by people in a hostile relationship with the Shang, while some submitted to Shang domination. Among the different fangs, the Qiang-fang interacted with the Shang most frequently. The term "Qiang," however, when it was not followed by the word fang, also referred to various foreign tribes to the west of Shang.[55] Thus it is both a name for a specific group of people, and a general appellation referring to a number of foreign tribes.

This situation further developed during the Zhou period, as some fixed terms were employed to designate the foreign tribes that scattered among and around the Central Plain states. These included Rong, Yi, Man, and Di—all general designations referring to the barbarian tribes.[56] They were probably not autonyms, but were names given by the Chinese. On the other hand, a barbarian tribe named Xianyun posed a great threat to the Zhou, and this term seemed to have remained a specific ethnic name.[57] Yet there is also evidence showing that Xianyun was used interchangeably with Rong. For example, in a bronze inscription we read:

Lord Bai said: Bu-Qi Yufang, the Xianyun are grievously troubling our western *yu*, (the Xi-yu). The king has ordered me to move forward and pursue them to the west, . . . you attacked the Xianyun with great force in my war-chariots, at Gaoling. You cut off many heads and took prisoners. The Rong gathered together and pursued you for a long way. You fought hard against the Rong and graciously did not fall into trouble with my chariots.[58]

Thus either the Zhou people confused the Xianyun with the Rong to the west, or the term Rong was used as a general term referring to the foreign barbarians. It was during the Eastern Zhou period that the terms Rong, Yi, Man, and Di began to be relegated to designate foreign tribes to the four cardinal directions, although by no means were these terms fixed to one direction. Thus we hear of "the northern Rong" in *Zuozhuan*,[59] and "western Yi" in *Mencius*, and "southern Yi" in some bronze inscriptions.[60] It may also be noticed that by the Eastern Zhou time the Qiang were considered part of the various Rong tribes.[61]

According to *Liji*, the *Book of Rites*, these designations corresponded to the four cardinal directions. One passage states that

the tribes on the east were called Yi, . . . those on the south were called Man, . . . those on the west were called Rong, . . . those on the north were called Di.[62]

Here the traditional terms of eastern-Yi, western-Rong, southern-Man and northern-Di are neatly formulated. As in the case of the Qiang in the Shang period, these terms are more of a directional than ethnic designation. We hear "the Nine Yi (tribes), Eight Di, Seven Rong, and Six Man"[63] or similar expressions in a number of texts, including *Mozi* and *Han Feizi*,[64] etc. The implication of such terms is that more than one group of people, regardless of their ethnic identities, were often seen by the Chinese as belonging to the same "foreign barbarians." The "Nine Yi," in particular, reminds us of the Egyptian use of the "Nine Bows" as foreigners. The closest term corresponding to "barbarian" in the Chinese concept, therefore, would be *"Man-Yi"* or *"Rong-Di."* Some of the terms used to denote these foreign people, such as Xianyun 獫狁, Di 狄, Man 蠻, and Mo 貊, carry derogatory overtone in that the characters contain radicals denoting animals.[65] The implication, therefore, was that these were nonhumans. Although, admitting a considerable degree of cultural pride, this need not imply a general xenophobic attitude.

The similarity between the expressions "Nine Yi-barbarians" and the "Nine Bow" is very interesting, which demonstrates that both Chinese and Egyptian had a tendency to lump all the foreigners into one common stock. The numbers nine, or eight, seven, six, for that matter, are obviously numerical metaphors for "many."

As a contrast to the idea of the "four barbarians," there is the expression "Zhongguo 中國," that is, the Central State(s), China. Scholarly opinions differ on exactly when this term came to be used in the sense of central state(s), that is, a geopolitical term denoting the state of Shang, Zhou, and their vassals located in the Central Plain area.[66] An early Western Zhou bronze inscription seems to be the earliest attestation of the term "Zhongguo" in the ancient documents. Here Zhongguo denotes the area around the city of Luoyang, where king Wu of Zhou built his capital.[67] However, it was not yet a term that referred to "the Zhou state." It was perhaps during the Eastern Zhou period that this term gradually came to mean the central state(s),[68] that is, the Chinese states that existed in the Central Plain area of north China. Yet this does not mean that a concept that saw the Zhou state as the center of the known world was not already in existence in the Western Zhou, as witnessed such terms as "four states (siguo)," "eastern state (dongguo)," "southern state (nanguo)," and "northern state (beiguo)," that suggest a contrasting central position of the Zhou.[69] It is even possible to trace this concept to the Shang oracle bone inscriptions where terms such as "eastern land (dongtu)," "western land (xitu)," "southern land (nantu)," and "northern land (beitu)" presuppose an idea that considered the Shang state as being in the "center."[70] It is doubtful, though, if the Shang people had already developed a strong Sino-centric perspective that considered the Shang state as the center of the world, the unquestionable leader of civilization.

While "Zhongguo" referred to the state as a political unity or area, the people residing in Zhongguo, as opposed to those barbarians of the foreign tribes, were called people of "Hua 華" and "Xia 夏." These two terms also came into frequent use during the Eastern Zhou period, when a heightened consciousness of the conflict between the Chinese states and the foreign tribes was prevalent.[71] The origins of these terms are obscure. The etymology of the character *hua* is "flower," with the extended meaning of "beauty" or "embellishment."[72] When applied to the people of Zhongguo, therefore, it might carry the meaning of "civilized people." Based on the pervasive flower decorative patterns on the potteries of the Yangshao Neolithic culture, it has been suggested that here might be found the origin of the term Hua as a designation for the people of Yangshao culture, who, according to this view, were the ancestors of the nuclear Chinese people.[73] This suggestion, though attractive, must be taken with caution, since it is a very subjective view and is extremely difficult to substantiate, more so since doubts have been raised on the identification of the decorative patterns as flowers.[74]

The original meaning of the character "Xia" is unclear. According to the interpretation of the Eastern Han lexicographer Xu Shen, it means "the people of Zhongguo," which is only a circular confirmation of the use of the term. Modern scholars on epigraphical grounds have long refuted his explanation of the structure of the character as "a man with a head, two arms and two legs".[75] To use the name of Xia, the legendary dynasty before Shang, as a designation for the people of the Central States, however, implies that these are people with a long tradition both politically and culturally. Thus the use of Hua and Xia together signifies that the bearers of these names are people with high culture and a long and glorious history, a sharp contrast to the barbarian foreigners.

Textual and Graphic Evidence

Representations of foreigners usually appear in contexts. It is necessary to analyze these representations as well as their contexts, either textual or graphic, to gain further understanding of the characteristics of the foreigners as seen from the perspective of those who left the evidence. It is, however, difficult to discuss people's representations of foreigners without also dealing with the attitudes reflected in such representations. In this section, I will try to limit my discussion to a number of direct textual and graphic representations of foreigners, and leave the more complex evidence concerning the attitudes toward foreigners for the next chapter.

The notion of culture versus nature, or we-civilized versus they-uncivilized in ancient Mesopotamia could be illustrated by a number of epics, including the epic of Gilgamesh. We are of course not really certain if the ancient scribes, when they composed, or better edited, the epic, made any conscious effort to formulate such a scheme. Yet, somehow, the result could be illuminating if seen through modern analytical glasses. In the *Epic of Gilgamesh*, as has been suggested, the wild man Enkidu represents the primitive, the uncultured beastlike human being, who was to be initiated into civilization. The attributes that make him a savage are his habitat, that is, desert and steppe; his ignorance of farming, with no bread and wine to eat; his lack of proper living style, with no house, and worst of all no bed, the symbol of civilization, family life, and procreation.[76] From the description of Enkidu, we could gain a picture of the "savage" in the mind of the ancient Babylonian writers:

> Enkidu, born in the hills—
> With the gazelles he feeds on grass,
> With the wild beasts he drinks at the watering-place,
> With the creeping creatures his heart delights in water—
> . . . .
> The barbarous fellow from the depths of the steppe.[77]
>
> The milk of wild creatures
> He was wont to suck.
> Food they placed before him;
> He gagged, he gaped
> And he stared.
> Nothing does Enkidu know
> Of eating food;
> To drink strong drink
> He has not been taught.[78]

It was the harlot who had introduced civilization, symbolized by sexual knowledge and food, to Enkidu:

> For six days and seven nights Enkidu came forth
> Mating with the lass,
> Then the harlot opened her mouth,
> Saying to Enkidu,
> "As I look at thee, Enkidu, thou art become like a god.
> . . . .
> Up, arise from the ground,
> The shepherd's bed!"[79]

Becoming like a god is, of course, the ultimate result of being civilized. Thus the situation of Enkidu before his initiation epitomizes the image of the barbarian in Mesopotamian literary representations. This image was carried over to, or resonated in, the descriptions of two groups of foreigners, the Amorites and the Gutians.

In the *Curse of Agade*, a popular text in the Old Babylonian period, the Gutians, who invaded Mesopotamia and caused the downfall of the Akkadian empire, were described in the following way:

> Not classed among people, not reckoned as part of the land,
> Gutium, people who know no inhibitions,
> With human instinct but canine intelligence and monkeys'
>   features—
> Enlil brought them out of the mountains.[80]

Here the Gutians were described as total strangers, people "not reckoned as part of the land (i.e., Mesopotamia)," with no civilized behavior, and having animal-like features. Other sources picture them as "serpents of the mountains" or "dogs."[81] In a word, they appeared inhuman or subhuman. Such expressions are understandably exaggerations, they nevertheless reveal a strong aversion toward the Gutians as fellow human beings. Other texts, however, reveal a concern over culture:

> Oppressive Guti, who were never shown how to worship god,
> Who did not know how to properly perform the rites and
>   observances.[82]

Here the writer was making a distinction of the Gutians as culturally ignorant: they did not know how to worship and perform rituals. Again this is a biased view from the standpoint of Mesopotamian culture. The Gutians certainly had their own tradition and custom in worshiping their gods. It nevertheless shows that the Mesopotamian writer tried to distinguish foreigners from himself on a cultural basis.

Descriptions of the Amorites were similar to those of the Gutians except perhaps in a more detailed way concerning their different cultural behaviors. One text states concerning the Amorite: "To the Amorite, who has neither city nor house, Enki presented livestock."[83] Their lifestyle, therefore, was that of the nomadic people. They were, not surprisingly, associated with animals and referred to as people "with instincts like dogs or like wolves."[84] In the Sumerian proverbial literature, moreover, we can also find evidence that refers to the contrasts between the civilized and the barbarian.[85] In the legends related to the king of Akkade, the enemies are described as people with partridge bodies and raven faces, both with human blood.[86] It seems that the most condescending way possible for the Mesopotamians to express their contempt toward the foreigners or enemies was by referring to them as animals. In this respect, Mesopotamia shared with China a similar sentiment, as we shall see below.

The above picture, however, was drawn mainly from official documents or texts of a public nature that express nationalistic sentiments. It should be balanced by texts of a more private nature. In a letter written just before the Gutian invasion, the writer, a rich land lord, cautions his tenant: "If the Guti attempt an attack against you, then bring all the cattle into town. Formerly (?) when the Guti men drove away the cattle I never said a word; I have always given you silver (for the damages.)"[87] It is interesting that private communications such as these seem to have already taken the encroachment of the Gutians as a normal fact of life, and that the Gutians, whether or not they were demonic or animal-like barbarians, did not seem to be of special concern to the writer. In any case, the writer did not utter a single anger-venting or racial-slandering word against the Gutians. The Mesopotamians might not like the invaders, but no surprise or cultural shock was experienced either.

Even in mythological stories, which usually represent sanctioned values, one could not always make clear the exact intention of the stories, or whether there is an exact intention to begin with. Take the myth of the marriage of the god of the Amorites, Martu (Amurru), for example. The god Martu is described thus: "In his life he has no house, he eats raw viands, when he is dead, he will not be buried. Why would you want to marry the god Martu?" This description of the Amorite god could be seen as a negative caricature of the nomadic lifestyle of, and prejudice against, the Amorites. It has been argued, however, that despite this rather negative caricature, the Babylonians did not really have any "racial" prejudice against the Amorites.[88] The myth of the marriage of Martu actually points to an acceptance, not rejection, of the nomad by the sedentary young girl.[89] To put it in a sociological perspective, it is suggested that the marriage represents a sign of the urbanization of the nomads,[90] although it is also true that the nomadic lifestyle evolved from the edge of the sedentary cultural sphere. The point has also been made that the racial discrimination against Martu, although reflecting an old prejudice, could only be a kind of literary device and therefore of no consequence in the poem.[91] This is of course one way to read and interpret the poem. But the description itself, for what it is worth, could still be an important testimony to a basic Mesopotamian mentality that posited a fundamental difference between the nomadic and the sedentary culture.

Figure 3.1. Cylinder seal showing a king (?) and defeated enemies,
after Frankfort, 1939: 23, fig. 6.

Thus one should recognize the fact that evidence of different
natures can reflect different attitudes in different situations, and, although prompted by the desire to paint a broad picture, one should
not lose sight of the nuances of reality.

The above impressions gained from texts, moreover, should be
counterweighted by graphic evidence. Even before the appearance
of writing, Mesopotamian people had already tried to express their
feelings and relationship with the world in the forms of paintings on
potteries and cylinder seal engravings. Among the earliest cylinder seals
found in the Uruk period, the craftsmen already tried to incorporate
scenes of his daily existence into the limited space on the surface of
the seals. The subjects represented could be categorized into several
groups: religious scenes, secular scenes, animal and heraldic figures.[92]
Besides peaceful scenes that depict ritual or secular life, they did not
forget to portray the violent aspects of their existence. A seal impression of this period shows a man with a spear, probably representing
a ruler, standing in front of several bound prisoners, with another
soldier holding a stick in the act of hitting one of the prisoners.[93] The
scene was very likely a commemoration of a certain historical event,
an important battle perhaps. It is a testimony indicating that conflicts
between groups of people were memorable. Other "heraldic" scenes
often show struggles between men and beasts, which are the prototype
of all the subsequent man-beast opposition motifs in Mesopotamian
artistic tradition. It is not historical in the narrow sense, because it
does not seem to commemorate a particular event. But it nevertheless carries a historical message: it reflects a consciousness of human
beings' existence in the world, an existence that demanded constant

efforts to subdue wild nature. This is expressed iconographically with scenes showing either the actual subduing of the animals by man, or animals walking in an orderly and tamed fashion. In other words, these scenes testify to the existence of a bipartite view of the world consisting of "we-human beings" and "they-wild nature, enemies." The appearance of some domesticated animals in the scenes could have been depictions of a stable life, or hopes for such a life.[94]

A number of scenes on the cylinder seals show conflicts between the gods, as some gods are being killed by others.[95] These kinds of scenes are usually explained as a reflection of the struggles between the various city-states, as the gods are representatives of the city-states. On the other hand, wars against foreign peoples were sometimes described in a form of myth, wherein Mesopotamian gods were victorious over foreign gods.[96] Thus the scenes could theoretically also have been depicting the conflicts between Mesopotamians and foreign peoples. Eventually, of course, it is almost impossible to clearly identify the "enemies"—whether in the forms of animals, humans, or gods—as people from outside of Mesopotamia and not from one of the city-states.

If cylinder seals could not be seen as "monumental art" that are invested with cultural and political significance, the victory stela of Naram-Sin surely must be counted as representative of the artistic expressions of the self-consciousness of the people of Akkad on a monumental scale. The stela commemorates the king's victory over the mountain people, the Lullubi. He is shown stepping on the corpses of his enemies while ascending a mountain. Before him is a dying enemy, perhaps the enemy leader, who is trying vainly to pull a spear from his neck. Behind Naram-Sin are his soldiers carrying spears and standards, also ascending the mountain. The entire scene, therefore, could be seen as an elaborate presentation of the above mentioned "historical" battle scene on the cylinder seal. Another scene, showing bound prisoners on a shell inlay on slate, was found in the audience hall of Palace A at Kish, again comparable to the seal impression with bound enemies mentioned above.[97]

What is noticeable is that in these iconographic representations the Mesopotamians did not make any remark on the foreigners' physical features. They were practically indistinguishable from the Mesopotamians except that they were often depicted as naked, a sign of defeat and low status. It was perhaps not necessary for the Mesopotamians to try to depict the physical characteristics of the foreigners or

Figure 3.2. The victory stela
of Naram-Sin. (Paris, Musée
Louvre), after Pritchard,
1954, fig. 309.

enemies, since they knew who the enemies were, and the purpose of
the representations was not identification, but commemoration. Thus
the fact that we could not easily identify the physical features of the
foreigners depicted on the monuments does not automatically imply
that the foreigners were of the same racial type as the Sumerians, or
the other way round.

In sum, when the Mesopotamian people drew distinctions between themselves and foreigners, what they cared about most was
not language and physical characteristics—criteria that some modern
theories on racial distinction deemed most important—but behavior
and lifestyle. What alienated people, then, was cultural difference, not
biological characteristics.

Figure 3.3. The Narmer palette (Cairo Museum), after Kamp, 1991: 42, fig. 12.

The Egyptians articulated their view of foreigners in a different way. The Egyptian artists from early on demonstrated their ability to depict the physical features of all kinds of beings, including that of humans. Their depiction of peoples around Egypt, that is, Palestinians ("Asiatics" or "Semites"), Nubians, and Libyans—although stereotypical, could serve as good indications of the actual physical characteristics of these peoples. Archaeological evidence shows that contacts between Egypt and the Syrio-Palestinian area went back to prehistoric times.[98] The earliest representation of Asiatics or Semites in Egypt is probably the Narmer palette, a commemorative slate palette from the late prehistoric/First Dynasty site at Nekhen (Hierakonplois).[99] On one side of this palette, Narmer wears the crown of Upper Egypt, a defeated enemy chieftain is kneeling before the king. It is very likely that he was a Semitic, since he is shown with long hair, a rather heavy beard, and a prominent nose, which are the characteristics of the standard Asiatics (i.e., Semites of the Syrio-Palestinian area) in Egyptian artistic representations. Another two defeated enemies in the bottom register of the same side also show Semitic characteristics. The key problem is the name of the chieftain. Whether it should be read as "Wa" or as "Wa-sh" has been the subject of debate. If it referred to "Wa," which could mean the border area of the Delta, later the "Harpoon district,"[100] then the scene on the palette would be a depiction of the struggle between the Egyptians and the tribes of Semitic extract in the Delta area.[101]

Similarly, the beheaded enemies depicted on the other side have beards and long hair. On the bottom of the same side, the king, represented by a raging bull, attacks a Semite and a walled city. It is possible that this enemy also represents a Semitic tribe that existed in the Eastern Delta, which was probably not yet under Egyptian control at this early stage.[102] In any case, the posture of the king versus the enemy clearly indicates a sense of Egyptian superiority over the Semite/Asiatic. This sense of Egyptian superiority was not only political, but also religious in its nature. On the Narmer palette, the figure of Horus-falcon is depicted with a rope in hand, while the other end of the rope was tied to the neck of an enemy. Complementing the figure of the king before the decapitated enemies, it indicates that the god of the Egyptians also controls the fate of the foreign foes.

The palette could have represented the culmination of a long development of group conflicts in Egypt. For the first time, it seems, order was established by the political force represented by Narmer. In this way, King Narmer, or whatever political force he represented, found a concrete way to draw a line between "us" and "others" and to formulate the "Egyptian" attitude toward the foreigners. Similar ideas are expressed on another archaic palette, "the Battlefield Palette," on which Nubians (identified by their spiral hair) are attacked by a lion (i.e., the king) and several vultures.[103]

Similar scenes showing the king smiting his enemy with a club are found in the wall painting of an archaic tomb (tomb 100 at Hieraconpolis), on some ivory cylinders from Hieraconpolis, on an early dynastic alabaster palette, and among some of the rock inscriptions found at Sinai, as well as in the funerary temples of Sahure and Neuserre.[104] Some of the enemies in the scenes appear to be Semites. This kind of scene was to become a standard expression of Egyptian dominance over the foreigners and the world at large in the subsequent development of Egyptian religiopolitical iconography down to the Graeco-Roman period.[105]

We are not sure, however, if these scenes of the king smiting the enemies can be interpreted as either commemorating Egyptian military victory, as symbolic representation of the king's power, or as apotropeic protection against foreign attacks.[106] There is no compelling reason to

Figure 3.4. A typical image of the Pharoah smiting the enemies,
after Hall, 1986, fig. 64.

assume that all such scenes should have represented the same meaning, and it is certain that in later eras they were mostly symbolic. If the
Narmer palette was "commemorative" of a certain historical event, the
archaic period scenes of the king killing enemies carved on the rocks
of Wadi Maghara[107] could hardly have been anything more than the
displaying of Egyptian presence at the area in a by then conventional
art style.

Another stereotypical representation of foreigners is the image of
the Nine Bows. They were either shown trampled under the feet of the
king, or as bound prisoners.[108] An extension of the motif of treading
on the enemies in the funerary setting was the custom of drawing two
bound enemies, usually one Nubian and one Asiatic, on the footboard

Figure 3.5. Bound foreigners representing various tribes
(New York, Metropolitan Museum of Art), after Robins, 1997: 137, fig. 155.

of the coffin. This is symbolic of the deceased's conquest of the enemies
in the netherworld, represented by Nubians and Asiatics.

The political as well as economic relationship between Egypt and
Nubia has already been studied extensively.[109] As Egypt and Nubia had
frequent and close contact since the prehistoric period, the presence
of the Nubian people in Egypt was a common phenomenon. In the
Egyptian official representations, whether of the Archaic period,
such as the ivory label of King Aha, which shows a Nubian prisoner,
identified by his bow, traditionally used to represent Nubians, or a
relief at Gebel Shaik Suleiman on which a Nubian prisoner is bound
to the prow of an Egyptian ship, with corpses lying in the water,[110]
or from the later Old Kingdom, such as the relieves in the temple
of Sahure and Neuserre, the Nubians are always represented as defeated enemies.[111]

The Libyans had been in contact with Egypt as early as the late
predynastic period, as testified by the famous Tjhenu palette.[112] On
one side of this palette was depicted several buttressed towns being
attacked each by an animal, obviously symbolic of Egyptian deities. On
the other side, oxen, donkeys, and rams are depicted walking peacefully,
while a hieroglyphic sign denoting _Thnu_ or "Libya" was also present.

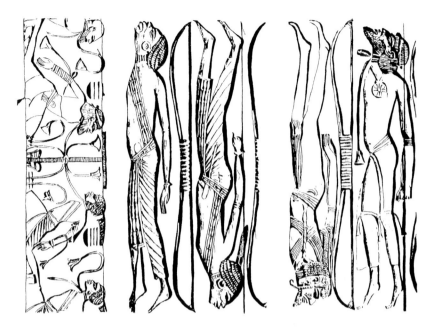

Figure 3.6. Nubians and Syrians representing the Nine Bows,
after Desroches-Noblecourt, 1963: 51.

Although it is uncertain if this signifies Egyptian conquest of Libyan
tribes or settlements during that time, there is no doubt that there
were contacts between them. Just about the same time period, Libyans
were also mentioned and represented as prisoners on a cylinder seal
of Narmer. This implies that they were conceived and treated by the
Egyptians not very differently from the Nubians and Asiatics.[113] Old
Kingdom representations of these people are from the royal temples,[114]
where the Libyans are depicted together with the Asiatics and the
Nubians as the defeated enemies, although we need not take these
symbolic representations as reflecting real historical events.[115]

Similar representations of the foreigners could be added end-
lessly for the Middle Kingdom and later eras.[116] We are, however, only
interested in pointing out that the stereotyped representations of the
Asiatics, Nubians, and Libyans as defeated enemies are only one way of
presenting the foreigners in Egyptian tradition. As Loprieno suggests,
in Egyptian literary representations of the foreigners, there are two
modes of expression, which he terms as *topos* and *mimesis*.[117] *Topos*
being the idealized representation that was ideologically charged,
with strong official, political, and theological implications. *Mimesis*,

Figure 3.7. Lybian people depicted as domesticated Egyptians in the temple of
King Sahure, Fifth Dynasty, after Borchardt, 1903, vol 2., pl. 1.

on the other hand, depicts more personal, daily-life situations, hence
less stereotypical and less ideologically charged. A similar situation
is evident in graphic representations. For example, besides being
represented as defeated enemies set in ahistorical situations, in real
life Nubians were shown either as household servants,[118] mercenary
soldiers, or as police.[119] The fact that they were tomb owners discloses
their social position: they were certainly not seen as enemies. Again,
such realistic representations of foreigners in later eras can be added
to a great extent.[120] We shall return to this in chapter 5 in connection
with the discussion of the social status that foreigners enjoyed in Egypt.
What needs to be emphasized here is that the official representations
of foreigners never seemed to have changed throughout the ages,
indicating a strong and persistent political ideology at work. As for
the more private representations of foreigners, since they were mostly
representations in their Egyptianized fashion, it is doubtful that they
were considered as truly foreigners any more.

      In contrast to the rich graphic sources from Egypt, archaeo-
logical discoveries in China have produced little material concerning

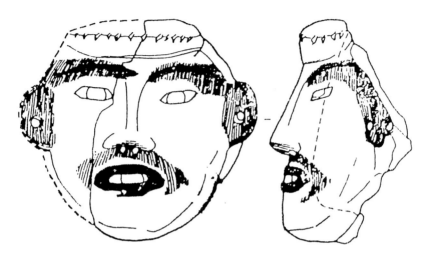

Figure 3.8. Human face with Mongolian type (excavated at Baoji),
after Zhongguo shehui kexueyuan kaogu yenjiusuo, 1983: 75, fig. 57:1.

human figures of any kind, let alone of foreigners. Neolithic human
faces/masks found in Shaansi and Gansu seem to indicate that the
depicted people were of the Mongolian type.[121] The same situation
occurs with the clay statues found with the Neolithic Hongshan culture
in northeastern China.[122]

Shang Dynasty evidence of human figures are equally meager. A
group of five kneeling figurines are found in the tomb of Fu Hao, the
wife of King Wuding.[123] The simplistic representation of the figures
made it difficult to investigate their identity, although the kneeling
posture suggests a subservient position. In terms of iconography, the
genre of human images found on Shang bronze objects that could be
considered as representing foreigners was found in the famous motif
of a tiger (or a pair of tigers) with wide open mouth that is engulfing
(or protecting) a human head of Austronesian extract (as could be
determined by the wide nose and thick lips).[124] K. C. Chang thinks
that this human figure (or human head) represents a shaman who
was communicating between the human and divine worlds.[125] Exactly
why a foreigner should be represented as a shaman, or whether he is
indeed a shaman, however, remains an open issue.[126] One such figure
was represented on a bronze axe, which could symbolize a "beheaded
foreigner."[127] The oracle bone inscriptions reveal that, as a result of
military actions, large numbers of foreign prisoners were brought

Figure 3.9. Human head of Austronesian type between two beasts, after Chang, 1983a: 360, pl. 6.

back. These prisoners were often sacrificed during Shang religious ceremonies.[128] Archaeological finds confirmed that human sacrifice was common practice during the Shang period at such occasions as the dedications of buildings, offerings to the gods, or royal funerals.[129] Rows of beheaded skeletons and heads were found in some of the tombs of the Shang Kings and separate burials.[130] It is impossible, however, to discern if the beheaded victims were from any distinct non-Mongolian type of foreign group.[131]

The recent discoveries at Sanxingdui, Sichuan province, unearthed a large number of bronze masks dated to the late Shang period.[132] The particular features of these masks, such as high and straight nose and high cheekbones, clearly indicate that they, whether human beings or deities, are not Chinese, not if we compare the figures of, for example, the Qin terracotta soldiers found in the subsidiary burial pits of the tomb of the First Emperor of Qin.[133] Since Sichuan was not part of China or under Shang rule at this time, the masks could serve as evidence of the image of certain foreigners from the Shang point of view. Suggestions that they represented people from Mesopotamia, however, are fantastic.[134]

In the subsequent era, representations of human figures usually appeared in funerary settings as surrogate figurines,[135] as part of a larger object or structure, such as the two human figures found in the early Western Zhou cemetery of the state of Yu,[136] or the supporting post of

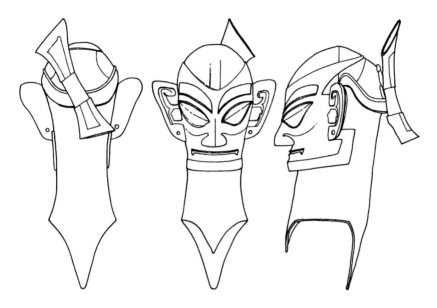

Figure 3.10. Bronze mask from Sanxingdui, after *Wenwu*, 1989, 5: 6, pl. 10.

the ceremonial bells of the Marquis Yi of Zeng, or as part of a lamp.[137] One has yet to find any sample of foreign people among such types of materials. A group of nude musicians, cast in bronze, both male and female, may represent people of southeastern China (present Zhejiang province). It is again uncertain simply by viewing the schematic representations if they could be the Yi-barbarian people.[138] Judging from the instruments they used, such as zither, drum, and mouth organ, they were Sinicized as far as their profession is concerned. Only two hairpins with human head decoration (of Scythian type) found in a Western Zhou palace foundation at Shaanxi suggest that people could have had contact, although uncertain in what capacity, with foreigners from central Asia.[139] It is therefore remarkable that, despite frequent contact with foreign tribes, the Chinese from the Shang Dynasty onward showed relatively little interest in depicting the images of foreigners in any elaborate way.[140] Representations of human figures increased on bronze vessels, lacquer ware, and silk embroidery from the Warring States period on, yet few could be identified with any certainty as representing people of foreign extract.[141]

Literary descriptions of the physical features and behavior of foreigners, on the other hand, were better represented. The best evidence

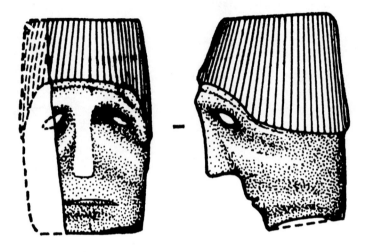

Figure 3.11. Human head of Scythian type (excavated at Zhaochen),
after *Wenwu*, 1986.1: 46, pl. 2.

came from *Zuozhuan*, a monumental work that recorded the events
of the Eastern Zhou period (c. 770–403 BC), known as The Spring and
Autumn period, following the title of a work by Confucius. Interactions
of various degrees of magnitude between the Chinese vassal states of
Zhou and the barbarians are preserved in *Zuozhuan*.

A prevailing opinion shared by those Chinese who could be
described as conservatives saw the barbarians as culturally backward
and never the match of the people of the Central Plain. The Rong, for
example, were described as "people without affection and friendships,
and are covetous,"[142] and the Di were people who lacked all the necessary virtues of civilization:

> He whose ear does not hear the harmony of the five sounds is deaf;
> he whose eye does not distinguish the beauty of the five colors is
> blind; he whose mind does not accord with the rules of virtue and
> righteousness is wayward; he whose mouth does not speak the words
> of loyalty and faith is a stupid chatterer. The Di approximate to all
> these four conditions.[143]

It is clear that the standards to evaluate whether a people could be
considered as civilized are those already adhered to by the Central
Plain states. A particular style of music employing "five sounds,"
mentioned in the above quoted passage, was supposed to be the rep-

resentative musical form of Chinese culture.[144] A passage said to be the words of Guan Zhong 管仲, the famous chancellor of the State of Qi, more or less sums up the contrast between the Chinese and the foreigners: "The Rong-di are wolves, to whom no indulgence should be given; within the Xia states all are nearly related, and none should be abandoned."[145] This obviously derogatory expression about the Rong-di could be seen as diplomatic rhetoric aimed at enhancing the unity of the Chinese states during the politically fragmented Eastern Zhou period.[146] Because of Guan Zhong's policy of "Revere the (Zhou) King and expel the barbarians," Confucius once praised him and said that "without Guan Zhong, I probably would have my hair disheveled and wear a cloth that folds from the left."[147] In other words, Guan was a cultural hero for Confucius. The Confucian thinker Mencius once characterized the cultural style of the northern barbarian Mo people thus: "In Mo all the five kinds of grain are not grown; it only produces millet. There are no fortified cities, no edifices, no ancestral temples, no ceremonies of sacrifice; there are no princes requiring presents and entertainments; there is no system of officers with their various sub-ordinates."[148] This characterization enumerated the basic elements of culture—dietary habit, living condition, religious belief, entertainment, and bureaucracy—the sign of an advanced stage of civic life—which are certainly very similar to the ones made concerning the Gutians and Amorites mentioned above.

Short of pictorial representations, the physical difference between the Chinese and the barbarians is vividly portrayed by a passage from *Liji*:

> The people of those five regions—the Middle states, and the Rong, Yi (and other wild tribes round them)—had all their several natures, which they could not be made to alter. The tribes on the east were called Yi. They had their hair unbound, and tattooed their bodies. Some of them ate their food without its being cooked with fire. Those on the south were called Man. They tattooed their foreheads, and had their feet turned in toward each other. Some of them ate their food without its being cooked with fire. Those on the west were called Rong. They had their hair unbound, and wore skins. Some of them did not eat grain-food. Those on the north were called Di. They wore skins of animals and birds, and dwelt in caves. Some of them did not eat grain-food.[149]

If we read carefully, however, the text never refers to the barbarians as physically different from the Chinese. The "difference" was seen basically in ways of dressing and bodily decoration, including hairdo and tattoo, dietary habits, and expressions of a different culture or way of life, rather than any biological diversity. By the late Warring States period and the beginning of the Qin empire, a synthetic work that represents the collective wisdom of the day, the *Spring and Autumn Annals of Master Lü* (*Lüshi chunqiu*) describes the people of the four directions outside China as having no rulers, that is, no "proper" rulers, and that

> their people are like the deer, wild birds, and the beasts, in that the young order the old about, the old fear the able-bodied, the strong are the "worthy," the violent and arrogant the "honored." They harm each other day and night, they never rest, and in this way destroy their own kind.[150]

The animal simile in these texts is of course only a figure of speech. It should be pointed out that in most of the pre-Qin texts, whenever someone is referred to as an animal, it is mostly a way to indicate the indignation of the one who made the comment with regard to the uncivilized behavior of the one who is referred to. The real gist of the discourse, therefore, is to demonstrate the barbarians' lack of proper cultural values. This lack of culture provided the legitimate excuse for China to impose on the barbarians the benefit of civilization under the rule of the Sage Kings. Consequently, not only were barbarians referred to as animals, anyone whose behavior was not up to a civilized standard could be labeled an animal. One of the most famous comments made by Mencius on the philosophies of Yang Zhu and Mozi reads: "Yang Zhu's idea was for the benefit of oneself, which means having no sovereign. Mozi's idea was to equally love everyone, which means having no father. Having neither sovereign nor father is a sign of being like birds and beasts."[151] Disregarding the erroneous idea that birds and beasts do not have a certain concept of parenthood, this equation between the recognition of the authority of father and sovereign on the one hand and civilization on the other, and the simplistic identification of "benefit for oneself" with "having no sovereign," point to an important cultural difference between the Chinese and the barbarians: whereas the Chinese valued social hierarchy, the barbarians were unstructured, therefore animal-like. Needless to say this difference is more the creation of the subjective value judgment of the Chinese (in this case Mencius) then any objective reality, since the barbarians were never unstructured socially and politically, and the Chinese were quite capable of acting like animals as Confucius's *Spring and Autumn Annals* judiciously renounces those treacherous acts and murders that took place among the Central Plain states.

To sum up, in Mesopotamia and China, foreigners were characterized as culturally different people, although they did not seem to have shown particular interest in depicting the physical features of the foreigners, literarily or graphically, in any extensive way. Monumental art in Mesopotamia proved to be more militant than the Chinese tradition, for in China it was only in the Warring States period that scenes of military action began to be depicted on bronze vessels, and only as small, almost schematic decorations.[152] The lack of representations of foreigners in China, moreover, was perhaps due to the artistic tradition of the Shang and Zhou period that to a large extent averted direct representations of human figures. We need, of course, to realize that the majority of the objects with any graphic designs are ritual bronze vessels, which are a highly specialized group of objects, and certainly not all that had ever been manufactured. The Egyptians, on the other hand, made the representation of foreigners—especially the defeated foreigners—one of the most important themes of their political expressions, and they had the ability and desire to clearly depict the physical features of the different groups of foreigners. They too, however, seemed to regard the foreigners as different mainly in a cultural sense. We have yet to find any literary reference to the foreigners and their cultures based merely on physical characteristics alone. On the whole, therefore, one could argue that all three civilizations displayed the tendency that considered the cultural characteristics of the inhabitants of the peripheral world "not only different but inferior to those in the central country. . . . The culture of the foreigners is viewed either as lacking the basic requirements of the civilized world or else as opposite to the normal (i.e., correct) behavior."[153] On the other hand, as we shall see, one cannot claim that cultural prejudice based on physical difference never played any role in forming a people's attitude toward foreigners. Exactly how each culture played out their relationship with the foreigners, and what their attitudes were toward the foreigners, need to be examined in more detail, as we shall venture to do in the next chapter.

4

Relations and Attitudes

Enlil brought down the Elamites, the enemy, from the highlands.
Nanshe, the Noble one, was settled outside the city.
Fire approached Ninmar in the shrine Guabba,
Large boats were carrying off its precious metals and stones. . . .
The province of Lagas was handed over to Elam.
>   —*The Destruction of Sumer and Ur*, Sumerian Text,
>   c. eighteenth century BCE

Enemies

In the records of the ancient civilizations, foreigners and foreign countries were very often considered as sources of hostility. A foreigner can be defined as someone who is from a place outside of the political and cultural spheres of a certain community. This concept of "foreigness," therefore, could represent what is unfamiliar, hostile, and exotic to the usually ethnocentric natives. The fact that the Sumerian word for foreigner (*kur*) was also used to designate "enemy" indicates that there was a tendency to identify foreigners with enemies in early Mesopotamia. The earliest Egyptian historical evidence, the Narmer palette, is usually assumed to be a commemoration of Egyptian victory against foreign enemies. In Shang China, many of the foreign tribes mentioned in the oracle bone inscriptions are regarded as enemies by the Shang.

Archaeological discussions of the cultural characteristics of the peoples of the Zagros mountains to the north and east of Mesopotamia have established a clear differentiation between the material culture of northern Mesopotamia and the Zagros group.[1] It has been suggested that because of this difference in lifestyles there existed a constant animosity between the Mesopotamians and the people of the Zagros mountains, notably Elam and the surrounding countries.[2] Textual evidence examined in the last chapter seems to support such an argument, although it is clear that texts could at best be seen as skewed representations of the reality, thus the expression "constant animosity" must be qualified by a consideration that peaceful coexistence might in fact have been the norm.

The first memorable event after the legendary flood in Mesopotamia was the war against the Elamite by King Enmenbaragesi of Kish, as the Sumerian King List states: "Enmenbaragesi, he who carried away as spoil the 'weapon' of Elam, became king and ruled 900 years."[3] Regardless of its legendary nature,[4] the story reveals the underlying mentality that the Elamites were the arch enemy of the Mesopotamians throughout the third millennium BCE.[5] As the Sumerian King List admits, after Enmenbaragesi, "Ur was smitten with arms, its kingship taken to Awan."[6] Although Sargon of Akkad (c. 2340–2284 BCE) conquered Elam, it was the Elamite invasion during the reign of Sharkalisharri (c. 2222–2198 BCE) that finally caused the collapse of the Akkadian empire and the Gutian takeover.

In the "Lamentation over the Destruction of Sumer and Ur," a Sumerian text dated to the early second millennium BCE, the Elamites are described as the enemy sent by Enlil to destroy Mesopotamia:

> Enlil brought down the Elamites, the enemy, from the highlands.
> Enlil brought down the Elamites, the enemy, from the highlands.
> Nanshe, the Noble one, was settled outside the city.
> Fire approached Ninmar in the shrine Guabba,
> Large boats were carrying off its precious metals and stones. . . .
> The province of Lagas was handed over to Elam.[7]

A similar text, the "Lamentation over the Destruction of Ur," again mentions Elamites and Subarians as destroyers of Ur.[8] The Gutians are also seen as the tool of Enlil to destroy Sumer: "On that day Enlil brought down the Guti from the mountain-land, whose coming is the Flood of Enlil, that none can withstand."[9]

The agonizing memory that the Elamites and the Gutians were "god sent" destroyers, and a deep feeling of an almost innate conflict between "our country" and "enemy country" could also be seen in other Sumerian epics from the Ur III period. These include "Enmerkar and the Lord of Aratta," "Enmerkar and Ensuhkeshanna," "The Lugalbanda Epic," and "Lugalbanda-Hurrum."[10] In these epics, as is common to many epic traditions that promote national identity,[11] the city of Uruk served as a symbol for "Mesopotamia" as opposed to the "enemy country." This is probably due to the historical position of Uruk in the effort to overthrow the Gutians and to reestablish Sumerian cultural and political hegemony. The reason for the promotion and continuous preservation thereafter of the epics by the Ur III kings, moreover, was presumably that these epics served to express national aspirations, or to boost nationalistic morale among the people. It is doubtful that they recorded any historical events.[12]

A text of the Old Babylonian period advised a prince thus:

> If he (the prince) improperly convicts a citizen of Sippar, but acquits a foreigner, Shamash, judge of heaven and earth, will set up a foreign justice in his land, where the princes and judges will not heed justice. If citizens of Nippur are brought to him for judgment, but he accepts a present and improperly convicts them, Enlil, lord of the lands, will bring a foreign army against him to slaughter his army, whose prince and chief officers will roam (his) streets like fighting-cocks.[13]

The text reveals the idea that the foreigners could be instruments of the just gods. Why foreigners and not people from other Mesopotamian cities? This is probably because of a deeply ingrained idea that foreigners were most likely those who could bring destruction to a Mesopotamian city, and whose behavior was difficult to predict, as was the wrath of the gods, as indicated by the phrase "the flood of Enlil."[14] According to the Mesopotamian idea of the nature of history, in the words of one scholar, "each succeeding dynasty was the instrument whereby the gods displaced the given incumbent. Occasionally, however, the gods might send a strange new people as a scourge,"[15] As will be mentioned below, the foreigners were often seen as demons from without, whose purpose was to destroy Mesopotamia.

In the Neo-Assyrian period, such official documents as the annals of the kings, presented a stereotyped image of foreign enemies. The enemies represent everything that was opposite to the Assyrian ideology.[16] They were seen as the antithesis of Assyria. The representation of foreigners and foreign countries, as it was influenced by this preconceived ideology, employed certain fixed literary *topoi* to describe the world beyond Assyian borders. These include descriptions concerning the natural landscape, the daily life of the foreigners, their material culture, and their sociopolitical institutions, personal behavior, and so on. As Assyria was basically a land of low plains, foreign lands were characterized by those features that are most alien to the Assyrian landscape, such as mountains, seas, marshes, and deserts. Thus people in the north are characterized as "mountaineers," people in southern Mesopotamia (the Arameans) are people who lived "in the midst of the marshes," while some of the nomadic groups are "tent dwellers" or "desert folk."[17]

In general, these qualifications of the habitat and the culture of the foreigners disclose the Assyrian ideology that enemies are fundamentally "abnormal." Moreover, abnormality is connected with moral debasement. As the royal inscriptions show, the enemies are described as people who are morally "bad" as opposed to the "good" Assyian king. They violate the oaths, are insubmissive, proud, insolent, speak words of hostility, act rebelliously, and so on. They are, in a word, the creation of an ideology that aimed at propagandistic affirmation of the justice of Assyrian kingship.[18]

In the case of Egypt, in view of the monumental nature of the illustrations on the Narmer palette, it is reasonably clear that it commemorates a basic political and historic situation of Egypt that involves military action, presumably against rival groups in the Delta that included some foreigners. Scenes of killing and displaying the corpses of the enemies are shown on the palette. As has been mentioned in the last chapter, a king victorious over his enemies became the established iconographical motif in the depiction of scenes related to Egypto-foreign relations.[19] This official ideology was not only expressed iconographically, but also in written texts. According to the royal annals recorded on the Parlemo stone, wars against the Nubians (*Nḥsyw*) and Libyans (*Ṯḥnw*) were fought during the reigns of an early dynastic king and the Fourth Dynasty king Snefru respectively. Snefru's campaign against the Nubians, although no further details are known, was said to have brought back seven thousand prisoners and two hundred thousand large and small cattle.[20]

A limited number of Old Kingdom biographical records bearing reference to Egyptian encounters with foreign people and countries provides us with a better perspective of the official image presented above. In the autobiography of Weni, a high official of the Sixth Dynasty, the expedition to the land of the Asiatics was described as the heroic annihilation of the foes and the destruction of villages and settlements:

> This army returned in safety, it had ravaged the sand-dwellers'
>   land;
> This army returned in safety, it had flattened the sand-dwellers's
>   land;
> This army returned in safety, it had sacked its strongholds;
> This army returned in safety, it had cut down its figs, its vines;
> This army returned in safety, it had thrown fire in all its
>   [mansions];
> This army returned in safety, it had slain its troops by many
>   ten-thousands;
> This army returned in safety, [it had carried] off many [troops] as
>   captives.[21]

It is useless to try to decide if this poetic expression of military success
was exaggerated or indeed true at all. The more significant point is
that this victory paean clearly demonstrates a hostile attitude toward
the people of the Syrio-Palestinian area. It was not enough to defeat
foreign troops; it was necessary to ravage their land and destroy their
crops. This hostile attitude should not be discounted on the ground
that it was expressed in a poetic way. Although one could say that the
autobiography was essentially a private document, it is also arguable
that, since the funerary establishment was as much a private as a com-
munal matter, the message contained in the autobiography would still
reflect the attitude of a wider spectrum of the Egyptian population,
admitting that this attitude was not necessarily a reflection of the reality of Egypto-foreign relations.

Another autobiography, of an expedition leader by the name
Harkhuf, also of the Sixth Dynasty, tells a rare story of the diplomatic
maneuver between Egypt and its Nubian neighbors carried out through
the cunning manipulation of Harkhuf:

> Now when the ruler of Irtjet, Setju, and Wawat (all Nubian areas)
> saw how strong and numerous the troops from Yam (another Nubian
> area) which came down with me to the residence together with the
> army that had been sent with me, this ruler escorted me, gave me
> cattle and goats, and led me on the mountain paths of Irtjet.[22]

Harkhuf used the cooperation of one Nubian tribe from Yam to induce
the submission of other Nubian tribes. The broad picture painted by
Harkhuf was that Egypt was very much respected by the Nubians. In
his own words, he was one who "brings the produce of all foreign lands
to his lord, . . . who casts the dread of Horus into the foreign lands."[23]

Just how true this claim was is difficult to evaluate. In his autobiography, Harkhuf said that he brought back to Egypt one pygmy, with limited "contributions" from the Nubians. Thus we could perhaps say that at the time Egypt was not really in control of the Nubian tribes in any substantial way. The expression "to cast the dread of Horus into the foreign lands" actually hints at the nature of Egyptian power in Nubia: it was such a distant place that only the rather empty and self-aggrandizing claim of "dread of Horus" could fullfil the Egyptian ego. A discrepancy between reality and ideal could be read between these lines.

Harkhuf's expeditions seemed to be basically peaceful, as he achieved his missions with diplomatic skills. A contemporary of his by the name of Pepinakht, on the other hand, claimed to have conducted campaigns in Nubia: "(I) slew a great number there consisting of chiefs' children and excellent commanders of guards. I brought a great number of them to the court as living prisoners."[24]

It is noteworthy, however, that Harkhuf's description of the Nubians and the land of Nubia was rather colorless and businesslike, with few personal reflections. There can be of course any number of explanations for this: the literary tradition for this kind of texts; the composer of the text probably not being Harkhuf himself; or simply Harkhuf's own personality. When compared with other biographical inscriptions of the Old Kingdom period, such as that of Weni and Pepinakht, we could sense a collective mentality of the Egyptian elite: the foreign lands, be it Nubia or Syria, were not places to cast a curious eye—the Herodotean spirit had not yet appeared. Only the letter of the boy-king Pepi II preserved in Harkhuf's biography revealed a youthful curiosity of the exotic pygmy-dancer.

The collective Egyptian animosity toward the Nubians and other foreign people is also shown by the so-called execration texts found at Giza dated as early as the Sixth Dynasty. These are small clay figurines on which were written the names of the enemies, many of them west Semitic, which were subsequently smashed as a magical act to inflict harm on the named.[25] Similar objects with the same intention are found in the Middle Kingdom period.[26] For unknown reasons, the Egyptians found it necessary to confront and to destroy certain foreign people with this extreme measure.

The Middle Kingdom official attitude toward the foreigners was announced in a hymn to King Sesostris III:

Land's protector who widens borders,
Who smites foreign countries with his crown, . . .
Whose terror strikes the Bowmen in their land,
Fear of whom smites the Nine Bows. . . .
His Majesty's tongue restrains Nubia,
His utterances make Asiatics flee.[27]

A similar attitude is expressed in a boundary stela of Sesostris III that characterizes the nature of the Nubians:

Since the Nubians listen to the word of mouth,
To answer him is to make him retreat.
Attack him, he will turn his back,
Retreat, he will start attacking.
They are not people one respects.
They are wretches, craven-hearted.[28]

The Nubians are worthless beings in this royal propaganda. Neither has the king any reservation as to his own prowess in conquering the foreigners:

I subdued lions, I captured crocodiles.
I repressed those of Wawat,
I captured the Medjai,
I made the Asiatics do the dog walk.[29]

Here the foreigners are mentioned in the same class as wild animals. This animal-foreigner equation is further demonstrated in a text designated as "The Satire of the Trades": "The courier goes into the desert, leaving his goods to his children; fearful of lions and Asiatics, he knows himself (only) when he's in Egypt."[30]

As the other side of the coin, the wretched enemies denounced in the royal propaganda could also become the most dangerous destructive force that threatens Egypt. In the didactic literature that plays on the idea of social and political disasters, foreigners are described as the agents that ruined the country, very similar to what has been seen in the Mesopotamian epics of the destruction of cities. In the "Admointion of Ipuwer," the "sage" Ipuwer announced his vision of the impending disaster: "Lo, the desert claims the land, the nomes are destroyed. Foreign bowmen have come into Egypt, . . . there are no people anywhere."[31] Whether the vision of the turbulence was historically based (and it may very well not have been so),[32] the historically true fact was the presense of the idea or the belief that the foreigners were destroyers of peaceful life. Similar expressions could also be found in the *Prophecy of Nerferty*:

> The land is bowed down in distress,
> Owing to those feeders,
> Asiatics who roam the land,
> Foes have risen in the East,
> Asiatics have come down to Egypt, . . .
> Desert flocks will drink at the river of Egypt.[33]

This image of foreigners as enemies was very much ingrained in the Egyptian mentality and expressed through both public and private literature.

The confrontations between Egypt and other parts of the Near East became a more prominent political phenomenon during the New Kingdom period. Foreigners were on the Egyptian scene constantly, and were seen not only as enemies, but sometimes also as allies and friends and partners in different situations. In terms of official attitude—that is, expressions found in royal inscriptions and figurative representations, as well as biographical texts of the officials—the foreigners, particularly those from the Syrio-Palestinian area, are as a group often referred to as ^{c}*3m ḥsi*, "the vile Asiatics." The interpretation of the adjective *ḥsi* has been the subject of debate, and it has been suggested that "vile" might not be a proper rendering of *ḥsi*. Often the meaning of "defeated" or its derivatives suit the context better, especially when it refers to a military action against foreigners.[34] There is no need to single out even the most famous texts that dealt with foreign enemies or to go over the long list of confrontations and wars the Pharaohs conducted throughout the centuries. Suffice it to say that this common usage of *ḥsi* expresses the prevailing attitude that foreigners were, or were perceived through political and theological viewpoints as, inevitably, in a defeated and downtrodden position in relation to the Egyptians. Iconographical evidence, such as bound prisoners from foreign countries, were displayed on royal monuments and temple walls all over the country. To give one example, on the funerary furniture of Tutankhamun, one of the least significant kings of the New Kingdom period in terms of military action, scenes of the slaughtering of Syrians and Nubians and captives of Nubians and Asiatics are depicted.[35] The motif of bound prisoners, usually one black and one Asiatic, trampled under the feet of the ruler, are all very familiar scenes.[36]

Unlike the relatively secured political situation of Egypt after its establishment, even long after the founding of the Shang Dynasty, different ethnic groups in and around the Central Plain were still in a state of constant confrontation with the Shang.[37] In the Shang oracle bone inscriptions foreigners, or people from other tribal groups, are often mentioned in contexts that suggest a hostile relationship with the Shang people. Records of wars fought between Shang and foreign tribes indicate that Shang was often in a defensive position.[38] At times the Shang would attack the foreign tribes, or form an alliance with neighboring tribes to subdue their mutual enemies.[39] Commemorative inscriptions on some late Shang bronze vessels also testified to military conflicts between Shang and foreign tribes.[40] As the oracle inscriptions are mostly short and factual, and their purpose being divination and not the accurate recording of history, no direct evidence concerning the Shang people's attitude toward these foreign enemies is available. One of the more elaborate inscriptions has the following words:

> The minor courtier, Se, participated in the military action, capturing (a number of) people of the tribes of Wei and Mei, and 24 men of (a certain tribe), 1570 men of the tribe of Er, one hundred . . . men of the tribe of . . . , 2 chariots, 183 shields, 50 armors, . . . arrows, . . . and sacrifice—to king Zu Yi, sacrifice Mei to king Zu Ding.[41]

From the treatment of prisoners of war, as the above passage reveals, we can at least learn something about the Shang view of "the others." We often see in the oracle bone inscriptions foreign prisoners, especially the Qiang people, sacrificed to the ancestors or deities during Shang religious ceremonies. Prisoners from other foreign tribes also met a similar fate, although with less frequency.[42] Most of the male prisoners were sacrificed. The cruelty of the act can best be demonstrated by the elaborate terminology related to human sacrifice. At least fifteen different terms of sacrifice are identified in the oracle bone inscriptions, and the ways of sacrifice include burning, drowning, beheading, or severing in half.[43] An extraordinary record has one thousand prisoners sacrificed on one occasion, as bloody a scene as one can imagine, if the record bears any truth.[44]

Archaeological finds confirm that human sacrifice was common practice during the Shang period on such occasions as dedications of buildings, offerings to gods, or royal funerals.[45] The implication, as should be clear, is that the Shang people did not have a high regard for foreigners as fellow human beings. The prisoners who were not sacrificed became household slaves or field workers.[46]

When the Shang state finally collapsed, the Zhou Dynasty, formerly a vassal of the Shang in the west, took over the Shang regime and began to expand its territory toward the east and the south.[47] Although, according to tradition, the Zhou originated from among the western barbarian tribes, they nevertheless had distinguished themselves culturally as the heir of the Shang, an agricultural people who grew grain for a living.[48] Their relationship with the barbarian tribes, once they assumed control of the Central Plain was also highly unstable. Later tradition mentioned that from the beginning of the dynasty, foreign barbarian tribes were involved in Zhou court politics and encouraged discontented vassals to rebel. These included the Quan Rong of the western region and Xu Rong (referred to in the bronze inscriptions as Eastern Yi or Southern Yi).[49] These traditions are more or less confirmed by contemporary evidence. Many bronze vessel inscriptions testified that the Zhou kings met strong opposition from tribes to the east, the south, and the north.[50]

An early Zhou inscription mentioned warfare against Guei Fang, a northern "barbarian" tribe that had appeared already in the Shang, probably located in present-day northern Shanxi and Shaanxi. The general who led the attack, a certain Yu 盂, mentioned the incident in a *ding*-cauldron thus:

It was the eighth month, after the full moon, the day was on *jiashen* [day 21] in the morning dusk, the three [officials of the] left and the three [officials of the] right and the many rulers entered to serve the wine. When it became light the king approached the Zhou temple and performed the *guo*-libation rite. The king's state guests attended. The state guests offered their travel garments and faced east.

Yu with many flags with suspended Guifang . . . entered the Southern Gate, and reported saying: "The king commanded Yu to take . . . to attack the Guifang [and shackle chiefs and take] trophies. [I] shackled three chiefs, took 4,8-2 trophies, captured 13,081 men, captured . . . horses, captured 30 chariots, captured 355 oxen and 28 sheep.[51]

Another bronze vessel, made by a general with the name Xi Jia, dated to the year 823 BCE, has the following inscription:

It was the fifth year, third month, after the waning half moon, day *gengyin*; the king for the first time went and attacked the Xianyun at Tuyu. Xi Jia followed the king, cutting off heads and manacling prisoners; the victory was without defect. The king awarded Xi Jia four horses and a colt chariot.

The King commanded Jia to regulate the taxes of the four regions of Chengzhou as far as the Southern Huai Yi. "The Huai Yi of old were our tribute money men; they ought not dare not to produce their tribute, their taxes, their presented men, and their trade-goods. They ought not dare not to come to the encampments and come to the markets. If they dare not to obey the command, then according to precedent strike and attack them. If it be the trade-goods of our many lords and hundred families, none ought not be brought to market, and they ought not dare then to send in illicit trade-goods, for then they will also be [held to] precedent.[52]

Here the northwestern barbarian tribe Xianyun and the southern barbarian Huai Yi were mentioned in one text, which indicated that relations with these foreign tribes were pressing matters for the Zhou. What is worth noticing, however, is that the inscription seems to indicate that there was a possible tributary relation between the Zhou and the Yi barbarians, at least from the Zhou point of view. Although so far there is no positive evidence to show that this relationship had existed before,[53] there is no evidence to deny what was claimed in the text. Subsequent actions against Xianyun and Eastern Yi were recorded in a number of bronze inscriptions.[54] In light of the "tributary system" that existed later in the imperial period, the so-called tributes from the barbarian countries were probably more often trade objects than gift-tributes. In any event, this text reveals an important message with regard to our understanding of Sino-barbarian relations: one should not perceive this relationship as a constant confrontation.

The view that the western Zhou had trouble with the barbarian neighbors was also revealed in some poems in the *Book of Odes* that describe the conflicts between the Zhou and the barbarians. For the fighting aristocrat-warriors the sentiments expressed in the poems are anxious and exciting:

> In the sixth month all was bustle and excitement,
> The war chariots had been made ready,
> With the four steeds, strong and eager;
> And the regular accoutrements had been placed in the carriages.
> The Xianyun were in blazing force,

And thence was the urgency.
The king had ordered the expedition,
To deliver the royal kingdom.[55]

On the other hand, the view of peasants was full of ambivalence, because war had torn families apart and obstructed farmers' work:

Let us gather the thorn-ferns, let us gather the thorn-ferns;
The thorn-ferns are now springing up.
When shall we return? When shall we return?
It will be late in the year.
Wife and husband will be separated,
Because of the Xianyun.
We shall have no leisure to rest,
Because of the Xianyun.[56]

In the "Yaodian 堯典" chapter of *Shang Shu*, or *Book of Documents*, presumably the earliest collection of political documents partly dated as early as the Western Zhou, it is mentioned that the ancient sage-emperor Shun had banished four of his worst officials to the four corners of the kingdom.[57] According to another tradition, preserved in the *Zuozhuan*, Shun had expelled the four "villains" to the four borders to "ward off evil spirits."[58] The stories imply that even the failed officials in the Chinese court could teach the barbarians the essence of civilization, presumably the Chinese way of life. The result, as it was claimed, was that the entire world became the subjects (of Shun). Although the date of "Yaodian" is disputed and probably should be assigned to the early Warring States period,[59] it could still contain some early tradition. Placed in a historical perspective, such stories tell more of the emergence of a cultural consciousness on the part of the Zhou Chinese than any historical fact of the remote era of the sage kings. Moreover, as has been pointed out above, there was a discrepancy between this subjective consciousness and the sociopolitical reality of the time.

Interactions of all kinds of magnitude between the Chinese vassal states of Zhou and the barbarians are preserved in *Zuozhuan*. Considered as a true or close-to-real record of the history of this period,[60] the *Zuozhuan* presented basically two kinds of views toward foreigners: one pacifist, the other militant.[61] The militant views took a more confrontational position and demanded the submission of the foreign tribes. This is represented by Guan Zhong's famous words: "The Rong Di are wolves, to whom no indulgence should be given; within the Xia states all are nearly related, and none should be abandoned."[62] The pacifist view, on the other hand, tried to accommodate the foreign tribes into an alliance, to maintain peace on the border. We shall return to this point later in this study.

It seems, therefore, the term for foreigner was often synonymous with "enemy." In this connection, one passage from the book of *Mencius*, the prominent Confucian thinker of the Warring States period, seems to have articulated very aptly the subtle relations between foreign enemies and the internal unification and survival of a state:

> If a prince have not about him his court families attached to the laws and worthy counselors, and if abroad there are not enemy states and foreign invasions, his state is bound to destruction.[63]

Mencius's original intention was to warn against the possible dangers that grew out of easy and wanton lifestyles during times of peace and prosperity. Foreign invasions are what stimulated people to be on guard against their moral lapse. Conversely, however, a presumed foreign enemy and rival state could become the pretext for a government to urge for internal unity, which often meant sacrifice of individual property and liberty for the sake of collective security. Mencius's insight inadvertently points to an often occurring political phenomenon that is certainly still valid even today.

Demons

Foreigners were sometimes real enemies, but this was not necessarily always so. Real enemies are oftentimes those close at home. Yet, as has been demonstrated above, there is clear evidence that distant foreigners were often treated and perceived as enemies. In more extreme cases, foreigners were equated with demons, symbols of evil.

In an article entitled "The Demonization of Foreigners and Enemies in the Ancient Orient,"[64] Volkert Haas argued that because of the two major factors that affected Mesopotamian history—namely the constant threat from the eastern mountains and the invasion of the nomadic people from the west—people in the cultural sphere of the Two Rivers developed a sense that tended to demonize foreigners and enemies. Fear of the unknown, distrust of the unfamiliar, distress over the destruction of the homeland, and dispair about the seemingly inevitable and cruel fate all contributed to the formation of a demonic "other." In the mind of the Mesopotamians, the mountain demon in the east and the storm demon in the west were the ravaging forces that from time to time devastated Mesopotamia. These could have been the personifications of wild nature, such as the storm demon of the desert "who pulverizes the land like corn," but they could also have been a metaphorical reference to the foreign enemies. Like the magicians, the demons spoke foreign languages, or were foreign gods.[65] The most popular and most feared demon in Mesopotamia, Lamashtu, was conceived as a foreigner: a Sutaen, or an Elamite.[66] This phenomenon, according to Haas, reflects an aspect of group psychology that identifies the unfamiliar and the hostile with demons and evil spirits.

One could, however, question whether the demonization of the foreigners was only the result of a group psychology that had risen from an unfamiliarity with the foreigners. It has been demonstrated that, as early as the late Neolithic period, the Mesopotamians began to establish outposts in faraway foreign lands. This was because of the fact that, due to a lack of resources, the lowland Mesopotamians had to acquire more resources from the neighboring highlands in order to survive.[67] By the second half of the fourth millennium BCE, Mesopotamia had already established complex and intensive trade networks with other parts of the Near East.[68] Thus at least the trade organizers of the Mesopotamian cities from very early on must have already had sufficient knowledge of the faraway countries and had engaged in business activities with the foreigners on a regular basis. This background is important for us to assess the attitudes toward foreigners as expressed through literary texts. When we hear the foreigners described in derogatory terms, we have good reason to consider the possibility that the Mesopotamians were not describing objective facts, but were deliberately instigating a sense of group self-identity by emphasizing a very different "other." Their descriptions are probably not the result of ignorance or fear of the unknown but, on the contrary, come from certain knowledge of the object and a desire to distort and exaggerate, for political, literary, or psychological reasons. Of course, in order for this strategy to work, a substantial number of "uninformed" people who were manipulatable, willingly or otherwise, had to be assumed.

This psychology was not peculiar to the Mesopotamians, however, for the Egyptians and the Chinese all possessed comparable attitudes. In ancient Egypt, Nubia was known as the land of magicians at least since the New Kingdom period, as evidence from this time onward suggests. In some mythological tales, the goddess Isis was called a

Nubian, and Amun was also thought to have come from Nubia.[69] This presumably is connected with Nubia's exotic position in history as well as in the imagination of the Egyptians. Indeed, this "Nubianization" of the Egyptian deities seems to be the opposite of the idea of demonizing the foreigners. Yet magical texts from the New Kingdom did mention demons with foreign names. These, however, are nearly all names derived from Semitic languages of the Syrio-Palestinian area.[70] This may still reflect the mentality shown in the earlier practice of execration texts where people from the Syrio-Palestinian area, as well as Nubia, were seen as evil opponents and were cursed. One literary text caricaturizes the Syrians thus: "The narrow pass (of Syria) is dangerous, having Shasu-Beduin concealed beneath the bushes, some of whom are of four or five cubits (from) their nose to foot and have fierce faces."[71] In the religious texts such as the *Coffin Texts*, *Book of the Dead*, and *Book of the Underworld*, numerous strange gods, spirits and monsters were vividly portrayed. One spell in the *Book of the Dead* reads: "Come thou to me, Re-Harakhte, to make me triumph over my enemies, when thou hast warded off the Disease Demons."[72] The identities of the disease demons are not known, but a magical spell against child disease has the following words:

> Run out, you Asiatic woman who come from the desert, you Negro woman who come from the wilderness! Are you a handmaid?—come in vomiting! Are you a noble woman?—come in his urine, come in the snot of his nose, come in the sweat of his body![73]

This spell betrays the idea that what is foreign often is connected with the demonic, the evil, because being foreign entails in Egyptian cosmological thinking being part of the chaotic world. Thus demons with foreign names often appear as causes of diseases. Although there might be the possible historical background that at one time epidemic spread from Syria and Palestine to Egypt,[74] the larger context of a general xenophobic attitude that blames things evil on foreign origins should be taken into consideration. Such sentiment can also be detected in a dream interpretation text, where it is said that when one dreams of an Asiatic garment upon him, it is a bad omen. It means his removal from office.[75] The rationale behind this interpretation, if it can be fathomed at all, was probably that the Asiatic garment symbolizes foreigners, downcast people without dignity. Therefore the wearing of Asiatic garments signifies one's becoming an Asiatic and consequently removal from office. Finally, in the realm of the dead, the enemies might be considered as comparable to the foreigners. In a spell in the *Book of the Dead*, the deceased says:

> O Cruel One who does this against me, begone from about Re and let Re see me. Let me go forth against my enemy and triumph over him in the Council of the gods in the presence of the great Ennead.[76]

To the deceased, in a sense, the enemies or demons that they were to encounter in the nether world were foreigners, as the realm of the dead was an a unfamiliar place, much as the foreign country outside the normal human world.

The idea that the "foreign devils" were from the edge of the civilized world also found its echo in the Chinese *Classic of the Mountains and Seas*, a text dated to the early Warring States period (fourth century BCE.), but probably reflecting concepts conceived in an earlier period. In the section entitled "The Great Wilderness," that is, barbarian territory at the edge of the known world, we find various descriptions of certain monstrous people:

> Some people are there who have bird beaks and wings and who fish in the sea.[77]
>
> In the Great Wilderness is a mountain called Great Wilderness Mountain, where the sun and the moon set. There are people here with three faces. They are the children of Zhuan Xu. They have three faces and one arm. The three-faced people do not die.[78]

These examples could have been created out of pure imagination or based on received mythological tales. Yet a number of examples demonstrate clearly the demonization of known foreign people, such as the Rong, a tribe to the west that had continual interaction with the Chinese:

> In the Great Wilderness is a mountain called Yung Fu Mountain. The Shun River enters it. There are people called Quan Rong (Dog Rong). The Yellow Emperor begot Miao Long, Miao Long begot Rong Wu, Rong Wu begot Nong Ming, Nong Ming begot White Dog. The White Dog has male and female (offsprings). They became the Dog Rong. They eat meat.[79]

Again, the southwestern minority Miao people, whoes descendants can still be found even today, were also mentioned:

> On the far side of Northwest Sea, north of the Black River, are people with wings, called Miao People. Zhuan Xu begat Huan Tou,

Huan Tou begat the Miao People. The Miao People are surnamed Xi and eat meat.[80]

The demonization of the foreigners formed in the *Classic of Mountains and Seas*, being combinations of mythological tales and imagination, however, serves no immediate political purpose. They nonetheless could be seen as betraying a deep-rooted attitude in the collective mentality of the Warring States period that was apprehensive to things unknown and exotic.

It should be made clear, though, that the monstrous peoples mentioned in the *Classic of Mountains and Seas* in general are non-confrontational with regard to China proper, in contrast to what we have seen in the *Zuozhuan* regarding the aggressiveness of Rong and Di. This is mainly because the *Classic of Mountains and Seas* was structurally a "description"—however imbued with imagination and mythologizing—of the faraway lands that had no immediate contact with China.[81]

There are in general two points in the descriptions that make these people monstrous: physical features and cultural behavior. They either have bodily features that bear animal resemblance, or behave like animals, characterized by meat eating, especially raw meat. Thus the basis for demonizing the foreigners was not entirely cultural difference such as living style, customs, and language, but also including considerations of physical features. The consideration of physical difference between the "Chinese" and the foreigners was usually not mentioned in the pre-Qin writings. As evidence from the medieval period onward indicates, physical features became an important indication for the Chinese to adopt a certain derogatory attitude toward the foreigners.[82]

Friends and Allies

It might not be surprising to learn that foreigners were often seen as enemies and demons, the products of hostile attitudes and insecurity when a people faced the unknown or the unfamiliar and were looking for excuses and targets to cope with the pressure. These attitudes are clearly cultural constructs that try to internalize and rationalize unfounded biases. Yet this could not have been the entire story. Reviewing the interaction of a people with "outsiders," or "other" peoples, one might find that in reality peaceful relationships far outweighed confrontations. The seemingly intensive animosity toward foreigners might have been confined to officially proclaimed policies and representations. The day-to-day interactions between a people and foreigners could not have been in a constantly hostile situation. In terms of real-politics, moreover, a peaceful relationship with foreigners was most of the time desirable for the political leaders. The Mesopotamian evidence concerning the attitudes toward the Amorites provides a good example. As has been shown, the Amorites were seen in Mesopotamian documents as barbaric and uncivilized nomads. In reality, though, a diplomatic relationship existed between the Ur III Dynasty and the Amorite kingdom. One text from Isin reads: "[leather products] for the envoys of the king who are going to the mountain, to the place of Šamamum, the Amorite."[83] It implies a reciprocal relationship between the two, as the envoys in the text were returning the visits of envoys sent by the Amorite king Šamamum. There is also evidence of intermarriage between Amorites and Mesopotamians.[84] The pattern here is similar to that which is found in the myth, mentioned in the last chapter, of the god Martu, who married a Mesopotamian girl, despite cetain doubts regarding his nomadic background.

The Egyptian animosity toward foreigners was also only one aspect of the relationship between Egypt and foreign lands. As Harkhuf's biography already indicated, the Nubian tribes were not really looking for confrontation as long as reasonable terms of contact with Egypt could be reached. It is also a prominent fact that already in the Old Kingdom Nubians were employed by the Egyptian government to serve as soldiers and on the police force. When Weni set out for his campaign against the Asiatics, it is said that

> when his majesty took action against the Asiatic Sand-dwellers, his majesty made an army of many tens of thousands from all of Upper Egypt: from Yebu in the south to Medenyt in the north; from Lower Egypt: from all of the Two-sides-of-the-House and from Sedjer and Khen-sedjru; and from Irtjet-Nubians, Medja-Nubians, Yam-Nubians, Wawat-Nubians, Kaau-Nubians; and from Tjemeh-Land (Libya).[85]

Here the Nubian tribesmen as well as Libyans were recruited to join the Egyptian expedition, which was impossible without a rather peaceful relationship and mutual understanding between the Egyptians and these foreigners. It also implies that linguistic barriers did not exist, or had little consequence with regard to the communication between the Egyptians and the Nubians. For another example, on the sea-going ships depicted on the walls of the causeway of Unas pyramid temple, and the pyramid temple of Sahure, we can see Syrian seamen paying hommage, presumably to the king. There must have been proper communication between the Egyptians and the Syrians, who most probably were hired laborers for the Egyptian ships.[86]

Evidence of peaceful interaction between Egyptians and foreigners can be found from time to time. The famous Beni Hasan wall painting of a group of "Asiatics" who came to Egypt, presumably to trade with the Egyptians, is revealing: the traders came in small groups, with women and children, which would indicate a very relaxed relationship between the Egyptian and the traders. The traders, moreover, were depicted as bearing their weapons, which was rather unusual, but could also be interpreted as their coming into Egypt as equals, that is, not having to have their weapons discharged as prisoners or slaves did.[87] In the *Story of Sinuhe*, the people of the Syro-Palestinian area were generally rather friendly toward Sinuhe, even welcoming him as one among them. Despite its fictional character, the story tells us that a friendly relationship between the Egyptian and the foreigner was not uncommon or extraordinary.

In terms of political alliance, it was only since the New Kingdom that international reality forced Egypt to take more practical moves in its dealings with foreign states. In the reign of Amenophis II, the rise of Mitanni forced Egypt to come to terms with it, and allowed the area of Syria to fall within the power sphere of the Mitannian kingdom.[88] In order to maintain diplomatic relationships with the Near Eastern powers, marriage alliances between the Pharaohs and foreign princesses were contracted.[89] This kind of alliance, nevertheless, was not concluded on the principle of equal status: foreign princesses were allowed to become consorts of the Egyptian king, but Egyptian princesses were not wed to foreigners. As the Babylonian king Kadashman-Enlil complains in a letter:

> [Moreover], you (Amenophis III?), my brother, when I wrote [to you] about marrying your daughter, in accordance with your practice of not gi[ving] (a daughter), [wrote to me], saying, "From time immemorial no daughter of the king of Egy[pt] is given to anyone." Why n[ot]? You are a king; you d[o] as you please. Were you to give (a daughter), who would s[ay] anything? Since I was told of this message, I wrote as follows t[o my brother], saying, "[Someone's] grown

daughters, beautiful women, must be available. Send me a beautiful woman as if she were [you]r daughter. Who is going to say, 'She is no daughter of the king!'?" But holding to your decision, you have not sent me anyone.[90]

This desperate message makes it clear that marrying the princess of another state was considered a special privilege, especially one from Egypt. This reflects the idea, at least for the ancient Egyptians and their Near Eastern neighbors, that taking women from another people as wives was a sign of dominance. Both Artatama and Shuttarna, kings of Mitanni, had been asked several times before finally giving their daughters to the Pharaoh.[91] There was, moreover, no problem of family hierachy involved. Amenophis III could therefore marry the sister of Kadashman-Enlil and still try to have the latter's daughter. As Kadashman-Enlil complains in another letter: "Here you (Amenophis III) are asking for my daughter in marriage, but my sister whom my father gave you was (already) there with you, and no one has seen her (so as to know) if now she is alive or if she is dead."[92] The same situation happened with the Mitannian marriage alliance, as Amenophis III married the sister and the daughter of Tushratta in succession.[93] It could therefore be said that not giving a daughter of a Pharaoh to a foreign prince was a sign of political arrogance.[94]

Another line of thinking about the marriage relations between Egypt and the foreign countries, however, stresses the nuances of political languages, as seen through the Amarna letters, and argues that the very fact that the king of Egypt was involved in marriage relations with other royal houses is already an admission of equal status. The foreign rulers were in fact happy to get what they wanted: to marry a daughter to the king of Egypt. Each side got what they thought was the better deal.[95] From the perspective of our present investigation, however, the attitude of the Egyptians is what we need to grasp. That attitude, of course, was one of clear Egyptian superiority: no Pharaoh's daughter was to be given away to a foreign prince. This line of thinking was just the opposite of the Chinese idea of marriage alliance. For being the father-in-law of someone else automatically raises him to a higher position, the rank of father, as the Chinese family ethics was equally honored in the political arena. By marrying a princess from the Di barbarian tribe, for example, King Hui of Zhou acknowledged his appreciation for the military support of the Di troops.[96] Here there is no doubt that the Di were the privileged party. The later history of

China shows that the Chinese court would send princesses to marry foreign rulers in order to keep a peaceful relationship, but would not accept foreign princesses as wives for a Chinese ruler.

Political treaties were another means to seal alliances, as the example of the Hittite-Egyptian peace treaty shows. The Hittite version of the treaty shows a spirit of equality by addressing both the Egyptian and the Hittite sovereigns as "the great king."[97] The Egyptian version, however, addresses the Hittite king as "the great chief of Hatti," which is a less honorific title usually applied to the Syrian and other foreign rulers.[98] It seems that the Egyptian official language could never have placed the supreme political-theological position of the Pharaoh below or even equal to any other earthly sovereign.

In the case of China, although it is clear that confrontations with foreign tribes during the Zhou Dynasty were frequent, it is also clear that not all the conflicts were destructive military actions. Sometimes inscriptions mention punitive expeditions to remind the vassal tribes to pay their tribute. Furthermore, the Zhou court also employed some "barbarian" troops in their military establishment, similar to what the Egyptians did by employing the Medja people.[99] A late tradition mentions that the Rong-barbarians were considered a faithful vassal state protecting the western frontier of Zhou—that is, before they finally rebelled, invaded and caused the downfall of western Zhou.[100]

Thus the Zhou and the barbarians were not necessarily always in a hostile relationship. This is important when considering the attitude of the Zhou toward the barbarians. They were probably more practical in dealing with the outsiders than later idealized records would have us believe. A simple model that portrays a constant antagonism between "we" and "they" is unlikely to reveal the historical reality.

From a diplomatic point of view, indeed, the Central Plain states of the Eastern Zhou period had always tried to keep a peaceful relationship with the strangers at the gate, since they had certainly learned that hostile relations could cause disasters, as in the downfall of western Zhou. As early as 721 BCE the Duke Yin of Lu held a meeting with the Rong. The Rong asked for an alliance, which was approved several months later.[101] In 570 BCE the state of Jin again made a peace treaty with the Rong. From the point of view of the Jin, to make peace with the Rong-barbarians was not that the Jin considered the Rong as having equal political or cultural status, but simply as a strategy to maintain a peaceful relationship at the border so as to concentrate military and political resources toward building a hegemony among the Central

Plain states. The advice offered to the Duke of Jin makes this point clear: "The Rong are animals. To conquer the animals but lose control of the Hua (Chinese states) is definitely not advisable."[102]

In 560 BCE, as the *Zuozhuan* reports, the state of Wu reported to its ally Jin that it had been defeated by Chu. Jin called for a meeting of a number of allied states at a place called Xiang to discuss measures to be taken against Chu on behalf of Wu. Fan Xuanzi, the Jin representative, however, accused Wu of misconduct and sent away its representative. Fan seized Wu-lou of Ju for his communication with Chu. Fan also intended to seize the leader of Rong, Ju Zhi, and accused him publicly at the meeting, to the effect that it was because the Rong had betrayed Jin that the states were not honoring the leadership of Jin. Ju Zhi replied:

> Formerly the people of Qin 秦, relying on their multitudes, were covetous of lands and drove out us Rong. Duke Hui (of Jin 晉) displayed his great kindness and considered that we Rong people were the descendants of the leaders of the Four Mountains (四嶽), and should not be abandoned entirely. He thus gave us the lands on his southern border. The territory was one where jackals dwelt and wolves howled, but we Rong extirpated the briars and thorns from it, drove away the jackals and wolves, and considered ourselves his loyal subjects who did not infringe upon his state or rebel against him. Nor to this day have we changed our allegiance.

He then goes on recounting the contribution of Rong in helping Jin to establish military power. Finally, he announced that since Jin did not trust the Rong people, he would withdraw from the meeting:

> We Rong people's food and garments are different from those of the Chinese (Hua 華) people, and we do not have diplomatic relations with the (other Chinese) states. Our language does not allow us to communicate (with the Chinese people). What harm could we have done? If we did not attend the meeting, we would have no regret.

He then sang the "Qing-sheng 青蠅" chapter of the *Book of Odes* and retired. This poem, appropriately refering to the virtue of a gentleman who honors his own promises, was used as a satire-cum-criticism directed at Fan Xuanzi, who, by accusing the Rong people, had tried to break the former alliance between Jin and Rong. Fan Xuanzi soon realized his error and asked Ju Zhi to attend the meeting, so as to fulfill the words of the poem (i.e., a gentleman does not listen to slander.)[103]

How should one understand the words of Ju Zhi as recorded by the author of *Zuozhuan*? I would consider these an imaginative reconstruction. The basic historical fact might simply be that the Jiang-Rong was excluded from attending the meeting and thus wanted to break their alliance with Jin. The author, however, reconstructed the situation by recounting the early history of the Jiang-Rong tribe, their relationship with the Qin and the Jin states. The entire speech, therefore, reflects the attitude of a Chinese author in trying to account for the Rong's action. It is a sympathetic view of the situation of the Rong tribe, yet the main thrust of the speech was a criticism of Fan Xuanzi's decision to exclude the Rong from participating in political affairs that were mainly among the "Chinese states." This act of exclusion, in fact, was not in conformity with the policy of Jin—that is, the 570 BCE peace treaty mentioned above—that the Rong Di barbarians should be kept at the border as allies.

The most interesting aspect of the entire story, though, is Ju Zhi's way of discourse, as he was represented as a well-cultured "Chinese diplomat." Hence, ironically, while he said that "We Rong people's food and garments are different from those of the Chinese (Hua) people, . . . our language does not allow us to communicate (with the Chinese people)," he was eloquent enough to state his case and to recite a poem from the *Book of Odes*, as was the usual diplomatic etiquette of the day, to make his point. We of course do not know if Ju Zhi was such a character in reality, but we can be certain that the author of *Zuozhuan* chose to represent this leader of the Rong tribe as a totally Sinicized person. The attitude reflected here is in sharp contrast with the evidence containted in the *Zuozhuan* and other sources that did not even consider the foreign "barbarians" as human beings, even if metaphorically.[104] Can we say that the author displayed a more sophisticated appreciation of foreign people and their culture? In view of the predominant perception of barbarians as uncultured tribes that should be subdued to serve the Chinese states, one is tempted to see this as a rather "enlightened" or "egalitarian" view. However, Ju Zhi's speech should perhaps better be understood as reflecting firstly the author's criticism against Jin Xuanzi, and only secondly a sympathetic view of the Rong. This sympathy was expressed not through an inside understanding of the feelings and cultural background of the Rong people, but by conceptually appropriating the Rong to act like the Chinese. Thus in the eyes of the Chinese, the Rong tribes' participation in certain battles involving interstates strife was a sign of submission of the

Rong as a vassal to the Chinese. This tells us nothing concerning the attitudes and considerations of the Rong tribes themselves: whether they fought for other reasons, or if they really felt compelled to act as "loyal subjects" to the Chinese state.

Given all the above considerations, one could still say that the author has demonstrated a keen reflective mind. For the author, who was of course a Chinese, expressed through the mouth of a "barbarian" the idea that cultural values are relative; thus the Chinese way of life was not the only way. The author also demonstrated a remarkable knowledge of the history of some of the barbarians, which shows a considerable interest in the non-Chinese peoples.[105] Here one is reminded of similar cultural psychology that prompted the comments of Ephoros about the Scythicans as exemplary, law-abiding people. It is obvious, to sum up, that the Rong were not always in a confrontational position with the Central States, and that they could be friends and allies of the Chinese.

The author of *Zuozhuan* was also capable of making fair judgments on the causes of disputes and conflicts between the Chinese and the barbarians, as he sometimes either wrote down the details of the events, leaving no doubt about who caused the conflict, or used the character *fa* 伐—"to punish by military action"—usually reserved for the military actions of the Shang-Zhou kings—to denote the military actions of the barbarians against the Chinese.[106] In those cases, therefore, it was actually the Chinese who were seen as the guilty party. The author of *Zuozhuan*, of course, was strongly judgmental not only regarding the difference between what was civilized and what was barbarian, but also regarding those states that did not live up to the moral standard of the ideal Zhou institutions. One could also say that, by asserting the idea of the relativity of cultural values and some of the demerits of the Chinese states, the author demonstrated strong confidence in the cultural values represented by Zhou court etiquette. The demerits of some of the Chinese did not imply the weakness of Chinese cultural values, but only as indications of the fact that some did not conform or live up to this value.

The interaction between the Chinese and the barbarians during the Spring and Autumn period was so intense, in fact, that the cultural barriers gradually melted away.[107] Intermarriages between Chinese princes and barbarian princesses were common. The mother of the famous Duke Wen of Jin, Chong Er, for example, was from the Rong tribe. This did not prevent him from becoming one of the great defenders of Chinese culture—symbolized by the Zhou court. At one time, the king of Zhou even married a daughter of a Di chieftain in order to repay military support from the Di.[108] Conversely, the sister of Duke Jing of Jin was married to the king of Rong.[109] Thus the marriage relationship between the Chinese and the Rong-di barbarians was not one directional. This and the previous story indicate that, despite the subjective view that Chinese were very different from the barbarians, there might not be a clear-cut boundary between the two parties, either culturally, liguistically, or geopolitically. Moreover, various legends about the ancestors of the barbarians being of the same descent as the Chinese also began to circulate at this time.[110] The words of Ju Zhi, for example, indicate that the "Rong people were the descendants of the leaders of the Four Mountains"; that is, they were the offsprings of an ancient Chinese royal house. The records in the *Classic of Mountains and Seas*, as we have also seen above, provide more evidence of this effort to trace the origins of the barbarian tribes to an ancestor common to the Chinese. These represented efforts to redraw boundaries between the Chinese and the barbarians. By creating a historical root that originated from the legendary Chinese ancestors, many of the barbarians could be legitimately included into the Chinese cultural sphere. The questions are, who created the legends, and why? Our evidence is of course mainly reflections of the Chinese point of view. It could have been provided to establish a legitimate cause for territorial expansion: since the barbarian tribes had the same origin as the Chinese, their being incorporated into the Chinese state would have been natural. One could also argue that perhaps these legends were created by the foreign tribes themselves in order to construct a relationship with the Chinese states. This presupposes that these foreign people already knew and absorbed much of the Chinese tradition, so that it would be less awkward for them to claim that they were culturally related to the Chinese.[111]

Finally, when the barbarian tribes, formerly scattered among and around the various Chinese states, were gradually absorbed and conquered by the Chinese, a new kind of cultural consciousness also began to appear. Instead of insisting on the barbarians' "animal" nature, this new attitude can be summarized in the idea that the distinction between Chinese and barbarian was based only on cultural differences. When the barbarians entered China (the Central Plain), as long as they accepted the Chinese way of life, they were to be considered as Chinese. This idea has indeed found its origin in the speech of the Rong chieftain Ju Zhi recorded in the *Zuozhuan*. The opposite situation, however, was not true. As we shall discuss later, except for a very few instances, it was unthinkable or at least unmentionable that the Chinese could adopt any barbarian culture.

From Apprehension to Appreciation

Although foreigners might be portrayed as hostile, foreign goods and objects were often highly praised and coveted, as the idea of foreignness also suggests exotic places and faraway paradise. Moreover, those who have access to foreign things are often those in power. Thus the possession of foreign things or even the demonstration of an appreciation of foreignness can be seen as a prestigious symbol of high social status.[112] The most interesting problem, however, is to observe if and when the appreciation of material objects, for their exotic and therefore "precious" nature, could be transformed, or elevated, to an appreciation of foreign ideas, or even foreign culture and a foreign way of life in general. Here we shall defer discussion of foreign objects and goods to the next chapter and concentrate on the appreciation of foreign culture.

Ancient Mesopotamian culture thrived on imported materials. An undeniable fact, however, is that there was a gap between the appreciation of foreign goods and interest in foreign culture. We can hardly find any reflection, in written form at least, on the nature of foreign culture in a positive manner.

It is exceptional, therefore, that one finds a number of remarks in the Neo-Assyrian royal inscriptions that could be considered to have a more objective interest in the character and lifestyles of the foreigners. One example is found in the description of the eighth campaign of Sargon II concerning horse training in Urartu:

> The people who dwell in this district have no equal in the whole country of Urartu for (their) ability in riding horses. Every year they take the young choice foals, native to his vast land, which they raise for his royal regiment. Until the horses are taken to the district of Subi—which the people of Urartu call the country of the Manneans—and their test performance can be observed, one sits upon their backs (i.e., rides the horses), and they are not taught how to advance, to turn around and go back, to be apt to battle: they are not assigned to teams.[113]

Another description concerns the irrigation system in the city of Ulhu in Urartu:

> Following his inspiration, Ursa, their king and lord, . . . revealed the water-outlets. He dug a main ditch which carried flowing waters [and . . . ; waters] of abundance he caused to flow like the Euphrates. Countless ditches he led out from its interior [and . . .] he irrigated the fields.[114]

This and similar descriptions of the prosperous condition of the country of Urartu seem to present a positive view of the enemy. Yet all these are eventually to be destroyed by the Assyrian army. Are we to consider this "positive" view as only a prelude to Assyrian conquest,[115] or to accept it as isolated case where the Assyrian king or whoever composed the annals was genuinely impressed by what he had seen or heard? In any case, occasional praise of the enemies' prosperity, such as that which the Annal of Ashurbanipal made concerning the palace of Susa,[116] could only enhance the prestige of the Assyrian king, for all these were for him to conquer.

On the whole, most of these records that show interests in foreign culture are sporadic and not meant to construct a coherent view or description of the "others." Instead, they serve as mirror reflections of the Assyrian self-image as a hegemonic and unique power over the rest of the world.

The Egyptians of the Old Kingdom period, on the other hand, recognized and depicted the foreigners in their art in a way that is far more elaborate than that produced by the Mesopotamians and the Chinese. What is uncertain for us is whether or not this recognition of the differences of physical features between the Egyptian and the foreigners prompted the Egyptians to explore further the cultural difference between Egypt and the foreigners. For example, except for the existence of some interpreters, there is little evidence to suggest that, before the Middle Kingdom, the Egyptians in general were interested in learning foreign languages.[117] This of course shows their more alienated attitude toward foreigners. It is true that, because of their unique interest in graphic representations, the Egyptians were able to delineate clearly the physical features of the foreign peoples. A closer look at the principle and structure of the graphic representations reveals, however, that the foreigners were depicted in traditional Egyptian mode and posture, which is to say, the Egyptians had employed their own frame of reference to represent the foreigners, so that they became part of the

Egyptian world. In this world, foreigners were either seen as enemies to be destroyed or as one among the servants of the Egyptians. In the latter case, they were given Egyptian names and represented just like their Egyptian counterparts. It has to be pointed out, nonetheless, that these are highly stereotyped representations, which did not have to conform to reality. The Egyptians are not necessarily hostile to all foreigners, and certainly many foreigners received fair treatment living in Egypt, as exemplified by the Nubian mercenaries who owned their own tombs and proudly proclaimed their status as good citizens in Egypt.[118] On the other hand, representations of Egyptianized Nubians are not direct evidence of an understanding of Nubian culture on the part of the Egyptians.

Another point worth mentioning is that in addition to depicting the physical features of the foreigners with great precision, the Egyptians also distinguish "us" and "others" in terms of cultural difference. We can observe that in certain documents of the Middle Kingdom period, cultural differences are emphasized as what separated Egyptians and foreigners. In "The Instruction Addressed to King Merikare," the author depicts the Palestinian area thus:

> Lo, the miserable Asiatic,
> He is wretched because of the place he's in:
> Short of water, bare of wood,
> Its paths are many and painful because of mountains.
> He does not dwell in one place,
> Food propels his legs,
> He fights since the time of Hours,
> Not conquering nor being conquered,
> He does not announce the day of combat,
> Like a thief who darts about a group.[119]

The author demonstrates a certain familiarity with the living environment and cultural behavior of the people of Palestine. It seems that these words betray an official, detached, unsympathetic view of the foreigners that was a continuation of the attitude we observe already in the Old Kingdom period. Yet it is also during the Middle Kingdom that evidence for a new sense of appreciation of foreign ways of life appeared in some literary works.

In the "Story of Sinuhe," the country of Yaa (Syria) and Sinuhe's experience living there were described in a serene and pleasant tone:

> Figs were in it (i.e., Yaa) and grapes. It had more wine than water. Abundant was its honey, plentiful its oil. All kinds of fruit were on its trees. Barley was there and emmer, and no end of cattle of all kinds.[120]

This was in stark contrast with what was found in "The Instruction Addressed to King Merikare," where, perhaps owing to its "royal," therefore official, nature, the Asiatic living condition was described with much disdain. A sympathetic appreciation of foreigners and their culture was clearly expressed in *The Story of Sinuhe*. There is of course no sure way to assess the extent of this attitude. Yet judging from the popularity that *The Story of Sinuhe* enjoyed in the later period, this kind of appreciation must have been accepted and circulated to some extent in Egyptian society.[121] A similar kind of appreciation of a foreign country can be found in the "Story of the Shipwrecked Sailor." In a fairytale-like way, the foreign country, an island in the midst of the sea, was described as a rather pleasant place to be: "There is nothing that is not in it; it is full of all good things." Even the snake monster-god, the Lord of Punt, was very friendly and helpful.[122]

The idea that a foreign deity could be friendly, as shown in the "Story of the Shipwrecked Sailor," can also be seen in the worshiping of foreign deities in foreign lands by the Egyptians. A report written by an Egyptian garrison scribe at Gaza, dated to the Nineteenth Dynasty, has the following words: "A further communication to my [lord: The offerings that you sent for] the festival of Anath of Gaza have all arrived, and I received your(?) [. . .] for the goddess."[123]

Sinuhe, to be sure, finally abandoned his possessions in the foreign land and sought for a more blessed old age and proper burial back in Egypt, therefore reassuring his readers that the Egyptian way of life was still more desirable than that of the Asiatics. Thus at one point the king says to Sinuhe: "It is no small matter that your corpse will be interred without being ascorted by Bowmen."[124] Sinuhe's final comment of his foreign experience was also indicative:

> Years were removed from my body. I was shaved; my hair was combed. Thus was my squalor returned to the foreign land, my dress to the Sand farers. I was clothed in fine linen; I was anointed with fine oil. I slept on a bed. I had returned the sand to those who dwell in it, the tree-oil to those who grease themselves with it.[125]

In other literary works of the same period, such as "The Prophecy of Nerferty" and "The Admonition of Ipuwer," people from the outside are still seen as the origin of trouble in Egypt:

All happiness has vanished, the land is bowed down in distress, owing
to those feeders, Asiatics who roam the land. Foes have risen in the
East, Asiatics have come down to Egypt.[126]

Lo, the desert claims the land, the nomes are destroyed, foreign
bowmen have come into Egypt.[127]

Despite the fictional nature of these works, the impression of the foreigners as troublemakers is indicative of a general attitude. Before the
New Kingdom, therefore, the view that Egypt was the only civilized
place in the world and that the Egyptian lifestyle was the only sensible
one guaranteed by Maat, while that of the foreigners was the equivalent
of chaos, still loomed large in many aspects of Egyptian mentality.[128]

    Evidence for Egyptian contact with foreign countries increased
dramatically during the New Kingdom. Foreigners, foreign languages,
and even foreign deities entered into Egyptian society on a scale un-
paralleled in the previous periods.[129] War and diplomatic correspon-
dences also forced Egypt to recognize the outside world in a more or
less egalitarian spirit. This is particularly obvious in a hymn to Aten:

O Sole God beside whom there is none!
You made the earth as you wished, you alone,
All peoples, herds, and flocks:
All upon earth that walk on legs,
All on high that fly on wings,
The lands of Khor and Kush, the land of Egypt,
You set every man in his place.[130]

Here Egypt was treated on the same terms as the foreign countries.
This of course may be seen as an exception, because the Aten worship
of Amenophis IV Akhenaten was the worship of a universal god.[131]
Nevertheless, the sense of equality was there. One can also cite the
Hittite marriage stela of Ramesses II, which states that the Egyptians
mingled with the Hittites in harmony.[132] This kind of evidence, however,
is still quite rare among official documents that are represented by the
heroic Ramesses II in the Battle of Kadesh, or the victorious Ramesses
III against the Sea People.[133] From the official Egyptian perspective, the
wars against the foreigners, no matter where they were fought or who
had taken the initiative to attack, were always "righteous" wars against
foreign invasions or rebellions. The foreigners, not surprisingly, were
variously described as or compared to crocodiles, lions, dogs, mice,
lizards, and the like. When they became prisoners, they were likened
to netted birds, or branded cattle.[134]

It was only with the "Report of Wenamon" that a new height of more objective and sophisticated description of a foreign culture was finally reached. This text, probably a literary rendering of a true story, provides us with an amazingly detailed and vivid view of the people and culture of the Syrio-Palestinian area at the end of the Egyptian New Kingdom period, around 1100 BCE. As an envoy of Amon of Thebes, Wenamon's mission was to fetch wood from Lebanon for the bark of Amon, and his presumably factual report was preserved in a single papyrus.[135] What interests us most is the section on the confrontation between Wenamon and the ruler of Byblos, which demonstrates a detailed and sympathetic understanding of the feelings of the people of Byblos. In a forceful pronouncement that defies Egyptian hegemony, the prince of Byblos said to Wenamon: "I am not your servant, nor am I the servant of him who sent you."[136] Although Wenamon argued for Amon's universal dominance, it is clear that the autonomous status of the prince of Byblos was fully appreciated. Before Wenamon left Byblos, the prince again demonstrated an upright character by forbidding the Tjeker people to harm him before eventually sending him off. Such a positive description of a foreign leader was almost inconceivable in official Egyptian documents.

It is illuminating that this new height of cultural consciousness, wherein the culture and history of the foreign countries were handled with respect, and wherein Egypt was not seen as the sole and uncontested master of the international community, only realized itself at a time when the political power of Egypt had begun to eclipse. Wenamon lived at the end of the Twentieth Dynasty and the beginning of the Twenty-first Dynasty, when Egypt was internally divided into two parts, the southern part being under the sway of the High Priest of Amon.[137] The days of Egyptian supremacy in Syrio-Palestine were gone, and Wenamon's report, though one of its kind, can be seen as an appropriate reminder of this fact.

During the Eastern Zhou or the Spring and Autumn period (c. 722–481 BCE), although the Zhou Dynasty was not as strong a political power as the Egyptian New Kingdom, its nominal position as the overlord of the Central Plain states still gave the Zhou king a high prestiege, and maintained a culturally superior attitude in relation to the "barbarians." In the period that followed the Spring and Autumn period, usually called the Warring States period (c. 403–221 BCE), the Zhou Dynasty was practically stripped of any political significance, China was divided among several strong kingdoms, while smaller states as well as barbarian tribes found it increasingly difficult to survive. Among the abundance of documents from this period, two examples concerning the Chinese attitude toward foreign culture may be singled out for discussion. One is the adoption of barbarian style of clothes and mounted archery by King Wuling of the state of Zhao (c. 313 BCE). This is because of King Wuling's desire to build a strong army to defend his country, and it was the barbarian style of mounted archery that was considered most effective. This idea was criticized by the king's advisors as an act of abandoning the "Chinese" tradition. But the king, determined to develop a strong military state, overruled his advisors and went ahead with his plan.[138] It was therefore a reverse of the Zhou court value and what the Confucian scholars had taught. This was not using Chinese culture to change barbarian culture, but on the contrary, adopting barbarian culture for survival's sake. It demonstrated that at this time it was still possibile for a ruler to follow a practical and nonideological sociopolitical course, and that Confucianism was not yet the incontestable norm. Another example is found in the book of *Mozi*, founder of a school of thought considered a major rival to the Confucians. In a discussion of burial customs, *Mozi* mentioned that some people of the west disposed of the body of their dead by crema-tion, believing that this was a filial act which could help the dead to ascend to heaven.[139] It is implied that the Chinese or Confucian way of rich burial was no more justified then the customs of these barbar-ians. Mozi's words showed a dash of modern anthropological insight in viewing culture as only a style of living among a group of people.

By the time of the late Warring States period, the "barbarians" of the Spring and Autumn period had already been mostly absorbed into the Chinese cultural sphere, or pushed to the nomadic area further inland to the west and northwest.[140] Instead, some new barbarians coming from the northwest—the Xiongnu—posed a major threat to the existence of the Chinese State. The new situation demanded some new strategies and attitudes from the Chinese statesmen in dealing with the problems. As this situation is in itself an enormous and often discussed subject, we shall be content in giving some basic reference and leave further discussion to another occasion.[141]

The above discussion of the relationships and attitudes toward foreigners reveals that, in different ways, evidence of a sympathetic understanding of foreign culture can be found in all three ancient civi-lizations. In Egypt, the abundance of private documents provides us with a unique opportunity to gaze into the mentality of certain writers who were obviously familiar with foreigners and foreign countries, perhaps through extensive traveling, and had developed an appreciation of foreign culture. At the same time, official representations of conquered, downtrodden foreigners remain unchanged even down to the Roman era. This official view can only represent the notion that, for political decorum as well as for theological self-fulfilling prophecy, there could only be one "correct" or "righteous" way of life—the Egyptian way. In order for this to be true, all related to the "non-Egyptian" way of life must be relegated to falsehood and injustice.

The Chinese material was mainly the product of a culturally highly self-conscious, intellectual-elite class. The examples we have seen show that, either for or against establishing a fair relationship with the barbarians, the intellectual-elites were the major forces in shaping the attitudes toward foreigners. The reality, it must be stressed, was that the Chinese political leaders did not reject communications and even marriage alliances with the "barbarians." Thus the problem of superiority of China verses Rong-di did not seem to be a paramount problem for the political elites, who might have different considerations on *realpolitik* than what the intellectual-elites had in mind.[142] The establishment of Confucianism as state ideology since the Han Dynasty, however, practically stopped any debate or critical thought about the assumption that Chinese culture was superior in comparison with any foreign people.

The Mesopotamian material concerning attitudes toward foreigners can be described as mainly official and propagandistic in nature, and foreigners were seen mostly in a disfavored way, except in cases where foreign royalty was involved. Occasional expressions of appreciation for foreign ways of life, however, indicate a possibility that, behind the official ideology, there could have existed some balanced attitude among the people in their daily life. Indeed, the day-to-day contacts between different peoples even in the ancient world might have been much more frequent than we suppose. The reality, or at least the other side of the story, concerning people's attitudes toward foreigners might therefore be gleaned from an investigation into the fate of foreigners inside a culture, as I will attempt to do in the next chapter.

5

Foreigners Within

Its (i.e., the temple) work house is filled with male and female slaves and with children of the princes of every foreign country that his majesty despoiled. Its store rooms [contain] goods that cannot be counted. It is surrounded by Syrian settlements, inhabited by the children of the princes.
　　　　　　　　　　—Stela of Amenophis III, c. 1410–1372 BCE

Social Positions

Textual and graphical evidence, as has been presented in the last three chapters, provided us with views of foreigners: their characteristics, their relationship with Egypt, China, and Mesopotamia, as enemies, friends, or allies. Yet these textual and graphical evidence, preserved on particular media with a limited spectrum of representation, run the risk of providing filtered and distorted messages. Any mentioning of foreigners, whether with a positive or with a confrontational attitude, has a great chance of representing only a particular, therefore partial, view of the reality. While keeping this in mind, it is time to investigate some evidence that were originally not consciously meant to provide any view of the foreigners but nonetheless could shed some light on people's attitudes towards them. We start by examining the social positions of foreigners, for these were the manifestations of the treatment and reaction that they received in a host country, and such treatment would inevitably have reflected the attitudes of the host people.

To begin to investigate this issue, however, we encounter a problem with the material at our disposal: there was no systematic evidence concerning the status of foreigners in any of the ancient civilizations.

In Mesopotamia, despite the prominent legal tradition, no extant legislative text can inform us of the condition of foreigners. Names of foreigners are indeed numerous, yet besides the dates and places where they were found, we know almost nothing of their juridical status.[1] In ancient China, towards the Warring States period and later, idealized Confucian works constructed a concentric image of the world, with foreign lands and peoples occupying the outer circle and with China in the center. Consequently there was no regular place for foreigners inside China proper. What follows, therefore, is necessarily an incomplete treatment of this issue.

One of the main sources of foreigners residing in ancient Mesopotamia was prisoners of war. The Mesopotamians treated their war prisoners in ways moderns would inevitably see as cruel: not only were they bound with ropes and put in neck stocks when captured and brought back for public display,[2] there is evidence that prisoners of war were blinded and made to do such manual work as grain grinding or water fetching.[3] It has been argued, however, that, mostly due to economic and considerations of upkeep, in early Mesopotamia prisoners of war in general were not made into full slaves but were settled on land, placed in the service of the temples, or employed as the king's bodyguards, mercenaries, or labor force.[4] Thus the status of prisoners of war, when settled in the country, was not that of slaves. This seems true also in the Old Babylonian period. In the city of Sippar, among the many foreign slaves bought from Subartu, an area roughly from the borders of Elam to northwest Syria, only a small number of slaves seem to have been prisoners of war.[5] One should not forget, of course, that early in the history of Mesopotamia slaves were brought from the foreign lands, forming the lowest stratum of society.

Another aspect of the fate of foreigners in Mesopotamia can be illustrated by a group of foreigners active in the Third Dynasty of Ur, the Amorites. As has been mentioned in the previous chapters, the term "Amorite" was almost synonymous with "barbarian" in the literary works. They were thought to be "uncultured" nomadic people, constantly pushing at the frontiers of Mesopotamia. Yet in the economic archives, the Amorites appear to be "as urbane as the bureaucratic organization to which we owe the record of their existence."[6] Evidence shows that Amorites were settled in Mesopotamia and acquired various professions, without any obvious hindrance. Examples of their professions include "envoy of the king," "mayor," "bodyguard," "soldiers," "conveyors," "lamenter," "priest," "brewer," "chief of the weavers," "farmer," "fowler," and so forth.[7] These professions clearly indicate that they were very much assimilated into Mesopotamian life and culture. Their social positions and the treatment they received, therefore, were presumably not much different from those of the native Mesopotamians. The indication of a rather egalitarian social status enjoyed by the Amorites could also be established by evidence of intermarriage between Amorite men and Mesopotamian women. Moreover, druing the Ur III Dynasty, no Amorites, or at least people with Amorite names, are so far found listed as slaves, which is another indication of the social status of the Amorites in Mesopotamia.[8] However, because they were still designated as Amorites, some scholars believe that they probably formed some more or less closed social groups.[9] The culmination of the Amorite infiltration into Mesopotamia was the establishment of the Babylonian dynasty. This would be as high as any group of "foreigners" could climb up the social ladder. We see a similar situation with the rise of the Libyan dynasties in post–New Kingdom Egypt.

A special feature of Mesopotamian mentality with regard to foreigners can perhaps be shown in the case of the Kassite experience. It is certain that the Kassites were a distinctive people both in the language they used and in their religious traditions. Yet their rule of four hundred years does not seem to have raised any opposition or apprehension. There is, for example, little evidence of hostility toward the Kassite kings. The Kassite rule was perceived, from what little textual evidence was preserved, as a completely legitimate regime.[10] This is comparable with the Amorite Dynasty of Babylon. The curious fact that they did not leave much trace of their own culture while in Mesopotamia inevitably reminds one of the case of the Hyksos in Egypt.

During the Neo-Assyrian period, when textual evidence became once more relatively abundant, we can trace the position of foreigners in Mesopotamia again. Due to mass deportations and the immigration of the surrounding areas, foreigners became a prominent feature in Mesopotamian society.[11] These included the deported, slaves, fugitives, merchants, and seasonal workers. The fate of the deported was not too cheerful, as high mortality, especially among the children and the young, lack of proper nutrition, and illnesses, often plagued them. However, as it was possible for deported men to own slaves, their social position was at least higher than that of slaves.[12]

The Assyrian imperial attitude toward foreigners was to see all deportees as Assyrians, yet there is evidence showing that for the "native" Assyrians, these deportees were still seen unfavorably.[13] Here official ideology was to try to incorporate a massive new population into the country, while the natives tended to view the newcomers as intruders. It could not be said, nonetheless, that the official ideology toward foreigners or foreign countries had changed from an antagonistic attitude to a more benign one, since the deportees were the result of Assyrian military victories. Their incorporation into Assyrian society was a practical means to consolidate the political and social harmony of Assyria. One scholar describes the Assyrian attitude toward the foreigners and foreign countries as "reasonably interested and knowledgeable. . . . (A)n Assyrian was reluctant to have a foreigner as a son-in-law, but he was willing to learn from him and tolerate him. Indeed, Assyrians could afford to tolerate foreigners, since they ruled most of those they knew."[14]

In this regard, the Assyrian state was gradually transformed by the newcomers, especially the Arameans. For example, the Arameans were identified as occupying various sectors in Assyrian society. They could serve as high officials in the civil government or as military commanders in the army. A bilingual text shows that an Aramaic leader of the Assyrian province of Guzana, while governor in the Assyrian system, was allowed to call himself king in the Aramaic version of the text.[15] This is a sign of the close symbiosis of the Assyrian and the Aramean people. Thus despite the fact that hostile attitude toward the Arameans was often expressed in Assyiran royal inscriptions, in reality the Assyrians had adopted a more lenient and practical strategy. Most significant, as evidence of the expansion and growing importance of the Aramaic people, the Aramaic language gradually gained the status of being the language of diplomacy and administration alongside of, or instead of, Akkadian.[16] Aramaic influence on Assyrian court life can be seen in the use of court prophecy as well as the loyalty oath that stipulated the political relations between Assyria and its vassals. It later expanded into other areas of relations such as that between the sovereign and his subjects.[17]

Despite the Aramean experience, the fact that many foreigners in Assyria were known by their gentilics alone (the Babylonian, the Arab), rather than by real personal names shows that foreigners were still seen as a separate social class. By inference, their social position could not have been the same as that of the Assyrians. An Egyptian living in Assyria, as one example suggests, could not find a wife in the normal way but had to buy a bride.[18] On the other hand, many foreigners, although still referred to as, for example, "the Aramean," nevertheless bore Assyrian names, indicating that they were in the process of being assimilated into Assyrian society. On the whole, the complex ethnic situation in Assyria can be summarized by the following statement:

> Politically the Assyrian empire was indeed Assyrian, linguistically it was largely Aramaic, but culturally and racially it was a complete mixture. In the beginning there were Hurrians, Assyrians, the descendants of Amorites, Kassites and Arameans; and by the end of the empire it was enriched by Arabs, Medes and Egyptians, as well as a motley sprinkling of Anatolians and Levantines.[19]

It has also been argued that the Assyrian kings, especially Esarhaddon, instead of using brute force, implemented a diplomatic, peaceful strategy to control the empire and tried to establish the image of a single "nation," combining both Assyria and Babylonia.[20] All these, however, should not obliterate the fact that, as royal propaganda, foreigners were most often identified as enemies in the Assyrian palace reliefs. Various scenes showing the captivity and slaughtering (beheading or flaying) of foreign enemies were among the favorite themes of the Assyrian kings.[21]

For Babylonia during the first millennium BCE, especially after the eighth century, the ethnic composition was even more complicated. The population consists of two principle groups. One is the Babylonian "native" stock, which is an amalgam of descendants of the ancient Sumerian and Akkadian people, plus the Amorites and Kassites, who by this time had already been assimilated into the local culture. The other is composed of more recent arrivals, including Arameans and Chaldeans.[22] Among the Arameans and Chaldeans themselves, many subgroups existed, some living in cities and towns, some occupying the countryside.[23] Many Aramean tribes were still semi-independent units that were not fully integrated into Babylonian society, although there was no apparent anti-Aramean sentiments on the part of other Babylonians.

Corresponding to the complex ethnic composition of society throughout history, then, the Mesopotamian evidence reveals a variety of different situations regarding the social position of the foreigners. This complex situation cannot be said to have existed in Egypt, where the ethnic mixture was never as extensive. On the other hand, throughout its long history Egypt had not only received numerous foreigners but also experienced foreign rulership on a number of occasions. As early as King Snefru of the Fourth Dynasty, royal annals recorded on the Palermo Stone mentions the capturing of seven thousand Nubians during a campaign to the south.[24] Presumably they were brought back to Egypt and employed as household servants or construction laborers. There is of course no way to acertain the truthfulness of this record. The implication, however, seems to be that foreigners could have been a visible element in Egyptian society even as early as the Old Kingdom.[25]

It has been suggested that institutionalized slavery gradually came into existence during the latter part of the Old Kingdom. The argument involves the reading of the meaning of "slavery" into the word *b3k*, to reduce to servitude, as it appeared in several biographical texts of the Sixth Dynasty period: "I have never reduced anyone to servitude (*b3k*)," or "I have never reduced one of your daughters to servitude."[26] However, the term often translated as "slave" was m *ḥm*.[27] During the Old Kingdom, *ḥm* was often used in compound nouns, most often *ḥm-nṯr*, god's servant, or priest. An expression *ḥm-nsw*, servant of the king, came to acquire the meaning of "slave" during the Middle Kingdom period.[28]

A papyrus from the late Middle Kingdom period contains the names of household slaves/servants (*ḥmw-nsw*) of a noble family.[29] Among the 79 names, 45 could be identified as "Asiatics (*ʿ3mw, ʿ3mwt*)." The majority of these foreigners were females working in the weaving room. Judging from the names of some children found in the list, the second generation of these foreign slaves were still slaves, although they could have already been Egyptianized to a great extent, since they adopted Egyptian names. The fact that they could be bought and sold makes it certain that their status could legitimately be called "slave."[30] This is evinced by a Middle Kingdom biographical text:

> The men at the service of my father, Mentuhotep, were born at home, the property of my father and mother. My men also come from the property of my father and mother, and apart from those who belong to me, there are others I have bought with my own means.[31]

As a form of property, slaves could be given to anyone at the master's will. A papyrus document from El-Lahun demonstrates this point:

> I am making this will for my wife. . . . I am giving her the four Asiatics whom my brother, the seal-bearer of the director of works, Ankhreni, gave to me.[32]

Figure 5.1. Nubian serving as household servant in Egypt, after Junker, 1929–55; vol. 2, 194, pl. XVI.

It has been suggested that slaves of foreign origin were treated the same as Egyptian slaves, as they could possess properties, and it was also possible for them to be granted freedom through various means.[33] In the course of time, especially since the New Kingdom, the status of slave (ḥm) was accorded only to foreigners, while Egyptians were referred to as "servants (b3kw)."[34]

Even if the phenomenon of slavery in Egypt is not entirely clear for modern researchers, one can still ask the question: How were foreign slaves/servants treated in Egypt? The above discussions only provide a view from legal and economic perspectives. Lack of evidence prevents us from learning more of their life, though imaginably not a happy lot, and, for that matter, not much different from slaves of Egyptian origin. However, not all the foreigners who came to Egypt were slaves. Already in the early Old Kingdom period Nubians were known to have lived in Egypt. A tomb relief showing a seated man with characteristic Nubian hairstyle and armbands indicates that people of Nubian origin could establish themselves in Egypt and had the means to acquire a typical Egyptian funeral.[35] That he possessed a tomb suggested that he had also achieved a certain social status. It is clear, despite his hairstyle and armbands, that this Nubian had been Egyptianized rather thoroughly; at least this was the message conveyed by the entire funerary establishment.

In the Old Kingdom, moreover, Nubians and Libyans were recruited by the Egyptian government to serve as mercenary soldiers in their military actions against the Palestinian Asiatics. Witness the biography of Weni:

> When his majesty took action against the Asiatic Sand-dwellers, his majesty made an army of many tens of thousands from all of Upper Egypt: from Yebu in the south to Medenyt in the north; from Lower Egypt: from all of the Two-Sides-of-the-House and from Sedjer and Khen-sedjru; and from Irtjet-Nubians, Medja-Nubians, Yam-Nubians, Wawat-Nubians, Kaau-Nubians; and from Tjemeh-land (i.e., Libya). His majesty sent me at the head of this army, there being counts, royal seal-bearers, sole companions of the palace, . . . from the villages and towns that they governed and from the Nubians of those foreign lands.[36]

Some of the Nubian mercenaries must have settled in Egypt, and traces of their existence were found in the neighborhood of Memphis. They were called "peaceful Nubians (*Nḥsyw ḥtpw*)."[37]

During the First Intermediate Period Nubian soldiers were known to have settled in Egypt in places such as Gebelein, Moalla, Dendera, Aswan, and Thebes.[38] From a number of tomb stelae of Nubian soldiers at Gebelein, it is suggested that inasmuch as they were willing and able to retain their ethnic identity (e.g., their holding bow and arrows, having dogs around), even though cast in an Egyptian outfit, they probably enjoyed considerable prestige in their local community as excellent hunters and soldiers. This is supported by a sentence in the inscription of Kedes, a Nubian soldier from Gebelein: "I surpassed this town in its entirety in swiftness—its Nubians and its Upper Egyptians."[39] This proud statement only makes good sense when we assume that Nubians in town were emulated and respected.

In the late New Kingdom, Libyans and Nubians were both in the service of the Egyptian police force against the Bedouins. The Libyans, for example, served as reconnaissance patrols, as witnessed by a royal letter dated to the Nineteenth Dynasty:

Figure 5.2. Tomb stela of a Nubian mercenary during the First Intermediate period, after Fisher, 1961.

> This royal decree is brought to you to say: What concern do you have with the Tjukten-Libyans of the Oasis Land that you should send out this scribe of yours to take them off their reconnaissance patrols?[40]

The Nubians, on the other hand, served as escort troops against the Bedouins, and received Egyptian supplies:

> List of the supplies that are destined for the feather-wearing Nubians and Nubians of the land of Akuyta who went as an escort troop against those Beduin enemies of Muked to cause the energetic arm of Pharaoh, L.p.h., to cast them to the ground."[41]

There is also evidence that shows that the Medjay-Nubian police were employed in the northern Delta area to fight against the invading Meshwesh Libyans, as a vizier in the reign of Ramesses XI addressed a commander:

> As soon as the captain of police Ser[montu reaches you, you shall] return at once with him and (with) all men of the Medjay-police

contingents that are with you in the town of Perhebit (in the northern Delta). And don't let a single man of them linger. (But) it is only
after you have properly ascertained the state of the Meshwesh-
Libyans so that you can return that I call them (the Medjay-police)
up according to their name-list, which I have in my possession
in writing.[42]

The composition of the army in the New Kingdom is in fact quite
complex, if the words of the author of a late New Kingdom text known
as the "Satirical Letter" can be trusted:

> You are dispatched on a mission to Djahy (Syrio-Palestine) at the
> head of the victorious army in order to crush those rebels who are
> called Naarin-warriors. The host of soldiers that is under your charge
> comprises 1,900 men (Egyptians), 520 Sherden, 1,600 Kehek, [100]
> Meshwesh and 880 Nubians, a total of 5,000 all told.[43]

Disregarding the numbers, the general idea of a multiethnic composition of the Egyptian army seems to be quite clear. Besides soldiers
and slaves, there are also foreigners who performed other tasks in
Egypt.[44] New Kingdom evidence shows that foreign craftsmen were
employed in the royal cemetery of western Thebes. Names of Hittite,
Hurrian, Semitic, Libyan, and Nubian origins are identified at the
workmen's village at Deir el Medina.[45] Although these were mostly
low-level craftsmen, they were at least treated as the equals of their
Egyptian colleagues. Moreover, foreigners in the greater Theben area
often occupied more important positions, such as "The Asiatic, chief
of craftsmen, Twti."[46] A scribe of the vizier, for another example, was
a certain Zabu, of Semitic origin.[47] In fact, Aper-El, a vizier under
Amenophis III, who had a tomb in Saqqara, was identified as a Nubian.
Another vizier, Paser, who served under Sety I, was a descendent of
a Hurrian.[48] It is also suggested, based on the trial records of tomb
robberies and records of land ownership,[49] that foreigners might have
spread to other parts of Egypt with mixtures of diverse groups not
unlike those found at Deir el Medina.

Evidence also shows that some foreign women worked in Egypt as
household servants and concubines in the New Kingdom period. A letter
of Amenophis II to his viceroy of Kush has the following words:

> O you [possessor of a] woman from Babylon, a maidservant from
> Byblos, a young maiden from Alalakh, and an old woman from
> Arapshka, the people of Takhsy (in Syria) are all of no account. Of
> what use are they?[50]

A stela of Amenophis II recounting the king's booty after an expedition to Syria mentions the capturing of foreign women and others that shows the extent of the inflow of foreigners into Egypt:

> His Majesty reached Memphis, his heart joyful, the Mighty Bull. List of this booty: maryannu: 550; their wives: 240; Canaanites: 640; princes' children: 232; princes' children, female: 323; favorites of the princes of every foreign country: 270 women, in addition to their paraphernalia for entertaining the heart, of silver and gold, (at) their shoulders; total: 2214; horses: 820; chariots: 730; in addition to all their weapons of warfare.[51]

Presumably the women were kept in the court or were given to the nobles and officials as gifts. Foreign women could also work as weavers in the harem.[52]

Since as early as the Old Kingdom foreign ladies could even marry a prince,[53] it seems that there was no limit for anyone, Egyptian or foreigner, to climb the social ladder. Herihor, the high priest of Amun in Thebes at the end of the Twentieth Dynasty, was probably a Libyan.[54] Indeed, the Twenty-second Dynasty was established by Libyan settlers in the Western Delta,[55] while the Twenty-fifth Dynasty was Kushite.[56] These "foreign rulers," however, seem to have been thoroughly Egyptianized, so that they would assume a traditional Egyptian attitude toward "foreigners." A statute of King Taharqa (690–664 BCE) of the Twenty-fifth (Nubian) Dynasty shows the king stepping on the "Nine Bows," traditional symbol of all foreign countries, including his own homeland Nubia.[57] We shall return to this with regard to the problem of cultural assimilation in the next chapter.

A special category of foreigners was the sons of the foreign princes. There was a long tradition that foreign children were brought to Egypt as captives of war and became slaves. Nevertheless, it was during the New Kingdom that sons of foreign princes were brought back to Egypt and raised in the court as a kind of hostages. The stela of Amenophis II quoted above is a good example. They were hostages while they were in Egypt, but potential allies in the future when they returned to their homeland to succeed their fathers.[58] A similar situation is described on a stela of Amenophis III concerning the temple at Thebes:

> Its work house is filled with male and female slaves and with children of the princes of every foreign country that his majesty despoiled. Its store rooms [contain] goods that cannot be counted. It is surrounded by Syrian settlements, inhabited by the children of the princes.[59]

Up until the New Kingdom, therefore, foreigners existed in Egypt in all sorts of social positions, and it seems that their presence in Egypt was felt as a normal phenomenon. It should be stressed that, unlike the situation in Mesopotamia either in the Old Babylonian period or during the Assyrian Empire, the foreign elements in Egypt were always a minor part of society, so that the main line of cultural development did not seem to deviate from the course established since the Old Kingdom. After the New Kingdom, however, as Egypt went through the chaotic Third Intermediate Period and experienced a succession of foreign dominance, the ethnic composition began to become more complicated on a par with later Mesopotamian society. We shall return to this period in the next chapter dealing with the issue of cultural assimilation.

In contrast to Mesopotamia and Egypt, relatively less information concerning the fate of foreigners can be gleaned from the Chinese source. Evidence concerning foreigners inside the Shang territory came inevitably from the royal city of Anyang where royal tombs and oracle bones were found. As a result of military actions, large numbers of foreign prisoners were brought back. We have seen in the last chapter how prisoners were sacrificed together with animals. It seems quite certain that the Shang people treated their foreign prisoners as a kind of sacrificial animal that could be slaughtered at will. Thus there is no doubt that the Shang people in general held foreigners in low regard.[60] There are, of course, some exceptions, since occasionally the Shang ruler also employed foreigners as officials. Some were responsible for preparing oracle bones, and some were in charge of the horses, presumably because they were expert horse trainers.[61]

Such information, however, is very scanty for the following centuries. We hear all sorts of interactions and wars between the Zhou or the Central Plain states and the foreign "barbarian" states. Undoubtedly prisoners of war were brought back, not to mention the exchange of personnel for marriage alliances between the Central States and the barbarians. No extant record, strangely enough, provides us with a glimpse of the lives of foreigners inside the Chinese states. Consequently all the information we have concerning attitudes toward foreigners is what we have already examined—that is, literary or archaeological evidence that discusses or represents foreigners as people living outside the Chinese cultural sphere. This is remarkable, especially in contrast to Egypt and Mesopotamia, but it is also understandable when we rec-

ognize that, to the Chinese world order, the barbarians were defined
as people living at the outskirts of the Sino-centric world together
with some criminals, as shown by a passage in the *Book of Documents*
(*Shangshu*), dated to the end of the Warring States period:

> Five hundred *li* (miles) constituted the Imperial Domain. . . . Five hun-
> dred *li* beyond constituted the Domain of the Nobles. . . . Five hundred
> *li* still beyond formed the Peace-Securing Domain. . . . Five hundred
> *li*, remoter still, constituted the Domain of Restraint. (Of these,)
> the first three hundred *li* were occupied by the tribes of the Yi-bar-
> barians; the next two hundred by criminals undergoing the lesser
> banishment. Five hundred *li*, the most remote, constituted the Wild
> Domain. (Of these,) three hundred *li* were occupied by the tribes
> of the Man-barbarians; two hundred, by criminals undergoing the
> greater banishment.[62]

This concentric world order, with China in the center, represents an
ideological construction that appeared in different forms. Consider
another passage in the *Book of Rites* (*Liji*):

> The people of those five regions—the Middle states, and the Rong, Yi,
> had all their several natures, which they could not be made to alter.
> The tribes on the east were called Yi. They had their hair unbound,
> and tattooed their bodies. Some of them ate their food without its
> being cooked. Those on the south were called Man. They tattooed
> their foreheads, and had their feet turned in towards each other.
> Some of them (also) ate their food without its being cooked. Those
> on the west were called Rong. They had their hair unbound, and wore
> skins. Some of them did not eat grain-food. Those on the north were
> called Di. They wore skins of animals and birds, and dwelt in caves.
> Some of them also did not eat grain-food.[63]

As we have seen in chapter 3, the idea that China was the "central
state(s)" could even be traced to the Shang period. What Chinese considered as "all under heaven (*tianxia*)," therefore, consisted of China in
the center, with barbarian states at the periphery. This ideology dictates
that whoever lives inside China should be seen as "Chinese," because
the world order prescribes that barbarians were located outside of the
Chinese cultural sphere. *The Rite of Zhou* (*Zhouli*) even designed a
special office to handle the "ambassadors from the barbarian states."[64]
The lack of any substantial evidence for the traces of foreigners living
among the Chinese, however, indicates that the Chinese literary and

artistic traditions, at least before the Qin-Han period, were not able or willing to depict non-Chinese people as participants of life in China. This Sino-centric ideology had, so to speak, successfully obliterated memories and records about the foreigners' existence in China.

Foreign Goods and Languages

One of the essential functions of warfare in the early states was the acquisition of booty. Human booty often became slaves; material booty, on the other hand, became treasures and symbols of prestige. The acceptance of foreign goods, whether through war or by trade, was always easy for a society to accomodate, as the possession of things foreign often signifies social, political, and religious status.[65]

The appreciation of foreign objects and materials was an inherent part of the Mesopotamian economic and industrial structure. Imported materials formed a very important part of the Mesopotamian lifestyle, including such crude material as limestone,[66] as well as such precious material as lapis lazuli and cornelian,[67] or precious metals like gold and silver.[68] It is no exageration to say that the splendors of Mesopotamian civilization relied heavily on imported goods. As early as the Old Akkadian period, for example, Sargon of Akkad boasted of having ships from Meluha, Magan, and Tilmun moored at his port.[69] Gudea of Lagash also reported the use of precious materials from various foreign countries in the building of the temple of Ningirsu:

> From Tidanum in the mountains of Martu he brought alabaster in great blocks and fashioned it into ur.pad.da-slabs and erected them in the temple as barriers. In KA.GAL.AD, a mountain (region) in Kimash, he mined copper and fashioned it into the Mace-of-the-Relentless-Storm. He imported esi-wood from the mountains of Meluhha and built [. . .]. He imported nir-stone and made it into a mace with three lion-heads; from the Hahhum-mountains, he imported gold in dust-form and mounted with it the mace with the three lion-heads. From the mountains of Melluha he imported gold in dust-form and made (out of it) a container (for the mace). He (also) imported abri, he imported willow logs from Gubin in the Willow Mountains and fashioned (them) into the bird (shaped part) of the SAR.UR-mace.[70]

Similarly, the Enmerkar-Lugalbanda epic cycle of the Ur III period depicted the region of the faraway Aratta as a kind of paradise, rich with all sorts of precious goods.[71] The correspondence of the Babylonian kings preserved in the Amarna letters also reveals a strong interest in foreign goods and especially precious items, which was expected of the royalty. An inventory of the gifts that the Egyptian king Amenophis IV sent to the Kassite king Burna-Buriyaš, for example, includes numerous items of gold, silver, bronze, fine linen cloth, ivory, and the like.[72] As can be imagined, the gifts were sent to answer the frequent requests of the Kassite (and later Assyrian and Mittanian) kings. An Assyrian king demanded that the Egyptian king send gold to him with a "justi-fied" claim: "Gold in your country (Egypt) is dirt; one simply gathers it up. Why are you sparing it?"[73] Records concerning the importation of foreign goods and material, whether as plunder or as merchandise, seem to be a recurrent theme of the Mesopotamian royal inscriptions. As has been pointed out, the foreign trade in Mesopotamia was always part of politics, and many of the trade objects were things that would enhance the prestige of the royal house.[74]

This attitude also seems to have been a natural course taken by the Persian kings to stress the variegated nature of the king's subjects. As Darius I claimed in a "foundation charter" of Susa:

> This palace which I built at Susa from afar its ornamentation was brought. . . . The Babylonian people—it did (these tasks). The cedar timber, this—a mountain by the name Lebanon—from there was brought. The Assyrian people brought it to Babylon; from Babylon the Carians and the Ionians brought it to Susa. The yaka-timber was brought from Gandara (Kabul region) and from Carmania (Kirman). The gold was brought from Sardis and from Bactria, which here was worked.
>
> The precious stone lapis-lazuli and carnelian which was worked here, this was brought from Sogdiana. The precious stone turquoise, this was brought from Chorasmia (lower Oxus), which was worked here. The silver and the ebony were brought from Egypt. The orna-mentation with which the wall was adorned, that from Ionia was brought. The ivory which was worked here, was brought from Kush and from India and from Arachosia (Kandahar region).
>
> The goldsmiths who worked the gold, those were Medes and Egyptians. The men who worked the wood, those were Sardians and Egyptians. The men who worked the baked brick, those were Babylonians. The men who adorned the wall, those were Medes and Egyptians.[75]

There is of course a sense of pride in this statement, as the employ-ment of artisans and materials from "all over the world" emphatically bears out the world dominance of the Persians. Nothing is clearer than this passage to show the truth that foreign objects, the value of which increase with distance and rarity, were symbols of prestige and sociopolitical status. The Persians were also proud of the fact that the empire consisted of many different people, now all under the rule of one dynasty. There was however no sense of a conscious cultural program to assimilate or to "Persianize" all the foreigners. Marriage unions nevertheless were practiced: we find in the reign of Darius a marriage contract between a Persian and the daughter of an Egyptian, witnessed by Babylonians, Arameans, Egyptians, and two Persians.[76]

Similar to the Mesopotamians, the Egyptians had also from the beginning of history been engaged in trade with outside peoples.[77] The trade in foreign goods was nothing extraordinary. Prehistoric archaeology reveals that precious goods were imported into Egypt from Elam, Syria, Palestine, and Nubia.[78] Although scholars have cautioned that in the prehistoric period in general precious goods were not necessarily used as symbols of social status, and symbols of status were not necessarily objects of foreign origin,[79] that they were precious, whether for politico-social status or for cultural and religious significance, was never in doubt. The Land of Punt, for example, had from the Old Kingdom been a place from where exotic goods were imported into Egypt.[80] Textual evidence for the adoration of foreign things as symbols of wealth and prestige can be found in the *Book of Kemit*, a school text compiled in the Middle Kingdom. The text adulates an enviable life of the noble, which "was salved with oliban of Punt and perfumes of God's Land."[81] As this was a very popular pedagogic text, the ideas expressed here presumably reflect prevailing social values. The idea that Punt was a place full of treasures was also indicated in the *Story of the Shipwrecked Sailor*, wherein the Lord of Punt—in the shape of a snake—laughed at the sailor's proposal to send him gifts: "You are not rich in myrrh and all kinds of incense. But I am the lord of Punt, and myrrh is my very own. That *ḥknw*-oil you spoke of sending, it abounds on this island."[82]

In the New Kingdom period, abundant graphic evidence gives us the unmistakable impression that foreign goods, whether from Nubia, Punt, Syria, or perhaps from the Mediterranean world, were so highly valued in Egypt that they received repetitive representations in the tombs of the nobles as well as on the temple walls.[83] Examples include the "tribute scenes" found in many of the New Kingdom tombs,[84] not to mention the famed scene of the "envoy" from Punt depicted in the temple of Hatshepsut at Deir el Bahari.[85] No matter if the representations themselves reflect what really happened or are merely copies of idealized scenes, the mere fact of the depiction of foreign goods is enough to demonstrate the value Egyptians placed on foreign imports. This is all the more true if we consider the royal attitude toward things foreign. Two examples suffice to demonstrate this point. When decorating the divine statues, Amenophis III proudly announced that "[He made his monuments] for his father Amon-Re, Lord of the Thrones of the Two Lands, . . . making for him the great gate . . . worked with electrum of the best of every foreign country."[86] Tutankhamun, similarly, claimed that he had used the best foreign imports to decorate the divine images: "His Majesty made monuments for the gods, [fashioning] their images with real electrum from the best of the foreign countries."[87]

With the influx of foreign goods, foreign languages were inevitably introduced.[88] While the knowledge and use of proper foreign names in writing was natural and perhaps even necessary for the New Kingdom scribes when dealing with foreign people and goods, the acceptance of expressions with cultural connotations was not in any sense prerequisite. Scholars discussing "loan" words in Egyptian documents, especially abundant during the New Kingdom period, have for a long time been interested in the exact origins of the words and their implication for the study of other Ancient Near Eastern languages.[89] More recently attention has been paid to the cultural import of these loan words: what are the areas of use of foreign terms (excluding proper names)? A study shows that vocabulary connected with environment was particularly common, as was the vocabulary of warfare, which is not unexpected for a time when Egypt often engaged in international warfare. Home life (diseases, injuries, conditions of the body, etc.), physical activities (terms like "to go astray," "to flee," "to flow," "to arrive," etc.), and abstract notions (terms expressing emotion, passion, and related actions), as well as terms of leisure and luxury, yield a relatively high level of foreign vocabulary.[90] It is suggested that

> the areas with heavier levels of borrowing reflect the expanded world
> of the Egyptian Empire, the introduction of new technologies in
> warfare and economic production, as well as a familiarity with quite
> a number of products employed in ordinary households and luxury
> goods enjoyed by the upper classes. In contrast, borrowing was very

slight where long established institutions are concerned: e.g., law, politics, and the kingship. These are, of course, precisely the areas in which the Egyptians no doubt felt little need for innovation.[91]

The textual genres in which foreign vocabularies appear range across almost every type of writing.[92] Although this is not proof that foreign terms occupied a significant portion in ordinary people's daily language, it nevertheless suggests that at least the elite stratum of New Kingdom society was fairly receptive to foreign expressions, either as a fashionable vogue and a sign of cultural sophistication, or out of business necessity. Exactly how the use of foreign vocabulary, especially those with cultural imports—terms such as "terror" "bless," "shame," "tremble," contempt," "surprise," threat," "forgive," and so on[93]—affected feelings and mentality, however, is an extremely interesting question awaiting further investigation. This investigation should go beyond the traditional "foreign influence" type of discussion[94] that only lists the foreign inventories without asking what exactly the influence was, and try to discern how the self-perception of the Egyptian changed with the acceptance of foreign goods, languages, and people. Such kind of inquiries, on the other hand, would be difficult to pursue in the Chinese case for lack of identifiable loan words.

Beginning from the early Shang, the bronze objects bear witness to foreign influence. It has been pointed out that a number of Shang bronze objects, including a kind of dagger and *ge* 戈, probably originated from the barbarian tribes to the north.[95] This shows that in the area of practical tools, especially those related to weaponry, the Shang people, just as the Egyptians of the early New Kingdom, were receptive to foreign imports, for the obtaining of such tools was vital for the survival of a society. On the other hand, objects related to cultural and religious life, such as ritual vessels, were less prone to change or adaptation to new ideas.[96] It seems that the negative values attached to the "barbarians," such as backwardness or lack of culture, were not associated with material goods coming from the barbarian lands. Instead, things of foreign origin carried with them an aura of exotic prestige. At times, for political purpose, foreign customs could even be encouraged. We have noted in the last chapter the example of the use of Barbarian-style clothes and mounted archery by King Wuling of Zhao for the purpose of winning wars.

Commercial activities between the Chinese states and foreign peoples must have existed to a certain extent, as witnessed by a passage in the *Zhanguoce*: "To the west of the great king's country (Qin) there are the abundant riches of Ba, Shu and Hanzhong, to the north there are the furs of the Hu-barbarians and the horses from Dai."[97] Further evidence apprears in a story in the *Mutianzi zhuan* (*Biography of King Mu*), a work of unclear origin but probably dated to the mid-fourth century BCE, where it is said that King Mu of Zhou received gifts of herds from the northern and western pastoralists.[98]

In the Han Dynasty, China had already clearly defined and established a view that saw the world as a construction of concentric cultural circles, with China in the center and less civilized peoples living in the circles further away from the center corresponding to their "cultural level." Yet the infatuation with foreign goods and materials only increased, as the opening of the silk road brought in exotica of every sort.[99] An early Eastern Han scholar Ban Gu, the author of the *History of Han*, thus described the richness of the palace park in the capital Chang'an as full of foreign imports:

> Within the park: there are unicorns from Jiuzhen, horses from Dayuan, rhinoceroses from Huangzhi, ostriches from Tiaozhi, traversing the Kunlun, crossing the great seas, unusual species of strange lands, arrived from thirty thousand *li*.[100]

Since the problem of East-West trade through the silk road has long attracted the attention of scholars of both sides,[101] we need not dwell on this topic at this moment, particularly because the time period under consideration is before the rise of the silk trade in the Han.

As has been demonstrated in the last two chapters, although prejudice against foreigners was indeed present, it seems that once the foreigners were admitted into Egyptian society, in general they were integrated into the local social fabric, whether as household slaves, servants, craftsman, or even officials in high positions. In other words, the reality of the attitude toward foreigners in Egyptian society was much more variegated and flexible than the impression one gains from officially proclaimed ideology. A similar situation is also found with Mesopotamian society. There is no denying that some foreigners, especially slaves or prisoners of war, were treated cruelly. Yet the basic structure of Mesopotamian society dictated that the population texture was quite fluid, as contacts with foreigners occurred very often and the influx of foreign population was a familiar fact of life. That we are able to know something about foreigners' fate in Mesopotamia and Egypt, moreover, at least indicates that the Egyptians and Mesopotamians could come to terms with the existence of foreigners in their society and were not averse to making references to them. In China during the pre-Qin period, on the other hand, we seldom find any reference to the life of foreigners inside the Chinese states. This must not be interpreted as meaning that very few foreigners actually went into "China" or the Central Plain states to stay for whatever reason. As I shall argue in the next chapter, I believe a mentality that tended to assimilate the foreigners into Chinese culture was the major reason behind this silence.

With regard to foreign goods, there is a common attitude among all the three civilizations concerned here. Foreign goods, by virtue of their rarity and the difficulty incurred in long-distance transportation, were unanimously seen as precious and as symbols of sociopolitical status. Whatever condescending attitudes toward foreigners expressed by these civilizations were obviously not applied to the objects that the foreigners used or produced. Bruce Trigger has made this point clear: "rulers maintained their authority by carefully regulating foreign trade and mining operations and turning their courts into centers for transforming exotic raw materials into luxury items that they could use to reward faithful followers."[102]

6

The Transformation of the Barbarians

When [King] Tang began his conquest, he commenced with Ge, and after eleven expeditions, there was no enemy left in the kingdom. When he fought in the east, the western Yi-barbarians complained, when he fought in the south, the northern Di-barbarians complained, saying, why does he make us last?

—Mencius, c. 372–289 BCE

To Assimilate or Not to Assimilate

Much as people tend to keep their own way of life and thinking, in reality their attitudes and mentality are susceptible to outside influence upon contact with others. When contacts are made, changes in both directions are usually expected. The extent of change, of course, varies from person to person, from culture to culture, and from time to time. While ideologically a culture may consider itself the center of the civilized world—all three in our study in fact did—and therefore culturally self-sufficient, in reality changes upon contact with foreign cultures are more or less inevitable. How or to what extent these cultures assimilate foreign cultures is the question addressed in this chapter.

The Confucian thinker Mencius once made a comment on cultural assimilation that later became the hallmark of the Chinese ethnocentric view: "I have heard of people using the Chinese (Xia) way to transform (*bian*) the barbarians, but I have never heard of any (Chinese) being transformed by the barbarians."[1] What exactly is the meaning of *bian*, which literally means "change" and is translated as "transform" here? What was involved in this transformation? What was the difference between Chinese and "barbarian" culture?

An often-cited passage in the Confucian *Analects* regarding the contribution of Guan Zhong, the chancellor of the state of Qi who advocated and carried out the policy of "expelling the barbarians and honoring the Zhou kingship," has the following comment by Confucius: "But for Guan Zhong, we should now be wearing our hair unbound, and the lappets of our coats buttoning on the left side."[2] Another passage in the *Zuozhuan*, cited in chapter 4 above, has the Rong-barbarian's confession that "We Rong people's food and garments are different from those of the Chinese (Hua 華) people, . . . our language does not allow us to communicate (with the Chinese people)." Language and lifestyle, including dietary habits and dress, seem to be the major differences that caught the attention of people when they thought about the cultural differences between Chinese and barbarians. However, it should be clear that Confucius's comment was only a figurative way of describing the condition under barbarian rule, for Guan Zhong's contribution was to uphold the pivotal position of the Zhou court, the symbol of the feudal system that Confucianism ascribed to. The real issue was therefore not hairdo or dress style, but the political and ethical system of *li* (ritual) and *yi* (righteousness), which were the central concern of the Confucian political philosophy. Thus when Confucius was distressed over the ruthless politics of the contemporary states, he was known to have opted to live in the land of the barbarians, not because he thought that the barbarians were more civilized, but because a "gentleman (*junzi*)" could transform the rustic into the sophisticated:

> The Master wished to go and live among the nine Yi-barbarian tribes. Someone said, "They are rude. What are you going to do?" The Master said, "If a gentleman dwelt among them, what rudeness would there be?"[3]

Confucius was also known to have said that "The Yi and Di-barbarians have their rulers, yet they still are not equal to the Xia states that have no rulers."[4] The implication was that Chinese culture, based on *li* and *yi*, was superior to the barbarians even during a time of political confusion.

The Confucian view of Chinese cultural superiority was followed by Mencius. In the above quoted passage, Mencius was referring to a Naturalist philosopher, Chen Xiang, who adopted the doctrine of another philosopher Xu Xing and advocated a simple and natural economy in which the prince cultivates the field together with his people and consumes the fruit of their own labor. Mencius denounced this philosophy as barbaric because both Chen Xiang and Xu Xing were from the state of Chu, the traditional southern Man-barbarian country. Mencius's denouncement not only focused on the impracticability of the naturalist economy, but also brought in the whole complex of Confucian sociopolitico-ethical values such as the five human relations and the concept of loyalty (*zhong*) and humanity (*ren*). Thus in a sense the contrast between the Chinese and the barbarian became the entire Chinese, or more precisely the Confucian, cultural foundation against the supposedly barbarian culture. This is obviously much more comprehensive and complicated than the mere adoption of living style and language, symbolically meaningful though they might have been. As a matter of fact, the barbarian Chu state was by this time already highly developed culturally, with strong influence from the Central Plain states yet maintaining its own characteristics. Recent archaeological discoveries also show that Chu was highly literate and extremely sophisticated in terms of material productions.[5] Thus the barbarian and simple economy advocated by Xu Xing was, comparable to the Taoist philosophy of Lao Zi, probably a reaction to the luxury and extravagant lifestyle of the elite class of both Chu and the Central Plain states. Mencius's criticism of Xu Xing, therefore, seems to be a deliberately distorted representation of what Xu was really advocating. Nonetheless, the critical remark still betrays a clear Sino-centric attitude that comprised a long-held prejudice on the mind of the intellectuals of Central Plain states.

In the context of cultural assimilation, Mencius also related a legend concerning the conquest of King Tang of Shang:

> When Tang began his conquest, he commenced with Ge, and after eleven expeditions, there was no enemy left in the kingdom. When he fought in the east, the western Yi-barbarians complained, when he fought in the south, the northern Di-barbarians complained, saying, why does he make us last?[6]

The story Mencius quoted was in circulation well before his time; thus he was not inventing but following a view that the barbarians were eager to be "conquered," that is, to be assimilated into Chinese culture. One of the earlier documents, the *Shangshu* or *Book of History*, has the following paragraph:

> After the conquest of Shang, the way being open to the nine Yi and eight Man, the people of the western tribe of Lü sent in as tribute

some of their hounds, on which the Great guardian made "The Hounds of Lü," by way of instruction to the king. He said, "Oh! The intelligent kings have paid careful attention to their virtue, and the wild tribes on every side have willingly acknowledged subjection to them. . . . When he (the king) does not look on foreign things as precious, foreigners will come to him; when it is worth which is precious to him, his own people near at hand will enjoy repose."[7]

The rationale here is that the "virtue" of the intelligent king would attract foreigners so that they come and submit willingly. This is shown in a typical expression found in the *Confucian Analects*: "If the foreign people are not submissive, then we should cultivate our virtue to entice them to come."[8] Here we find an expression that since became the official program of cultural assimilation, which also reflected confidence in the superiority of Chinese culture. As long as the foreigners are "transformed (*bian* 變)" or "acculturated (*hua* 化)," there is no problem with them being "Chinese." Race or physical characteristics did not seem to have been a concern in the open discourses.

The motif of the barbarians' yearning to become Chinese can also be found in other contexts. The *Spring and Autumn Annals of Master Lü* has the following observation:

> One who masters the art of rulership shall cause the Man and Yi barbarians who speak with garbled tongues, and whose customs and habits are different (from those of the Chinese) to submit to him. This is because his virtue is paramount.[9]

The willing assimilation of foreigners, therefore, had become a ready symbol of the virtuous and righteous nature of Chinese rulership, since the ruler was supposedly the representative of "correct" cultural values. Although such a claim might seem idealistic and ethnocentric, in reality the assimilation of non-Chinese into the Chinese cultural sphere was a verifiable fact. We have already mentioned in chapter 4 the process through which the "barbarians" were integrated into the Chinese cultural sphere.

Archaeological discovery provided further evidence on this point. For example, the tombs excavated at Jundushan to the north of Beijing have been identified as belonging to the Mountain Rong people of the Eastern Zhou period.[10] Bronze daggers with ram's head decorations at the end of the handle characterize the owner as seminomadic people. Yet in the tombs are also found bronze vessels similar to those found in contemporary "Chinese" tombs at Luoyang.[11] This phenomenon indicates that the Rong-people had acquired certain cultural artifacts from the Chinese, which fact in turn indicates that their lifestyle was more or less modified according to the Chinese way.

One rare graphic example of this process of acculturation can be found in a special group of hand-hammered bronze vessels, with incised figures of humans and animals in the contexts of hunting, dancing, ritual offering, archery contest, and battle, dated to the fifth century BCE and originated from the lower Yangtze Valley, the land of the Yue-barbarians.[12] It has been suggested, with good evidence, that the content of the scenes on these bronze vessels, showing a mixture of Central Plain social and ritual practices and local Yue customs such as sitting and dress style, and bodily tatoos, indicates a process of the acculturation of the Yue people.[13] Another prominent or "exotic" foreign culture around China was the eastern Yi culture, which was later absorbed or evolved into the Chu state.[14] A recent discovery at Sichuan province of a bronze culture (late Shang period), apparantly non-Chinese at this time, yet showing clear technological and stylistic connections with the Shang bronze culture, might have been the ancestral civilization of the later Shu state, eventually part of China. This is another example that shows the complexity of the formation process of China as a cultural entity.[15]

In the north, a good example is the Sinicization of the state of Bai Di-barbarians located to the north of present-day Peking, known as the state of Zhongshan (中山, literally "central-mountain"). The state of Zhongshan was known in documents as being established by the Di-barbarians and was culturally "backward" at the beginning. Since the end of the fifth century BCE, as it was defeated by the Chinese state of Wei and was subsequently ruled by ministers from Wei for twenty years, this "barbarian" state began to transform into a "Chinese" state.[16] Archaeological discoveries made since the late 1970s show that by the late fourth century BCE it was already an avowed "Confucian" society, at least as shown by funerary architecture, bronze objects, and most interestingly, bronze inscriptions recovered from the tomb of King Cuo, which mentioned such Confucian ideals as *ren* (humane), *li* (ritual, propriety), *zhong* (loyalty), *ci* (kindness, charity), and *ai* (love).[17] What is ironic, however, is that this Sinicized state, having abandoned their warlike cultural characteristics, was later destroyed in 296 BCE by the state of Zhao under the leadership of King Wuling, who adopted "barbarian clothes" and mounted cavalry.

Thus cultural assimilation occurred in both directions. However, the "barbarianization" of the Chinese was rarely mentioned as a positive sign, and the overwhelming majority of the documents attest to the necessity of the Sinification of the barbarians, for the culture of China was an absolute value that was not subject to the changing conditions of people and places. This is why Confucius could assert with confidence that "if a gentleman dwelt among them (i.e., the barbarians), what rudeness would there be?"

Rooted in such confidence, moreover, is also a very deep sense of cultural pride—if not chauvinism—for it was never admitted that foreign culture, the barbarian way of life, could ever have been a viable choice. This pride has been canonized by the famous sentence from Mencius quoted at the beginning of this chapter: "I have heard of people using the Chinese way to transform the barbarians, but I have never heard of any (Chinese) being transformed by the barbarians." Yet underneath this pride was perhaps a sense of insecurity, a logical phenomenon that went together with pride and prejudice. It was perhaps because of this sense of insecurity that the Chinese mind seems to have been prevented from appreciating foreign culture beyond a superficial grasp of material novelty.[18] The adoption of barbarian mounted cavalry by King Wuling of Zhao, to pick the most famous example, was in fact not a complete adoption of barbarian culture, but a convenient borrowing of the superior tools of war. As we have seen, even this superficial borrowing caused heated debate among the courtiers. Here it might be added that this sense of insecurity later developed into a material form: the building of the Great Wall, the purpose of which was to keep the barbarians out, with no intention of incorporating them into the Chinese world.[19] Thus the wall was also a symbol that defines a new self-image of China as an integrated country politically, socially, and culturally.[20] It was as much a wall to keep the Chinese people in as it was to keep enemies out. This self-image is best illustrated by a letter sent to the Xiongnu by Emperor Wen of Han in 168 BCE:

> According to the decree of the former emperor, the land north of the Great Wall, where men wield the bow and arrow, was to receive the commands from the Shan-yu (i.e., the king of Xiongnu), while that within the wall, whose inhabitants dwell in houses and wear hats and girdles, was to be ruled by us.[21]

A clear demarcation line is drawn along the cultural difference between the nomadic and the sedentary lifestyles. On this point, it is interesting to note similar efforts in Egypt and Mesopotamia to build walls as defense against invasions. The "Wall of the Prince" mentioned in the story of Sinuhe—if we can trust that the background of the story was historically true, was located in the eastern edge of the Delta as a division line between Egypt and the foreign land. The "Amorite Wall" that Šu-Sin, king of Ur, built, probably stretching for more than two hundred kilometers from the Euphrates above Sippar to the far side of the Tigris in the region of Baghdad, was also a defensive wall to keep the Amorites from invading the south.[22] While the Egyptian Wall of the Prince might have also been a dividing line between the "civilized" and the "barbarian," the Amorite Wall seems to be more of a military defense line than a cultural line, since the northern part of Mesopotamia at the time of Šu-Sin was already culturally part of the greater Mesopotamian culture. In any case, the two walls did not seem physically to last long enough to exert any further influence on the history of either Egypt or Mesopotamia.

It should be emphasized that the so-called attitude was not something that can be read from the sources without ambiguity. An interesting story, which casts a sarcastic eye on the achievement of "civilization," amply shows the complexity involved:

> [In about 625 BCE,] the King of the Rong-barbarians dispatched Youyu to Qin. Youyu was a descendant of a Jin native who had fled to the Rong and who could speak the Jin language. Duke Mu of Qin, a reputed ruler, showed Youyu his wealth. Youyu was unimpressed and said "If one employed spirits to make these sort of things, it would be toilsome for them. If one employed people to make these sort of things, it likewise would be miserable for them." Duke Mu found this strange and asked him: "In the Central States we rely on the classics, the rites and music, and laws and regulations to govern, yet still, from time to time, there has been chaos. Now the Rong people do not have these things. How do they govern? Isn't it very difficult?" Youyu smiled and said, "This is why the Central States are chaotic. When Huangdi, the sage king of antiquity, created rites, music, laws and regulations and made precedents of his own behavior, he could barely attain a minor degree of order through these things. In later generations, the kings became more arrogant and licentious day by day. They sheltered themselves behind the awesome power of the laws and regulations to instruct their subjects below to take on their responsibilities. When those below were extremely exhausted, they harbored rancor against those above on the grounds of humanistic and ethical principles. Those above and below contended in their

resentment, usurping and assassinating one another until they ex-
terminated whole clans. In every case this was due to this sort of
[lack of constraining principles]. The Rong people are not like this.
Those above embody genuine virtue in receiving those below; those
below cherish loyalty and sincerity in serving those above. Governing
the entire country is like ruling oneself. We are not aware how it is
ruled. This is truly the way a sage king rules." At this point Duke Mu
retired to ask Liao, the Scribe of the Capital, "We have heard that
a sage in a neighboring country is a concern for its rival state. Now
Youyu is worthy. This is Our bane. What shall We do about it?" Liao
said, "The king of the Rong lives in obscurity and has never heard
the tones of the Central States. Your Lordship could test him by
sending him female musicians, thereby to divert his mind from his
work; ask the king for favors for Youyu and thereby estrange them;
detain Youyu rather than send him back and thereby cause him to
return late. When the king of the Rong notices something unusual,
he will surely suspect Youyu. When there is a distance between the
lord and his vassal, then we can capture them both. Moreover, when
the king of the Rong indulges himself in music, he will surely neglect
his government." Duke Mu said, "Well put!" . . . Accordingly, . . .
the Qin presented the king of Rong with sixteen female musicians.
The king of Rong accepted them and found them enjoyable. For an
entire year he did not return them [to Qin]. Thereupon Qin then
sent Youyu back. Youyu admonished [the king] several times, but
he would not listen. Furthermore, Duke Mu on several occasions
covertly sent someone to invite Youyu. Youyu subsequently left the
Rong and turned to Qin. Duke Mu honored him as a guest and asked
him about the feasibility of an attack on the Rong.[23]

This story reveals the delicate situation for anyone attempting
to try to interpret the "attitude" of individuals toward foreign culture
and, for that matter, toward their own. It indeed could be read as a
sarcastic criticism of the corruption and treachery of the "civilized
people" who, by introducing their own corrupted lifestyle, destroyed
the innocent "noble savage." Yet on the other hand, it could also be
read as a puritanical indictment on the undesirable sociopolitical
extravagance of the Central States. The "virtue" said to belong to the
Rong people can equally be seen as good Confucian values. Thus one
could turn around and say that the central ideology of the story is still
a propagation of the Chinese (Confucian) culture value in the disguise
of the virtue of the Rong-barbarians. In other words, whether the Rong
really possessed superior virtue or not is not really the concern of the

story. It is a case of moralizing comparable to what Ephoros had to say about the Scythians discussed in chapter 1. Judging from the fact that various versions of this story were incorporated into different ancient texts, this story must have been circulated quite widely among the intellectual circle during the transition from the Warring States to the Qin and Han empires.[24] The main reason for the popularity of the story could equally have been either the sarcastic or moralizing effects that it contained or the intriguing political tactic that was displayed in it.

The idea that foreigners should be acculturated when they enter China might have produced two results: one, the foreigners, if they came into the Chinese sphere of influence, were not given the liberty to retain their cultural identity, since Sinification was the only equivalent of a worthy lifestyle. Two, even if they could somehow maintain their cultural characteristics, the Chinese would probably have ignored them. To give foreigners Chinese names, for example, was the first step to Sinicize them, no matter if in reality this would make no difference to the foreigners' cultural affinity or self-identity. Even today many Chinese are still most happy to conjure up worthy names for their foreign friends or acquaintances. From the Eastern Zhou period down to the Han Dynasty, however, there existed very few references to the existence of Sinicized foreigners in China. A famous example is Jin Mi-di, a Xiongnu prince who surrendered to the Han Dynasty when he was fourteen.[25] Jin, literally "gold," was a Chinese surname. Because of his loyalty to Emperor Wu, he rose to high position and was finally bequeathed a marquisate, just as any other successful Han subject. He could have gone down in history as a Chinese noble if we were unaware of his ancestry. His biography in the *History of Han* (*Hanshu*), however, indicated that he did not forget that he was a foreigner. He was also referred to by his Chinese competitors as "the barbarian boy." Whether or not he was still attached to Xiongnu culture did not seem important for the Chinese biographer, who noted in a conventional manner that his descendants inherited his marquisate and had considerable success in the Han court, some as military leaders, some as Confucian scholars.

One could of course ask whether the lack of evidence of the activities of foreigners in China reflects historical reality or only represents the lack of interest on the part of those who left the records. Even if the latter were true, the complicated processes of cultural interaction and assimilation could be shown by a number of cases that occurred

around the borders of the Han empire; namely, the gradual incorporation of the Southern and Eastern Yue kingdoms into Chinese territory,[26] and the long, drawn-out conquest-domination-coercion process
that went on between China and people on the Korean Peninsula, the
Southwestern Yi tribes, and the Western Qiang.[27]

The ideology of a "heavenly court" based on impeccable moral
standards that the barbarians could only hope to become part of, of
course, was firmly established by the early Western Han. This Sino-
centric view gained strong ideological support with the adoption of
Confucianism as the state ideology in the Han Dynasty. It was most
explicitly expressed in the various parts of the *Zhouli* or *The Rites of
Zhou*, the reconstructed and idealized government institutions of the
Zhou Dynasty, which was probably compiled in the Warring States
period, and reedited during the Western Han.[28] One only needs to point
out that, in this idealized government, various offices were created to
handle affairs related to the foreign barbarians who were identified as
vassal states surrounding China. For example, the office of Xiangxu
象胥 was created to "take charge of the emissaries of the countries of
Man, Yi, Min, Lo, Rong, Di, and to take charge of transmitting and
explicating the royal decrees in order to make peace with them."[29] The
way that these barbarian countries were arranged in the system of
Zhouli, however, shows its fictional character. Though indeed kept at
the borders and having engaged in various types of interactions with
the Han state, as the records in *Shiji* and *Hanshu* suggest,[30] the foreign
barbarians hardly ever existed in the manner suggested by the *Zhouli*.
In the office of *zhifang* 職方 in *Zhouli*, for example, the official's duty
was to "take charge of the maps of the entire world, to be in control
of the entire land, to specify the people of the [feudal] states, cities,
countrysides, four Yi, eight Man, seven Min, nine Lo, five Rong, six
Di, and the account of their wealth, nine grain, and six beasts."[31] The
numbers of the barbarian countries are of course nonspecific expressions that convey the basic idea of "many" or "indistinguishable" and,
by extension, not worthwhile to have more knowledge about their
individual characters. There was no evidence, moreover, to show
that the Chinese government had ever had the ability to oversee the
internal affairs and wealth of the barbarian countries. The history of
the relationship between Han and the surrounding peoples, especially
with Xiongnu, with several humiliating defeats of Han and subsequent
marriage alliances, however, points to the hard reality that the early
Han Dynasty could only maintain a fragile balance of power at the
northwestern borders.[32]

This reality did not and could not prevent the Chinese elite in the Confucian tradition from constructing their ideal state. An early Western Han scholar Jia Yi (c. 201–168 BCE) once advised emperor Wen thus: "Now Han rules China (Zhongguo), it is advisable to appease and subdue the four barbarians with profound virtue, and to show the foreign lands enlightenment and justice. This way everywhere boat and wagon could travel and everything human power could achieve would all become our asset, and who dares to disobey the will of Your Majesty?"[33] During a court debate in 81 BCE, a Confucian scholar makes the following comment: "Concerning the barbarians and their barren land, what is there to be bothered? And where comes from the worry of warring states? If Your Majesty would not forsaken them and bestow on them virtue and benevolence, the northern Yi-barbarians will certainly turn to us and call at the border fortresses. Then we could make them our foreign subjects while they keep their barbarian institutions."[34] It is interesting to note that these words were spoken with full knowledge of the reality of the impact of the Xiongnu conflict. Jia Yi even went so far as to devise detailed diplomatic strategy to decompose Xiongnu's morale and integrity and instigate internal strife, much as we have seen in the Youyu story. The scholar at the court debate, furthermore, was well aware of the difficult financial and military burden the Han government was facing. The rosy picture of a grandiose Han Central Kingdom with the willing submission of the foreign barbarians was simply not there.

Nonetheless, a similar position is represented by an essay written by the Eastern Han scholar Wang Fu:

> It is obvious that people are the basis of the state, and the poor are the foundation of the rich. Therefore the sage-king would nourish the people and love them as his own sons, and care for them as members of a family. He would appease the threatened, secure the desperate, rescue the plagued, and remove disasters. Therefore the conquering of (foreign state) Guifang was not because of militarism, and the occupying the state of Xianyun (a state to the north, the later Xiongnu according to some) was not because of a greed for land. The actions are aimed at protecting the people and nurturing virtue, so as to tranquilize the borders.[35]

Wang Fu's idea of the relation between China and the foreign tribes was that the Chinese wars with the foreign tribes were not meant to expand territory because of a militant expansionism, but to secure peace within the country. This extremely patronistic assumption, therefore, was that the foreigners were those who disturbed the country's peace and prosperity. He further claims that, since ancient times, the guardians of the Son of Heaven were the four barbarians. Thus it is clear that Wang Fu has fully embraced the Sino-centric stand that sees China as the center of civilization, while the four barbarians are the political subjects and admirers of Chinese culture.

The end of the Han Dynasty marked a watershed for the disintegration of Chinese political hegemony, which led to the collapse, albeit temporarily, of the Sino-centric view of the superiority of Chinese culture. During the Northern Dynasties (fifth century CE), for example, some Chinese in the north, to the great dismay of the conservatives, began to learn the Hu-Barbarian language, in order to work and please the foreign overlords who at the time ruled northern China.[36] This is a good example of how time and the sociopolitical reality had changed people's long-held cultural values. To a certain extent, this is similar to the situation of Egypt during the Ptolemaic period when native Egyptians began to learn Greek in order to find employment in the Ptolemaic regime.

The most important contact with foreign culture was the incursion of Buddhism into China. To be sure, China had also contributed to the formation of "Chinese Buddhism" during the transmission process.[37] The process of the Chinese response and acceptance of Buddhism, whether intellectually or emotionally and sociopolitically, is a very complicated story. For the intellectuals who raised flags against Buddhist teachings, the reasons were mainly cultural differences: the destroying of the body (i.e., shaving of hair) that was the gift of one's parents; the renunciation of family life and the chance of procreation, which was extremely unfilial to the ancestors. From the perspective of the officials and government, the monks presented a potential threat to the political order: since they were concerned with matters of a nonsecular nature, they claimed that they were not obliged to pay homage to the secular authority, nor were they the subjects of the kings.[38] The complication, however, is that an increasing number of intellectuals found the Buddhist idea attractive, and a substantial portion of the common people also found their salvation in the teaching of Buddha. The question of whether or how to assimilate Buddhism into China, in fact, is still an ongoing issue in the modern era. But these issues have to be discussed on a separate occasion, for our present study of the Chinese attitude towards foreigners and foreign culture is mainly about the Sino-centric world view that was largely formed before the rise of the Qin and Han dynasties.

If the Chinese showed an interest in assimilating the foreigners, the Egyptians were far less inclined in that direction. There are of course numerous graphic representations of foreigners in Egyptian source, which indicates that the Egyptians paid considerable attention to the physical differences of foreigners. However, one aspect of these representations betrayed the Egyptian mentality regarding the foreigners: they were seen and represented as belonging to the Egyptian world, either as defeated enemies, as tribute-bringing envoys, or as servants. Only very infrequently were they shown as Egyptianized citizens, such as in the tomb relief of the soldiers from Gebelein discussed in chapter 3. It seems that graphic representations of foreigners, especially in public circumstances, were restricted by certain conceptual frameworks and representational methods, so that they followed a rigid and limited formula in that the foreigners are mostly shown in a negative spirit as captives or beaten enemies. On the other hand, textual evidence, as we have explored in the previous chapters, indicates that the relationships between the Egyptians and the foreigners were not necessarily and not always mutually hostile. Despite the fact that the foreign population became increasingly prominent in Egypt since the New Kingdom, and that contacts with foreign countries were frequent, which must have resulted in cultural assimilation in both directions on a considerable scale, it seems that no explicit discourse was formulated on an active assimilation of the foreigners or foreign cultural elements into Egypt. The Egyptian sources, that is, did not reveal any clear intention to promote the idea that Egyptian cultural values should be adopted by all who entered Egypt.

Thus, contrary to the Chinese response, the Egyptians never seem to have developed a real need or passion to Egyptianize the foreigners, to teach them the true way, so to speak. It is nonetheless true that, similar to the Chinese, the Egyptians also considered their way of life the only reasonable way and that the superiority of the Egyptian culture was a self-evident "truth." This was guaranteed by the Egyptian cosmology according to which the world is governed by Maat, who repels evil and establishes order. This order, being the only one in the cosmos, is Egyptian. Why then did they not want to Egyptianize the foreign barbarians? Short of a satisfactory answer, one can only suggest that the Egyptians probably felt that there was no need to Egyptianize the foreigners who were basically in the same world order, whether as friends or as foes. Thus the image of the king smiting foreign enemies, which was ubiquitous throughout Egyptian history, did not reflect any intention of cultural assimilation. The destruction of foreign enemies can be construed as a religious and therefore legitimate act.[39] At the same time, however, the existence of foreign foes was a necessary condition for the continuous operation of Egyptian theology and political ideology.

Despite the theological or political necessity for the existence of the foreigners, the Egyptian sources occasionally reveal certain aspects that touch upon the problem of the assimilation of foreigners in Egypt. The *Instruction of Any*, for example, presents a view that is perhaps more of a "taming of the wild" than a concern with cultural assimilation:

> The savage lion abandons his wrath, and comes to resemble the timid donkey. The horse slips into his harness, obedient it goes outdoors. The dog obeys the word, and walks behind its master. The monkey carries the stick, though its mother did not carry it. The goose returns from the pond, when one comes to shut it in the yard. One teaches the Nubian to speak Egyptian, the Syrian and other foreigners too. Say: "I shall do like all the beasts." Listen and learn what they do.[40]

Here the scribe Any was urging his son to study diligently, and, unwittingly perhaps, he seems to have placed the training of animals on the same level as instructing foreigners in the Egyptian language. One may surmise that in the mind of the author, the foreigners' status, comparable to that of the animals, was not very high. The famous *Hymn to Aten* admits to the fact that different peoples each have their own language, which is prescribed by the god:

> O Sole God beside whom there is none!
> You made the earth as you wished, you alone,
> . . . .
> The lands of Khor and Kush,
> The land of Egypt.
> You set every man in his place,
> you supply their needs;
> . . . .
> Their tongues differ in speech,
> Their characters likewise;
> Their skins are distinct,
> For you distinguished the peoples.[41]

This theological conception, although without claiming the superiority of Egypt, eventually places all the foreign peoples under the auspice of Aten, the deity of the Egyptians. This is in unison with our observation above concerning the Egyptian way of life, which is guaranteed by the Egyptian cosmology and world order under the auspices of Maat. Again, being the only one in the cosmos, the order is Egyptian.

Whether the teaching of Egyptian language, a fact that must have been necessary for the settlement of foreign population in Egypt, can be considered as an act to acculturate the foreigners, however, cannot be answered without further investigation into the actual content of the material taught and the purpose of the teaching. To teach the foreigners the basics of the language in order to follow orders and to act as servants, for example, hardly constitutes an acculturation program.

The lack of a policy to actively assimilate foreigners, nevertheless, does not mean that cultural assimilation did not happen. We have seen the Old Kingdom examples of Nubians serving as Egyptian household servants or as soldiers. The way that they were shown in the tomb paintings of Egyptian lords or in their own tombs indicates that, except for some ethnographic details such as hairdo or skin color, they had been Egyptianized rather completely. Or at least they were represented as being Egyptianized. Textual evidence of the New Kingdom period confirms that a large number of foreign people lived and worked in Egypt as part of the Egyptian population. An inscription of Ramesses II at Abu Simbel states that the king, after defeating his enemies, "brought the Nubians to the north, the Asiatics to the south, placed the Shasu-beduins to the west, and established the Libyans to the east."[42] This seems to be a program that relocates the enemies to an unfamiliar environment for easy control. That the Egyptians indeed tried to teach the Egyptian language to foreign prisoners, now settlers and servants, is confirmed by an inscription of Ramesses III, although it is unclear whether it was a systematic program:

> He (i.e., the king) has captured the land of the [. . .] Libu and Meshwesh, he made them cross the Nile, carried off into Egypt; they are settled into strongholds of the mighty king, they hear the word of the Egyptian people, serving the king; as he makes their language disappear, he changes their tongues.[43]

Such forced assimilation no doubt could have been effective. The aim of the action, nonetheless, was still utilitarian in nature: the foreigners were taught Egyptian so that they could serve the king. It was never spelled out that it was because of the superiority of the Egyptian culture that the foreigners should be educated in the way of Maat. On the other hand, it should also be noted that the influx of foreigners inevitably brought in foreign languages and, with the languages, new concepts and attitudes. As has been discussed in chapter 5, a large number of loan words, mostly Semitic, appeared in Egypt during the New Kingdom period. The semantic fields of these loan words range from environment, military affairs, home life, leisure, and luxury, to some abstract notions expressing emotion and passion. Regardless of how one interprets the cultural significance of these loan words, it is clear that, with the addition of new words and terminologies, the mental world, which has a reciprocal relationship with language, also entered into an irreversible process of change and expansion. The social psychology of adopting foreign language or foreign terms is complicated, though it might not be far off the mark to suggest that, just like the possession of foreign goods, to be able to use foreign language or foreign terms might be a symbol of social prestige. The author of "The satire on the trade" obviously makes the use of foreign terms an opportunity to show off his knowledge of the outside world.[44] A modern counterexample would be the Japanese incorporation of foreign words since the Meiji reformation, which transformed Japanese culture from a traditional and rural one to a modern, technologically oriented one.[45] To put it another way, the Egyptians were quietly absorbing foreign culture and entering a new stage of cultural development with new sentiments and a new outlook on life. The full details of this Egyptian transformation, however, have yet to be explored.

A symbol of the decline of Egyptian prestige in international politics was the marriage of the daughter of King Siamun of the Twenty-first Dynasty to Solomon, king of Israel.[46] Never before was a daughter of the Pharaoh married to any foreign prince, and this act certainly pointed to the emergence of a new self-image of the Egyptian royalty: the blood of the sun god Re was not inalienable from Egypt. The internal evolution of politics, on the other hand, created some fundamental changes in the ethnic background of the political leaders.

Documents from the Libyan period—that is, from the Twenty-second to the Twenty-fourth Dynasty—betray little of the rulers' Libyan characteristics apart from their names.[47] The Libyan kings were represented on monuments with the attributes—iconographical as well as titulary—of traditional Egyptian Pharaohs. They also adopted Egyptian religious beliefs in a traditional manner and used the Egyptian written script. Thus officially the Libyan rulers were "Egyptianized" or "acculturated," although it is still uncertain what kind of spoken language they employed. Given the fact that the Libyans had been infiltrating and living in Egypt, especially in the western part of the

Delta, for a long time before gaining political sovereignty, the cultural assimilation seems necessary and inevitable. Of course, the continuous use of the titles "Great Chief of Ma(shwesh)" and "Great Chief of the Foreigners" also indicates that cultural assimilation was not complete and that the Libyan rulers probably had a different cultural identity than that of the Egyptians. Osorkon II, for example, prayed in one inscription dedicated to the god Amun that his descendents should become not only the great sovereigns of Egypt but also the Chiefs of the Meshwesh-Libyans and the Chiefs of the Foreigners (ḫ3styw).[48] The wife of King Schoschenk I is given the title "King's Daughter of the Great Chief of the Foreigners" (s3t nswt n wr ʿ3 n ḫ3styw).[49] This kind of title indicates an affinity that was non-Egyptian, and thus casts doubts on the real extent of "Egyptianization" of the Libyans.[50]

The Twenty-fifth Dynasty was established by an Ethiopean court based at Napata near the Fourth Cataract. As a foreign regime, nevertheless, the Ethiopeans were very much in favor of orthodox Egyptian culture, as they also accepted Egyptian religion and script, rebuilt Egyptian temples, and emulated traditional Egyptian art forms. This is not merely a demonstration of the extent of their Egyptianization, since the area of Nubia had been in the sphere of Egyptian cultural influence ever since the Old Kingdom, but also an attempt to establish their legitimacy as the true rulers of Egypt. They were in a way more "orthodox" than the Egyptians. A parallel situation has been noticed between the Ethiopean Dynasty and the Manchu Dynasty in China in their upholding of the traditional culture of the conquered country.[51] However, just as the Libyan dynasties before, there is also doubt as to the real extent of the "Egyptianization" of the Ethiopeans. It has been observed that the iconography of the Twenty-fifth Dynasty ruler demonstrates both their southern ethnotype and the composition of the regalia (crown, costume). Their southern origin was not only iconographically emphasized but was also propagated in the more complex terms of theological speculation in that they were portrayed as the savior of Egypt from the south.[52] Thus the Egyptianization of the Ethiopeans was a complex phenomenon: on the one hand, they needed to be seen as a traditional Egyptian dynasty; on the other, their Egyptianization was so successful that they could utilize the subtle language of Egyptian theological and mythological discourse to assert their own identity.

By the time the Twenty-sixth Dynasty was founded, the Pharaoh, who was also of Libyan descent, was hard pressed to establish his legitimacy as the true descendent of the ancient god Re. As has often been discussed, the Pharaohs of the Twenty-sixth Dynasty launched a campaign to restore the culture of the old days, in art, literature, religion, and so on.[53] This cultural "renaissance" very appropriately served as a landmark for the eventual loss of traditional Egyptian culture.

By this time, foreign elements had infiltrated not only the Egyptian ruling machine; few of the major ethnic groups of the surrounding countries had failed to have made their presence felt in some way, at one time or another.[54] In such an environment, the attitudes of the Egyptians toward foreigners could be nothing but diverse. As one scholar puts it: "The Egyptian reaction [to these foreign groups was] marked by a complex interplay of prejudice, ideology, pride and self-interest."[55] While the court might find foreign mercenaries and merchants necessary to keep military and economic forces strong, native Egyptians found the situation repulsive, as witnessed by the mutiny against King Apries and the foreign mercenaries in the Twenty-sixth Dynasty.[56] When Herodotus visited Egypt, which was actually under Persian rule, the feeling he gathered from the people concerning their national identity was that cultural behavior, rather than ethnic origins, was the most important factor in constituting the Egyptian people. Thus the Egyptians paid meticulous attention to detailed everyday behaviors: eating habits, language, and religious ceremonies.[57] At the same time, anyone who could not speak Egyptian was regarded as a foreigner, and the Greeks were considered especially repulsive, as they were ritually unclean in Egyptian eyes.[58] Thus what Herodotus found was a mixture of cultural superiority and distaste toward foreigners, which was actually in conformity with traditional Egyptian attitudes. It has been pointed out that, although Egypt in the late period was infused with foreigners—and there is evidence of the influence of foreign languages as well as that the foreigners show "a consistent pattern of adaptation to, and adoption of, Egyptian culture and ways of thought"—the demotic script, developed during this period, largely excludes foreign influence.[59] This could be seen as a sign of the Egyptian idea of keeping a "pure" Egyptian script despite foreign influences.

During the first Persian period (525–404 BCE), a certain Udjahor-resene recounted his service under Cambyses. In his biography, he was said to have received the appointment of Cambyses to become the high priest of the temple of Neith, the rebuilding of which was sponsored by the Persian king.[60] Udjahorresene did not express any harsh feelings regarding the rule of the foreign king. Was he an opportunist? Or was it because of outside pressure that he could not openly express any personal discontent? We may never have the answer. What we can tell from his biography, however, is that he did not thank the king for giving him his position. Furthermore, he more than once emphasized that it was he who had taught the king to recognize the great power of Neith, so that the king paid homage to Neith, just as all the Pharaohs of former times:

> His majesty (Cambyses) did every beneficence in the temple of Neith. He established the presentation of libation to the Lord of Eternity in the temple of Neith, as every king had done before. His majesty did this because I had let his majesty know how every beneficence had been done in this temple by every king, because of the greatness of this temple, which is the seat of all the gods everlasting.[61]

Thus, in a sense, Udjahorresene (or Egypt) conquered the conqueror with his own religion, "to subsume the conqueror in the ideal of Egyptian kingship."[62]

During the second Persian occupation, a certain Somtutefnakht, who began his career under Nectanebo II, witnessed the coming of Alexander and the defeat of Darius III. He then returned to the temple of Harsaphes and served as a priest until the end of his days, perhaps in early Macedonian occupation. In his biography, he admitted that he received priestly office from the Persian court, although, like Udjahorresene before him, he did not express any gratitude toward the Persian king.[63] Yet we may also question if he were able to openly express his true thoughts with the Macedonians now in charge.

A most remarkable person at the turn of the dynasty was Petosiris, a high priest of Thoth, of Hermopolis. In his biography, we cannot find any disproval of the rule of the new ruler whom he referred to as "ruler" rather than "king." Presumably this was Philipp Arrhidaeus— Alexander having left Egypt by then, the man in charge should have been Ptolemy, yet to become king of Egypt. This of course betrays a view that the legitimacy of the new ruler is of some doubt in Petosiris's (or the author's) mind. Nor did the biography give any prominent position to the ruler or elaboration of Petosiris's relationship with the ruler in his biography, which is rather atypical from a traditional Egyptian point of view for a man of his status.[64] Only two sentences mention the Ptolemaic ruler: "I was favored by the ruler of Egypt. I was loved by his courtiers."[65] What is worth noticing, however, is the decoration in his tomb.[66] It was very clearly influenced by the Greek style of painting, most noticeably in the tunic dress, the cone cap, and the facial representations of the people in the paintings. This indicates that Petosiris, and presumably his family also, had a keen interest or appreciation of Greek art and even lifestyle. If we cannot be sure whether or not Ujdahorresene and Somtutefnakht were loyal to the Egyptian tradition, politically or culturally, there is little doubt that Petosiris represented a new breed of Egyptian intellectual who, whatever their political positions, had little difficulty in appreciating a new and foreign culture. It is particularly noteworthy that in the funerary inscription for his young son, Thothrekh, there is a tone of sadness and mourning for death, which, as has been pointed out, betrays a sentiment that was closer to Greek epitaph than to Egyptian traditional funerary text.[67] If this is true, we can find an Egyptian family that was considerably Hellenized in their outlook of life and death. The Petosiris phenomenon, however, involving the complex story about Egyptian attitudes toward foreigners in the last of Egypt's independent days and in the Graeco-Roman period, inseparably intertwined with the problem of the decline and fall of Egyptian culture, is sufficiently complex to warrant a special study.[68]

Compared with China and Egypt, the Mesopotamian evidence concerning the assimilation of foreign people into Mesopotamian society stands on another plain because of the complex ethnic composition from the beginning of its history. Since the relationship between Sumerian and Akkadian is itself a much discussed topic, as has been demonstrated in chapter 2, suffice it to say that the land of Mesopotamia was a melting pot for different peoples ever since the beginning of history. The Gutians, for example, who succeeded the kingdom of Akkad and held political power in Mesopotamia for over a hundred years[69] and who were labeled by subsequent Mesopotamians as the typical barbarians (see chapters 3 and 4), were in fact well assimilated into Mesopotamian culture, at least with regard to their political ideology. A text of the Gutian king Erridu-pizir, written in Akkadian, claimed that he was the "king of four quarters," a traditional Mesopotamian royal ideology, and that he also worshiped Enlil, the principle god of Nippur.[70] If he was indeed the first of the Gutian kings,[71] the rate of assimilation of the Gutians was rather speedy.

This does not mean that the incursion of foreigners in Mesopotamia did not cause problems. While some scholars maintain that the assimilation process was constant and natural, as the assimilation of the Amorites seemed to have been,[72] others point out that groups of foreigners residing in Mesopotamia, depending on their location, were under tight surveillance and no sign of integration on the part of the local government could be detected.[73]

The Kassite period marked the longest period of foreign rule in Mesopotamian history, if the term "foreign rule" is still meaningful. For it is so far commonly admitted that the Kassites, despite the fact that we are still not clear about their origin, were, after a long period of interaction with the Mesopotamians since the Old Babylonian period, completely immersed in Mesopotamian culture. They worshiped Mesopotamian deities, as witnessed by a sales contract that took oath on the following deities: Anu, Enlil, Ninlil, and Shuqamuna. Among these only Shuqamuna was a "Kassite" god.[74] The Kassite rulers also encouraged traditional Mesopotamian cultural activities such as the studying and copying of ancient literary works. Except occasional evidence of Kassite elements in artistic expressions—such as the molded brick wall—and the appearance of the name of a Kassite deity, the lack of things Kassite, whether texts written in Kassite, or other cultural artifacts, indicate that the cultural assimilation of Kassite into Mesopotamia was rather complete. In addition, the Kassite king was never seen or talked about as "foreign ruler" but only as "king of Babylon."[75]

In the mid-ninth century BCE, when the Neo-Assyrian empire reasserted itself as the uncontested master of Mesopotamia as well as the periphery area, many of the Aramaean states also became part of the Assyrian empire. Yet the Aramaeans themselves, at least for a period, still felt that they were distinctively different. In a bilingual text, an Aramaean leader was said to serve the Assyian states as a governor in the Akkadian text, yet in the Aramaic text he referred to himself as a king in relation to his subjects. The text reflects a practice whereby, according to Khurt,

> [members] of local Aramaean families were appointed to rule their states by the Assyrian kings and, as officially designated Assyrian dignitaries, were fully integrated into the Assyrian system of public honors and office. . . . So while the celebratory form of many Assyrian royal campaign-accounts dictated that Aramaean states were presented as hostile, to be crushed and devastated ruthlessly, and their populations deported, the historical reality is reflected more clearly by the Fehkeriye statue (the bi-lingual text). It shows a policy of recruiting distinguished Aramaeans into the highest echelons of Assyrian government, so creating a state where the division between rulers and ruled was not drawn along ethnic lines.[76]

This refers not only to the upper echelon of society, for the use of Aramaic language and script in the eighth century was an indication that Aramaeans constituted a significant proportion of the Assyrian population at all levels of the sociopolitical structure. In fact, the mixture of various groups of peoples in the Assyrian empire at this time makes it possible to see it as a multiracial state.[77]

Another aspect of cultural assimilation on the part of the Assyrians is the use of monumental lion gates in royal palaces. It has been pointed out that the idea ultimately derived from the lion gates of the Hittite empire. Archaeological discovery suggests that the Hittite style had influenced the art works of the Northern Syrian states, and it was possibly due to the contact of Tukulti-Ninurta II (890–884 BCE) and his son Assurnasirpal II (883–859 BCE) with North Syria that inspired their building program at Nimrud.[78] It is noteworthy that the Assyrian adoption of the lion gate motif was not a simple takeover, but rather a transformation based upon the native tradition, since the detailed feature of the lion, as well as the use of the lions at gateways in palaces, is different from the Hittite original.[79] Moreover, the Assyrian kings were very consciously incorporating such building components as parks and architectural forms of North Syria into their palaces.[80] These borrowings and adoptions in artistic and architectural forms point to an appreciation and a willingness to accept, at least partially, foreign taste.

Between Ideology and Reality

On the whole, one can conclude that we find no positive evidence that shows an active interest on the part of the Mesopotamians, official or private, to elaborate on a concept that justifies, either on political, social, or religious grounds, the assimilation of foreigners. Yet the evidence we have shows that people of foreign origin were constantly assimilated into Mesopotamian society throughout history. It has been pointed out that "rulers of non-Mesopotamian background, typically belonging to only recently acculturated groups, contribute energetically and effectively toward maintaining the cultural continuum once they assume political power."[81] This willing assimilation or acculturation, of course, was not a pronounced policy but the result of practicality and necessity. It was nonetheless clear that by posing himself as the heir of Mesopotamian culture, the foreign ruler gained his legitimacy as part of Mesopotamian society. He then could use this newly acquired legitimacy to discriminate against the "foreigners," that is, the enemies. Thus in the Old Babylonian—by origin Amorite—Dynasty, the fact that texts such as the *Curse of Agade* could be written down or copied indicates a certain sense of official approval of the denigrating descriptions of the foreign enemies contained in the texts. Such descriptions, it could be argued, could somehow enhance the solidarity within the political realm. On the other hand, there is also no lack of evidence that shows the use and appreciation of foreign goods and the adoption of foreign artistic motifs and lifestyles. This, of course, is in stark contrast to the stereotypical image of foreigners as the worst of enemies. What needs to be noticed is how far, underneath the political claim of unity, the coexistence of different ethnic groups could or did lead to cultural assimilation. Despite our observation that the Assyrian empire can be seen as "multiracial," we are not really sure to what extent these different ethnic groups were mutually assimilated with each other. A study of Babylonia during the seventh century BCE, for example, shows that different groups of people, though coexisting, "rarely acted as a cohesive unit."[82]

With regard to the question of whether or not the foreigners were willingly assimilated, similar situations existed in Egypt, especially from the Twenty-second Dynasty onward. The Libyans and the Nubians, as has been shown above, were Egyptianized foreigners who became more orthodox, at least in a political-theological way, than the natives. The effect of Egyptianization, whether or not a complete transformation from the "barbarian" into the "civilized," had one particular result similar to the Mesopotamian example: it gave the Egyptianized foreigner a legitimate cause to continue repressing "the vile foreign enemies," whoever those enemies might have been. Thus the adoption of Egyptian culture does not signify a reflection on the part of the adoptee that indicates a more open attitude toward cultural differences. Cultural value was still a tool to distinguish the we-group from the they-group. It should be noted that all these cases of acculturation did not indicate any conscious plan or policy on either side. The absorption of foreign culture, from the Egyptian standpoint, was something that could be done but not justified.

Unlike the Mesopotamians and the Egyptians, the Chinese developed an active attitude and willingness to acculturate the foreign barbarians. The openly proclaimed idea was that once a barbarian adopted Chinese culture he was considered a Chinese. The content of "Chinese culture," though never defined clearly, usually refers to the prevailing "Confucian" value represented by the all-inclusive term *li-yi*, propriety and justice. The Chinese, for their part, were never lacking in cultural values and thus were never in need of outside reference. In essence, therefore, the Chinese did not promulgate any openly apprecia- tive attitude toward foreign culture in general, which is comparable to the Egyptians. The historical reality, on the other hand, may have been more complicated, for it is questionable whether the assimilation of the barbarians ever happened as a result of free will on the part of the barbarians. It is also questionable whether the Chinese—particularly those who claimed to be the followers of Confucian values—treated the newly acculturated barbarians as their equals, or if they did, how long it took to acculturate them. The extent to which Chinese culture was influenced by the various so-called barbarian tribes to the west, south, and southwest, moreover, remains to be investigated.

With the coming of the end of the Warring States period, the idea of China being the center of the civilized world gained more strength among the Chinese—mainly intellectuals and statesmen, who had no doubt of the cultural superiority of China. That Chinese culture had the power to absorb and assimilate the foreigners once they came into China—and willingly because they admired Chinese culture—was a prevailing attitude and belief. On the other hand, since the end of the Warring Sates period, the emergence of Xiongnu to the north and northwest of China posed an unprecedented threat to the people of Central Plain. Thus in the minds of some intellectuals and states- men, perhaps even the same group of people just mentioned, there was formed a mentality that did not really want to have any contact with these barbarians. They had no interest in trying to seduce the barbarians into China. This exclusive attitude was best illustrated by the formation of the Great Wall. Thus there was an ambivalent feel- ing: the barbarians were welcome to China because of the superior value of Chinese culture, as it should be; yet on the other hand the barbarians were not welcome, because their power of destruction grew ever stronger and the Chinese were able to hold them back only with tremendous effort.[83] There was, to sum up, a dichotomy between ideology and reality, a phenomenon that needs to be reckoned with.

7

Conclusion

Thus the evolution of Chinese history from the Two Hans to the
Sui-Tang, and down to Song-Ming, one follows another like a string
that never breaks. Even those that lived surrounding us either
melted into us and became assimilated, such as the people of Liao,
Jin, Mongol, Manchu, Tibet, and Xinjiang, or they accepted our
culture and lived besides us from ancient times, like mount Liangfu
in relation to Taishan, such as Korea, Japan, and Vietnam.

—Qian Mu, 1895–1990

This study begins with a simple question: What can we know about
the attitudes toward foreigners in ancient Mesopotamia, Egypt,
and China? The intention that prompted this question, as already explained in the introduction, is a desire to better understand the ways
in which social groups perceived each other, and thus, hopefully, to
better understand the characteristics of these ancient civilizations. It
became clear during the process of investigation that the answer to
this question cannot be a simple one.

First of all is the ever-present problem of how or whether it is possible to re-present the "attitude" of peoples so far removed from us. How
far can or should one trust what the ancients have left us concerning
foreigners? What was their real attitude and what was only decorum?
Even when it is only decorum, could it not have reflected certain truth
about their attitudes? Is not decorum a particular attitude? Is there a
constant attitude to be identified, or is it that attitudes changed with
the historical forces that pushed them along? Even in the same historical period, was there any indication that there should be a unanimous
attitude toward foreigners for a given culture? Not to be intimidated
by such apparent obstacles, I have tried to maintain a more optimistic
view that, by placing our evidence in its proper historical and cultural
contexts, we could at least identify certain aspects of the attitudes of

the people who produced the evidence. As complete re-presentation is an ideal impossible to attain in practice, what can be reconstructed from the evidence at least shows us the range of the possibilities.

To answer the question I posed, moreover, involves an investigation of the formation of cultural identity, for the attitude toward others inevitably reflects the self-image of a given culture. In order to grasp such attitudes, it is necessary to discuss the textual and archaeological representations of foreigners in the cultural context of each civilization. As comparisons of ideas or actions cannot be separated from the physical environment, and because people always perceive foreigners in the context of their physical existence, the geographic and linguistic background needs to be dealt with in the first place. Moreover, the circumstances under which people perceived foreigners are also important to know—who, at what time, looked at which kind of foreigners? Different answers could be provided when source materials from different sociopolitical contexts are considered. Of course, "context" is not a fixed thing either—it varies when the one who makes the observation takes a different position. Thus I tried to investigate the attitude toward foreigners by tracing its manifestation in different contexts, such as what has been demonstrated in chapters 3 through 6.

By looking at the problem in a comparative way, furthermore, I am not only trying to understand the attitudes of individual civilizations toward foreigner and foreign cultures, but also hope to knock at the door that leads to a more general understanding of human society through a particular angle. In the following conclusion, I shall first try to give a summary of the main points of this study, followed by a discussion of certain key concepts that have eluded discussion in the previous chapters.

The Illusive Others

Were the ancient people, whether Chinese, Egyptian, or Mesopotamian, in general xenophobic? Questions such as this can no longer be posed without more precise qualifications in light of previous discussions. In the Ur III period, for example, the Amorites were given allotments of rations by the government just as were the natives. In the Old Babylonian documents recording daily activities, again, there is no sign that the Amorites were regarded as a hostile group of uncivilized foreigners.[1] The derogatory statements made against the Gutians and

Amorites—that they were animals—therefore, should probably be seen as the result of a mixture comprising residue of historical conflicts that might have happened in the past, as well as specific contemporary political motivations to dramatize the contrast between the Meso- potamian (including, in fact, some Semitic groups or even Amorites themselves) and the invaders. Thus although some Amorites had long become part of the Mesopotamian sedentary society, the "typical" Amorite in the literary representations, especially those with a public or official nature, remained nomadic—people who had neither city nor house, had no burial, and so on. This shows that, despite the reality of relatively peaceful ethnic interactions, a stereotypical view of certain foreign ethnic groups, especially the Gutian and the Amorite, as the ever-present enemies, remained a convenient literary topos for the Mesopotamian writers. In other words, even though Mesopotamia was a multiethnic society, there was still a sense of the unity of a "Mesopotamian/we" people, as opposed to "foreign" or "enemy/they" people. The enemies, real or imagined, therefore, were needed by the Mesopotamians in order to construct a cultural identity. Most impor- tantly, when the Mesopotamians tried to characterize the foreigners, they focused mostly on the latter's different cultural traits.

Although relatively isolated geographically, Egypt was never completely cut off from the outside world. Foreigners can be found in Egyptian society throughout history. The Egyptians allowed foreigners to reside in the country, and, as far as we know, with very few restric- tions either socially, economically, or politically. They came to Egypt as workers, traders, slaves, or mercenaries—some even rose up as queens and kings. By the time of the New Kingdom, foreigners were already a prominent feature of the entire population.[2] It should be clear that Egypt in the New Kingdom was a very cosmopolitan place that had a long history in dealing with foreigners politically, commercially, and culturally. Despite this, when the Egyptian texts mentioned a foreign people or country outside Egypt, they often employed stereotyped and hostile expressions to characterize the foreigners.[3] To account for such hostile expressions, it might be useful to consider two lines of official representations of Egypt's foreign relations, one political, another theological. From the political line of representation, to depict a very different and hostile outside enemy was one way to strengthen domestic solidarity, even when the threat of the foreign enemy was largely only imaginary or less serious. In the theological line of representations, the foreigners were of necessity the evil force from without, just as

Seth, who personified the perennial enemy of Egypt, was the chaotic force that threatened the order of Egyptian kingship.[4] A magical curse against Seth has the following words:

> Behind, O rebel vile of character
> Whose advance has been blocked by Re! [. . .]
> You will come near Egypt no longer.
> You will die wandering in foreign lands,
> You will penetrate no more the banks of Horus,
> The kingdom that had been granted to him![5]

Thus when the foreigners were described as "wretched enemies," or depicted as defeated, bound, or trampled under the feet of the Pharaoh on various monuments, they were only seen as part of the cosmological scheme of how things should have been. A political-cum-theological stock parlance that used derogatory terms against foreigners, therefore, became widely employed. Besides a generally stereotypical representation, it is notable that in reality the foreigners were distinguished from the Egyptians mainly on cultural rather than racial or physical grounds. There was, moreover, a progressive change of attitudes toward foreigners and foreign culture as revealed in some private documents. The change can be related to the growth of self-consciousness in certain individuals that corresponded to sociopolitical situations. As mentioned in chapter 4, most of the documents from the Old and Middle Kingdoms, except for very few examples of sympathetic description of the foreign land, presented the political and theological lines of hostility toward foreigners. A more realistic and objective view of and interest in foreign culture appeared at a time when a strong centralized political power had diminished. Here we refer to the *Report of Wenamon*. Egypt in the time of Wenamon (i.e., the end of the Twentieth Dynasty) was certainly not a strong and unified political power. Whether this could be seen as a general trend that, during a sociopolitical crisis, pride in one's own culture and prejudice toward things foreign could be reduced considerably, while interest in foreign culture could be enhanced, or as only a personal reflection, of course, cannot be easily decided. The decision to adopt barbarian clothing and cavalry by King Wuling of Zhao, although not without cultural significance, was basically a political and military move when he saw the decline of the fighting power of his troops. In any case, Wenamon's report pertains mainly to the attitude of the culturally more sophisticated elite class. The official attitude held by the court was still belligerent as ever toward the foreigners. In fact, even the Greco-Roman rulers, or their representatives in Egypt, found no need to discontinue the traditional hostile or condescending attitude. It seems that xenophobia exists at all times, and that the appearance of a more sympathetic attitude toward foreigners in a time of decline shows the softening of a more rigid mentality that usually comes with a strong government control.

It is possible that the Egyptian priestly/intellectual class that co-operated with the Greco-Roman conquerors might have agreed with the ancient Chinese idea that "when the barbarians entered China, they should be Sinicized." Udjahorresene, for example, introduced the Persian ruler to the Egyptian way of worshiping, which could be seen as an effort in "Egyptianizing" the king. Yet Egypt had never had a program or a conscious plan to Egyptianize the foreigners. Thus when the foreigners became the dominant force in Ptolemaic Egypt, Hellenization was inevitable. The decline of Egyptian culture was only a matter of time and might be attributed, at least partially, to the failure of the Egyptians to assimilate the invading Greek culture, as they had done in the Hyksos period, and to fuse native and foreign cultures in such a way as to uphold the Egyptian tradition in a world in which they were no longer politically dominant.

The Chinese attitude toward foreigners during the Spring and Autumn period, when enough evidence is available, shows a strong tendency to stress a particular "Chinese" cultural value—that is, the values represented by the politico-social ethics of the Zhou court, later know as "Confucianistic," as opposed to "barbarian ways" of life. Yet it is not certain, even today, who the "barbarians" were. According to the record of *Zuozhuan*, the barbarian tribes were scattered among different Central Plain states having close interactions with one another. The ancestors of the Zhou people, according to some, were descendants of the western barbarians rather than from the "Chinese" line of the Xia Dynasty.[6] On the other hand, it is also suggested that the various barbarian tribes were in fact "rear-guard detachments lingering in territory into which the Chinese culture was expanding. They may not have been ethnically distinct from the Chinese. Possibly, and even probably, they were backward, less developed groups of the same stock anciently holding the whole of North China."[7] In any case, before the Zhou people established themselves as the dominating force in China, they probably had close contact with the Rong and Di. The *Shangshu* (*Book of Documents*) mentioned that when King Wu of Zhou was attacking the Shang, a number of barbarian tribes came to help him.[8] The record could of course have been a literary embellishment to show the paramount virtue of King Wu that could attract even the barbarians. At the core of the story, it demonstrates an underlying mentality that did not refrain from associations with the barbarians.

Beginning from the Zhou, an agricultural lifestyle, as opposed to a nomadic one, gradually became a shared self-identity of the Zhou people and other groups that were integrated into the Chinese cultural sphere.[9] The distinction between Chinese and foreigners, henceforth, was largely based on cultural differences: agricultural subsistence that defined the lifestyle of the people, and the Zhou court ritual and social ethics that spread among the ruling strata of the vassal states later known as "Confucian" ideology. This cultural distinction between the Chinese and the barbarian became more articulated in the course of the Spring and Autumn period and finally was "canonized" in the Confucian classics, such as the *Liji* passage quoted in chapter 3, where the lifestyles of the barbarian peoples of the four directions are described as either "do not use fire to cook food" or "do not eat grain":

> Thus the people of China (Zhongguo), Yi, Man, Rong, Di all have their own way of living, taste, costume, technology, and tools. The people of five directions cannot communicate with each other because their languages are different, and their hobbies and desires are also different.[10]

Similar formulations could be found in such texts as *Zhouli* (周禮 *The Rites of Zhou*), in which a government official was put in charge of the emissaries of the barbarian states;[11] or *Yizhoushu* (逸周書 *The Apocryphal Book of Zhou*), in which a concentric and layered world system, with China (i.e., the Zhou kingdom) in the center and the vassals and barbarians in the outer circles, was constructed.[12] This world system, although an ideal construction that never existed in reality, nevertheless became the basic political rhetoric of subsequent governments and ruling elites regarding the relationship between China and foreign cultures and peoples. It is no surprise that this idiosyncratic perception of the outside world would produce numerous imponderable misunderstandings and prejudices in the course of China's long history.

Official Ideology and Private Sentiments

Despite the prevailing egocentric attitude that was found in the civilizations we have discussed, we can still discern two general levels of attitudes—one official, the other private—toward foreigners and foreign cultures. The official attitude tends to denigrate foreigners, which reveals one aspect of human society: for political decorum the political elites often tended to debase other people in order to boost the morale of their followers and to claim their legitimacy of power, for the logic was that those who claimed to be able to subdue the foreign threat were those who should be entrusted with power. But it is the unofficial attitude, the private expressions, however fragmentary the picture they may have provided, that reveal the more reflective side of a culture. There one finds thoughts and voices that advocated or expressed a more sympathetic understanding, a more open and appreciative and less egocentric attitude toward foreigners. Sporadic glitterings of such attitude can be found in the *Story of Sinuhe*, the *Report of Wenamon*, or in the speech of the Rong leader Juzhi in the *Zuozhuan*. However, the main current was always the official attitude, which, though disruptive and destructive in nature, seems to have taken control of most of the activities of societies ancient or modern. The balanced yet private attitude, exactly because it was private and thus lacking the means to become a constructive force, seems never to have had the chance of exerting major influence on history. These two attitudes, despite a certain degree of oversimplification, could be seen not only as constituting part of the "group psychology" but also as symbolic representations of the ambiguity of human nature. It is perhaps only by admitting the complexity of human nature (that despite individual revelations of the equality of humanity, taken as a whole, human society does not always act in its own best interest) that the attitudes toward foreigners presented by the ancient cultures as a group phenomenon becomes more comprehensible.

The Comparative Gaze

This book sets out to be an experiment in comparative study. The most demanding question of the whole inquiry, as one comes to realize, is a simple one: what can we learn from this exercise that could not have been learned without comparison? It is particularly worth pointing out that by simply asking a question and posing an issue one cannot claim that there is indeed something comparable, or worth a comparative study, among the ancient civilizations. One should not assume, for example, that there was a single concept of "foreigner" that was equally valid for all civilizations, or that any source that could reveal an "attitude" should be considered as having equal significance and cultural import. This realization in fact is one of the useful results of comparative study, for perceptions of this nature would normally not be entering our discussions.

To elaborate on the question of what constitutes a foreigner, it can be stated that, in all three civilizations discussed in this study, the foreigners were distinguished mainly on cultural rather than racial grounds. This is significant for the understanding of the early stage of ethnic conflicts in human society. "Racial" difference, in the sense of discrimination based on biophysiological features, seems to be a late development in the discourse of group conflicts. At least, it does not seem to have been an innate element in early societies. How it developed and even became the major element in group conflicts in each society remains to be further investigated. This is not to place any value judgment on whether racial consciousness is good or bad. Cultural consciousness, to be sure, also lies in the root of many group conflicts. In fact, a sense of cultural superiority existed in all the three civilizations studied here. One can hardly deny, therefore, that this sense of cultural superiority was a common feature of "civilizations" and often led to wars and conflicts. It is of course mainly a production of self-aggrandization, a group psychology that was claimed to be essential in maintaining solidarity. That it seems to have existed mainly with the "great civilizations" in the ancient world, however, is more likely only an illusion caused by the availability of evidence. The "winners" (i.e., the great civilizations) take all the glory of the "achievements" as well as the blame for the harm that the achievements had done to the "barbarians." In any case, cultural superiority was a production of psychology, not of reality, which could equally find its place in any cultural group, civilized or not. As pointed out by Norbert Elias, prejudice and group consciousness (i.e., the construction of we-group and they-group) as well as a denigrating attitude toward others, could exist even between groups of the same cultural, social, and ethnic background, let alone between people of different cultural backgrounds.[13]

This comparative investigation, to be sure, also shows a number of differences. The most striking one is the different interests in assimilating the foreigners into one's own culture. It becomes clear, if we review the cases, that a sense of cultural superiority did not necessarily prompt the need or interest to assimilate the foreigners. The "Mesopotamians," itself a term for a mixed group of peoples, showed no obvious interest in assimilating "foreigners," yet the reality was that foreigners were constantly assimilated into Mesopotamian society out of practical needs. As Akkadian was the *lingua franca* of the ancient Near East for a long time, the cultural supremacy of Mesopotamia was not challenged until the rise of the Persians, who, instead of being assimilated, devoured Mesopotamia. Unlike the Mesopotamians, the Confucianists posed the ideal of Sinicizing all the barbarians as one of the main goals in the political-cultural life of the nation. With such an attitude the Chinese obviously did not have a high regard for the "barbarian" way of life. Neither did the Egyptians have a high regard toward the foreigners. This, however, did not lead them, as it did the Chinese, to the conclusion that it is better for the foreigners to be Egyptianized. A possible explanation may be found in Egyptian theology, in which the world is governed by Maat, who repels evil and establishes order. This order, being the only one in the cosmos, is Egyptian.[14] There is no need, therefore, to Egyptianize the foreigners who are basically in the same world order, whether as friends or as foes. The different attitudes in assimilating foreign cultures may indicate the later development of each of these civilizations.

In trying to account for these different attitudes toward assimilating the foreigners, we may take notice of a particular psychological factor—beside the obvious explanation that it was because of a strong confidence in its own cultural value that the Chinese deemed it beyond debate that the barbarians should be Sinicized, and not the other way round—that is, whether there was also a sense of insecurity or a lack of confidence that lay deeper in the psychological background. For example, on the one hand Confucius could say with confidence that "when a gentleman dwells in a barbarian country, how could it be uncouth?" On the other hand, the remark by Confucius that "without Guan Zhong, I probably would be having my hair disheveled and wearing a cloth that folds from the left," betrays a sense of insecurity. Otherwise, there is no reason to fear a barbarian invasion since wherever a gentleman dwells it would be a civilized place. Thus it was arguably because of a lack of confidence or fear of the others that the Chinese placed great emphasis on the superiority of Chinese culture, which also prompted the demand for others to be assimilated into China.[15]

Whether this observation was true in China can be cross-examined by the Egyptian case. The reason why the Egyptians felt no need to Egyptianize the foreigners was probably because they had a sense of security, for the Egyptian religion provided them with a world order that was guaranteed by truth and justice. There was no need to assimilate the foreigners, as they were part of this world order in which only the Egyptians were the triumphant.

When we also look at the Mesopotamian example, the situation becomes even more interesting. So far as we can see, the Mesopotamians did not seem to be interested in actively assimilating foreigners. This, however, had little to do with whether they had confidence in their own culture or not. It was perhaps because of an open geographic position that forced the Mesopotamians from early on to accommodate the invasion of various foreign groups, in addition to the complex ethnic situation in Mesopotamian society from the beginning, that made Mesopotamian civilization one that surpassed the mentality of single-ethnicity. In other words, the problem of cultural assimilation was simply not an issue in the Mesopotamian case, though, as mentioned earlier, this does not mean that foreigners were free from social and political discrimination.

The Problem of Great Civilizations

There is, however, another level of meaning to the endeavor of comparative study. Ever since the nineteenth century, the names of the "Great Ancient Civilizations" have occupied the attention of writers and readers. Egypt, Mesopotamia, and China: these are the pinnacles of human civilization in ancient times.[16] Rarely, however, has anyone asked, What is common among them that warrants their place on the same glorious platform? Since they were not of the same age, their commonality must lie in the magic word "civilization." As has been demonstrated in this study, these ancient civilizations all deemed themselves superior to their neighbors. They were, according to their own terms, the most civilized people in their times. This presumption logically implies that other peoples were "less civilized." This was not only something that the privileged of these ancient civilizations held as true, it is also held as true, at least for most of the time, for the modern (nineteenth to twenty-first century) onlookers, writers as well as readers. Some may say that it is not even modern since, as we pointed out at the beginning of this study, the Greeks had already expressed their fascination with the civilization of Egypt. A number of recent studies have illustrated the paradoxical process of how, on the one hand, the Greeks sought to trace their culture to another ancient tradition, such as Egypt, on the other hand relegated the non-Greek world as part of the barbarian world, thereby revealing an attitude of the central importance of their own culture.[17]

The admiration for these great civilizations, moreover, should not be characterized as a naive sentiment. From among the eulogies offered to them, there is a sense of belonging, because admiration implies the desire to become like the admired, to identify oneself with something great and magnificent. To be able to understand and bring back the glory of these ancient folks, as scholars and antiquarians had tried so diligently to accomplish, gives one the thrill of high achievement, as if one had relived the past. In the back of one's mind there is perhaps even a secret voice: through reconstructing these great, lost civilizations, we can also be great. In other words, one who has the ability to understand or the taste to appreciate the greatness of the ancient people shares their glory and authority. History, or ancient history, for quite a while, has served this function of providing admirable memories and "evidence of civilization" for many. The acceptance and propagation of the greatness of the ancient civilizations by moderns, moreover, was in line with the rise of modern nationalism and colonial expansion, since the ancient civilizations, once their lineage with the modern states was established, could help lend legitimizing credentials to authenticate these new forms of hegemonic order. This is why the modern nation state needs to have access to the writing of history in all possible manners. For history constructs, or, as we hear more and more, fabricates, the meaning of a people's existence.[18] This meaning of existence, moreover, has to be positive for the benefit of the nation and its continual survival.

Still, what was the commonality among these great ancient civilizations? Language? Script? Religion? Philosophy? Art? Any expert in one of the disciplines involved in the study of these civilizations could detail their unique characteristics and conclude that none of them are comparable. History, as is often argued, is about particularity, not commonality. If one accepts this view, however, then the term "great" is not really appropriate anymore, since there are only differences among the civilizations, which fact renders moralistic evaluations such as "great" and "small" meaningless. If one views the history of humankind as one phenomenon, on the other hand, the particularities must be seen as variations of a central theme—the survival of people through time. One way of probing this central theme, to explore the commonality of the ancient civilizations, is to examine their state of existence, especially in relation to the "uncivilized" people that they had to encounter. This brings us back to our subject of attitudes toward foreigners.

If the ancient civilizations were civilized as they claimed to be, it was only possible because of the existence of those foreigners that they deemed less civilized. The civilized, in other words, could not become civilized without identifying someone else, the foreigner, as the uncivilized. The question is, who had the right to decide who should be counted as civilized or uncivilized? What does it mean to be civilized?[19] As far as the evidence shows, it is usually those who left enough documents and monuments that claimed or implied that they were civilized. It is clear, however, that these are at best one-sided stories if not fabrications. The civilizing process, moreover, is also a process of hegemonic expansion. When one civilization conquered another, it would hardly be appropriate to describe the situation as one "better" than the other, or one "more civilized" than the other. It is more adequate to say that the "winner" demonstrated stronger determination and more effective tactics, military or otherwise, in destroying or engulfing the "loser." The foreigners, enemies, and barbarians, then, were the necessary component of this drama. Civilization, in other words, should be seen not as a morally or aesthetically justified state of existence, but as a set of intricate strategies that presupposed a hegemonic order aimed at the continual survival of the community in opposition to the foreigners. The survival of a community seems to be a justified aim for itself, yet the necessity of survival often cannot be separated from narcisstic self-importance and damage to the others.[20]

This study of the attitude toward foreigners in three ancient civilizations allows one to reflect upon the nature of civilization, as the attitudes shown by these civilizations betray some commonalities that are not normally known. Moreover, the differences they exhibit are even more interesting, as they show the range of possibilities of human cultural development. The significance of these findings can be appreciated further when we consider their modern counterparts—that is, the modern attitude toward foreigners based on racial discrimination. It is too obvious not to mention that the racialized modern attitude toward foreigners—that is, placing a constructed and therefore fictional racial difference as the major factor that separates one people from another—is in stark contrast to the ancient attitude so far discussed in this study. In China in particular, the modern construction of ethnicity and racial consciousness, with its intense emphasis on physical features (yellow, white, black, etc.) has taken precedence over cultural factors such as language, religion, or custom. Arguably, it was prompted by an urgent need felt by the modern Chinese intellectuals of the late nineteenth and early twentieth centuries when facing the threat of foreign powers that a simple and clear argument for a national identity based on "race"—that is, physical features—was probably the most effective way to defend the nation and save it from destruction.[21] The history of Sino-foreign relations, however, shows that it was always perceived as a cultural problem. The identity—if there ever was a coherent one—was a cultural identity and not a racial one.

Traditional Chinese scholars, up until the early twentieth century, or even perhaps not long ago, often held a common conception that the special character of Chinese culture was its unique power of assimilation. This power of assimilation, according to this conception, was simultaneously the reason and cause of the superiority of Chinese culture. It is because of this power of assimilation that, throughout the centuries, foreigners came into China, became Sinicized, and contributed to the growth and development of Chinese culture. This opinion can be represented by the following words of a prominent twentieth-century scholar, Qian Mu, in his *Guoshi dagang* 國史大綱 (*An Outline of Our Nation's History*), which is still read by college students today:

> Thus the evolution of Chinese history from the Two Hans to the Sui-Tang, and down to Song-Ming, one follows another like a rope that never ends. Even those that lived surrounding us either melted into us and became assimilated, such as the people of Liao, Jin, Mongol, Manchu, Tibet, and Xinjiang, or they accepted our culture and lived besides us from ancient times, like mount Liangfu in relation to Taishan, such as Korea, Japan, and Vietnam.[22]

Qian Mu's statement can be situated perfectly in the context of early twentieth-century Chinese cultural nationalism that went hand in hand with racial nationalism. By constructing an unbroken cultural heritage, the Chinese race could claim a legitimate position in the modern world. Setting aside the problem of how to assess the truth of this unbroken cultural heritage, his view takes no account of the fact that, as a result of cultural interaction, assimilation usually happened both ways. Ignoring the ambiguous meaning of "Chinese," the fact that

Chinese culture has throughout the centuries absorbed many foreign elements means that there is not an unchanging Chinese culture. To insist on the existence of a unique and unchanging Chinese culture that acquired its uniqueness by continuously absorbing other cultures, therefore ever changing, seems to be a self-contradictory concept. What Qian Mu's statement reveals, nevertheless, is a near fossilized mentality from the pre-Imperial era that regards Chinese culture as the center of the civilized world. Such a close resemblance in the attitudes toward foreign culture between Qian Mu and the *Zhouli*, and numerous intellectuals in between that upheld similar attitudes, obviously needs a good explanation. While recognizing, as pointed out above, a nationalist feeling that prompted a need to keep a "warm affection and reverence"[23] toward China's past and to embrace a cultural identity superior to its neighbors, one cannot but begin to wonder about the implications of this phenomenon and ask, In what ways did the Chinese attitude—as it was manifested at any given point in time—toward foreigners and foreign culture influence the cultural development of China throughout the millennia until now? What was assimilated, what was not, why, and what was the result? Some of these issues, including the acceptance of Buddhism during the Six Dynasties period and the absorption of foreign food, music, and artifacts during the Tang,[24] the coming of Christian missionaries,[25] as well as the complicated problem of foreign rule in China,[26] are better known and studied, although the vast majority of them remain to be explored.

One example, however, reveals a very interesting and ironic situation in the assimilation of Chinese culture by its southern neighbor Vietnam. As a recipient of Chinese culture, Vietnam began to adopt Chinese style of government at least since the eleventh century, and during the fifteenth century the Vietnamese elite who were highly educated in Chinese Confucian learning began to construct their own ethnocentric view.[27] As a result the term Zhongguo (the Middle Kingdom, China) was used to refer to Vietnam, and the Chinese Ming Dynasty was denounced as "bandits" or even "yidi-barbarians."[28] The fact that the Sinicization process was so successful in Vietnam created an unexpected backlash for the Chinese view of assimilating the barbarians. Now the barbarians were assimilated and Sinicized, the "real" Chinese were made into barbarians. Nothing more powerful could illustrate the fact that the entire bipartite division between we/civilized/center and they/barbarian/periphery is a relative concept that could be employed by any social group to suit their need.

To sum up, what we have done in this study is to examine ancient documents concerning attitudes toward foreigners. Some documents reveal to us that the ancient people often thought that there were people out there who were not their kind and who were hostile to them. Other evidence shows that their attitudes were not always hostile toward foreigners or aliens. Thus we should not present a simplified picture of any "unified" attitude toward foreigners. Neither should we give a simple answer to the question of whether the ancient's attitudes were based on any historical reality. Conflict between groups was part of the human condition, yet it is uncertain if conflict was the reason or the result of hostile attitudes toward others. We are unlikely to solve this problem as long as the origin of group conflict remains a prehistoric phenomenon. It has been suggested that, before the time when resource became a problem, primitive societies tended to live separately without much competition. Conflict, or for that matter complex society, or agricultural society, arose as a result of resource competition.[29] When conflicts between small and closer groups were resolved as time progressed, and as larger "cultural spheres/states" were formed, resource competition began a new phase and turned into a competition of cultural values—that is, the construction of we-group versus they-group based on cultural differences—between states, though this need not have excluded the earlier aim of fighting for material resource. Here the possibilities exist for real or imagined conflicts, as well as a mixture of both. The beginning of documented human history, as I see it, falls into this second phase of competition. This explains why our evidence shows that the attitudes of the ancient Mesopotamian, Egyptian, and Chinese toward foreigners or foreign lands are basically cultural evaluations. The third phase of competition—that is, racial conflicts—was a fateful turn of cultural conflict that injected biological determinism into cultural values. This, however, is an entirely new situation, itself an often discussed subject in modern scholarship of humanity and social sciences, which falls outside of the scope of the present investigation—an exposition of the prelude to the human conflicts of the modern world.

Notes

Chapter 1. Introduction

1. John B. Friedman 1981.

2. Friedman 1981: 5–25; James S. Romm 1992: 82–120.

3. For example, it is suggested that in Strabo's view, the geographical totality is the totality of the human world. Thus knowledge about geography is part of the knowledge of humanity. See Ch. Van Paassen 1957: 18–20.

4. James S. Romm 1992: 1–8.

5. Friedman 1981: 3.

6. Yüan Ke 1981: 194, 232; R. Mathieu 1983. R. E. Strassberg 2002. For the textual and chronological problems related to early Chinese texts in general, see M. Loewe ed. 1993; E. L. Shaughnessy ed. 1997.

7. See E. Hobsbawn and T. Ranger eds. 1983.

8. I use "culture" and "civilization" interchangeably. Needless to say, this is only an expiedient way to get around a lengthy definitional pronouncement regarding the meaning of these terms. See Nobert Elias 1982.

9. A. Momingliano 1990. See discussion below.

10. For the effort of proselytism by Jews in late antiquity, see Louis H. Feldman 1993: 288–341.

11. See, for example, R. MacMullen 1984; R. Fletcher 1997: 39.

12. For example, Norbert Elias and John L. Scotson 1994.

13. Van Paassen 1957: 246–58.

14. John R. Gardiner-Garden 1987: 2–3; Van Paassen 1957: 257–58.

15. Gardiner-Garden 1987: 2.

16. Gardiner-Garden 1987: 5–6.

17. F. Hartog 1988: 7.

18. R. E. Holloman and S. A. Arutiunov eds. 1978; M. Banton 1987; T. H. Eriksen

1993; S. J. Shennan ed. 1989. For a discussion of the terms "ethnos" and "race," see Malcolm Chapman, Maryon McDonald, and Elizabeth Tonkin 1989: 11–17.

19. F. Barth ed. 1969; B. Anderson 1991. For a recent exposition of this theory in the study of Greek ethnic identity, see Jonathan M. Hall 1997.

20. T. Shibutani and K. K. Kwan 1965: 47; T. H. Eriksen 1993: 4; K. A. Kamp and N. Yoffee 1980: 85–104, concurs with this view. See also J. M. Yinger 1994: 1–37, for a sociological discussion of race and ethnicity. For a recent study of the Chinese minorities using this theory, see Wang Mingke 1997.

21. L. A. Despres ed. 1975: 192–93; C. F. Keyes 1976: 202–13.

22. Richard. S. Cooper, Jay S. Kaufman and Ryk Ward 2003: 1166–70; Michael J. Bamshad and Steve E. Olsen 2003: 50–57.

23. J. Blackburn 1979; G. Jahoda 1961.

24. F. Dikötter 1992: viii.

25. F. Dikötter 1992: 14–17.

26. A. B. Lloyd 1988: 215–53, esp. 218.

27. Jonathan Hall 1997: 47. See also Edith Hall 1989; Pericles Georges 1994; Wilfried Nippel 2002.

28. David Lorton 1973: 65–70.

29. There is a long history of discussion about the credibility of Herodotus, see, for examples, W. Spiegelberg 1927 ; A. B. Lloyd 1993; E. M. Yamauchi, 1997.

30. Zhao Tiehan 1965: 314–347; Hu Houxuan 1972; Tian Qianjun 1965: 17–24, 35; Wang Ermin 1977: 41–480; Yü Xingwu 1981; Yü Rongchun 1986; Chen Suizheng 1993. For a recent discussion of the historical background of the early Chinese perceptions of these foreign peoples, see Nicola Di Cosmo 2002: 93–126.

31. As shown by the title of a famous work, J. B. Pritchard 1969. M. Lichtheim 1983: 43–52, compares Egyptian wisdom literature with other traditions, notably Hellenic and Biblical ideas. Her treatment, nevertheless, is confined to several specific points of contact of shared values. Other significant works include W. S. Smith 1965; W. Helck 1971. D. B. Redford 1992 is so far the most comprehensive treatment of the relationship between Egypt and the Palestinian area. The approach, though a great achievement in its own right, is still a positivist inquiry into the actual contacts between the two areas. For the Egyptian relationship with foreign lands in general, see D. Valbelle 1990. In the field of Assyriology, the conference volume of Hans-J. Nissen and Johannes Renger eds. 1982 seems to concentrate on a specific topic. Yet being a collection of essays there is less integrating discussion to cull all the studies together and form a synthetic overview.

32. Some of the notable works are B. Schwartz ed. 1975; S. N. Eisenstadt ed. 1986; G. Cawgill and N. Yoffee eds. 1986; the most ambitious one is Bruce G. Trigger 1993. Most recently, Janet Richards and Mary Van Buren eds. 2000. See discussion below.

33. My preliminary attempts are Poo Muchou. 1994; 1998a; 1999.

34. Romila Thapar 1971.

35. Marshall G. S. Hodgson 1993: 268.

36. Hodgson 1993: 268–69.

37. George M. Fredrickson 1997: 5.

38. Fredrickson 1997: 8–9.

39. For a convenient summary of his arguments, see A. J. Toynbee 1957: 380–430.

40. A. Kroeber 1944.

41. Hodgson 1993: 270–77.

42. Trigger 1993.

43. Trigger 1993: 15.

44. Trigger 1993: 17.

45. G. E. R. Lloyd 1996; idem, 2002; Lloyd and Sivin 2002.

46. Lloyd 1996: 3–5.

47. Steven Shankman and Stephen W. Durrant eds. 2002; Lisa Raphals 1992.

48. Janet Richards and Mary Van Buren eds. 2000.

49. Baines and Yoffee 1998: 199–260.

50. Baines and Yoffee 1998: 204.

51. Owen Lattimore 1951: 337–50.

52. Baines and Yoffee 1998: 203.

Chapter 2. In Search of Cultural Identity

1. For a recent discussion of the origins of city-states in Mesopotamia, see Marc Van de Mieroop 1997: 23–41.

2. J. Oates 1986: 12.

3. A. W. Sjöberg and E. Bergman 1969; Van de Mieroop 1997: 46–47.

4. N. J. Postgate 1992: 34.

5. J. S. Cooper 1983a; Robert McC. Adams 1981: 244–45.

6. See, in general, A. Kuhrt 1995: 36–44.

7. Cooper 1983a: 7.

8. Postage 1992: 3.

9. Adams 1981: 11.

10. Cooper 1983a: 244–45.

11. Kamp and Yoffee 1980: 94. For theoretical considerations, see F. Barth ed. 1969. M. B. Rowton 1973: 247–58.

12. Trigger, Kemp, O'Connor, and Lloyd 1983: 1–4; N. Grimal 1992: 22–23; Ian Shaw ed. 2000: 65.

13. Karl Butzer 1976: 4ff.

14. For example, R. D. Givens, and M. A. Nettleship eds. 1976; D. Riches ed. 1986.

15. Chang Kwang-chih 1986: 214ff.; idem, 1999.

16. Su Bingqi 1997: 28–84.

17. Su Bingqi 1997: 28–84.

18. S. J. Shennan 1989: 1–32; Jonathan Hall 1997: 111–42. Ian Hodder 1991.

19. Chang Kwang-chih 1980: 248–59. See chapter 3 below.

20. Zheng Jiexiang 1994: 157ff.

21. Wang Guanying 1984, 5: 80–99. See also D. Keightley 1983: 523–64; Chang Kwang-chih 1980: 158ff.

22. Harold Haarmann 1986; W. B. Gudykunst ed. 1988.

23. Postgate 1992: 23–24.

24. See I. J. Gelb 1960: 258–71; J. S. Cooper 1973: 239–46; idem, 1999: 61–77.

25. J. S. Cooper 1983a: 8; also see V. Katz 1993: 18–21, for a brief survey of the supposed conflict between Semites and Sumerians.

26. See now the discussion of the process, H. Vanstiphout 1999: 141–59 in H. Vanstiphout ed. 1999: 141–59.

27. Gelb 1960: 266.

28. Gelb 1960: 266.

29. Gelb 1960: 270.

30. For an assessment of the problem of Sumerian-Akkadian bilingualism even after the disuse of Sumerian as a daily spoken language, see H. Vanstiphout 1999.

31. J. S. Cooper 1999.

32. See Antonio Loprieno 1995: 1–8.

33. Hoch 1994.

34. Lichtheim 1973–80: vol. I, 25.

35. Lichtheim 1973–80: vol. II, 44.

36. A. K. Bowman 1986: 122–24; R. S. Bagnall 1993: 230–60; P. Bilde et al. eds. 1992; J. H. Johnson ed. 1994.

37. Qiu Xigui 1978, 3: 162–71; W. Boltz 1994: 35–39; idem in M. Loewe and E. Shaughnessy eds. 1999: 108–9.

38. E. G. Pulleyblank 1983:411–66; esp. 413.

39. Pulleyblank 1983: 416–23. For discussion of the relationship between Chinese and Tibeto-Burman languages, see W. H. Baxter 1995; W. Boltz 1999: 74–81.

40. For details, see chapter 4 below.

41. From an archaeological point of view, the origin of the predynastic Zhou culture was complicated, consisting of various elements from the Shang, the northeastern, and the western regions. How one should combine this picture with linguistic evidence is not clear at this time. See Zou Heng 1980: 297–356.

42. Pulleyblank 1983; W. Boltz 1999: 81–83; Tsu-lin Mei and J. Norman 1976.

43. Teng Rensheng 1996; E. L. Shaughnessy 1997: 223–83.

44. See Tsuen-hsuin Tsien 1962.

45. See Adolf Erman 1966: 197.

46. See William K. Simpson 1977: 346.

47. *Zuozhuan* 32/10b, year 14 of Duke Xiang. See chapter 4.

48. Mangzi 5b/5; Legge 1985, vol. II: 255.

Chapter 3. Representations

1. Cf. B. J. Kemp 1991: 29–31.

2. A. Piankoff 1964: 56–59.

3. T. G. Allen 1974: 97–99.

4. K. Oberhuber 1990: 54–55; *CAD*, "ahu."

5. K. Oberhuber 1990: 284–85; *CAD*, "nakru."

6. H. Limet 1972.

7. F. R. Kraus 1970: 47–52; H. Limet 1978.

8. G. Buccellati 1966: 324.

9. Buccellati 1966: 324–32.

10. Cooper 1983b: 30ff.

11. In the reigns of Naram-Sin and Šar-kali-Šari, see Douglas Frayne 1993: 85, 183.

12. G. Buccellati 1966: 235–47; R. M. Whiting 1995: 1231–41.

13. I. J. Gelb 1961: 29–47.

14. J. R. Kupper 1957. Robert. M. Whiting 1995: 1231–41.

15. Kamp and Yoffee 1980: 95–96.

16. For the following discussion, see Katrien de Graef 1999a: 1–46; 1999b: 1–17.

17. Katrien de Graef 1999a: 44–46.

18. P. Steinkeller 1980: 1–9.

19. Jean Bottéro 1975, esp. 108.

20. Elena Cassin 1987.

21. H. Limet 1978: 1–12; G. Steiner 1978.

22. *ANET* 265–66.

23. W. Horowitz 1998: chapter 2.

24. See related discussion in P. Michalowski 1999: 305–15.

25. R. Giveon 1971.

26. *Wb* III, 234, 16–235,1.

27. See a general treatment, W. Helck 1971. On the term "Asiatics (ʿ3mw, Styw:" see Phyliis Saretta 1997: 13–66.

28. Lichtheim 1973–80: vol. I, 227.

29. A. Nibbi 1981: 151ff., maitains that *Nhsy* refers not only to the Nubian people, but also people who lived to the east of Egypt.

30. W. Hölscher 1937.

31. W. F. Petrie 1953: pl. A. 3.

32. Gunn 1927: 183.

33. D. Valbelle 1990: 46–47; E. Uphill 1967.

34. *Wb* I, 559, 2–14.

35. R. A. Faulkner 1969: 50.

36. Uphill 1967: 394.

37. Uphill 1967: 395.

38. Uphill 1967: 395–400.

39. *Urkunden* IV, 85.

40. *Urkunden* IV, 792.

41. See J. Vercoutter et al. 1976: 97, fig. 80.

42. See J. Vercoutter et al. 1976: 109; figs. 126–29.

43. *Wb* I, 3, 2.

44. H. Goedicke 1960; 1966; W. Helck and E. Otto eds. 1975–89: vol. I, 116, "Dolmetscher."

45. *Wb* II, 421, 9–424,18. See Loprieno 1988: 22ff.

46. Merer stela, MNK-XI-999, 7–8; quoted in Loprieno 1997: 196.

47. BM stela 1628, 13–15; quoted in Loprieno 1997: 196.

48. *Wb* II, 423,4.

49. E. Hornung 1990: fig. 107–9; idem, 1991:122–23; pls. 58–59; F. J. Yurco 1996.

50. For the meaning of *T3-mri* in the Ptolemaic period as "land of inheirtance," see M-Th. Derchain-Urtel 1992: 55–61.

51. H. Goedicke 1979: 14–17, argues that *T3-mri* represents the garrison towns and the landed property connected with them.

52. A. J. Peden 1994: 8–15.

53. Chen Mengjia .1956: 255–59; Li Xiaoding.1982: 693–96.

54. See Li Xueqin.1959: 61ff.; Yao Xiaosui and Xiao Ding. 1985: 92–108; D. N. Keightley 2000: 66–72. See Nicola Di Cosmo 1999: 907–9.

55. Li Xueqin 1959: 77–83; Gu Jiegang 1980, 1: 117–52. For a discussion of the Qiang from a linguistic point of view, see E. G. Pulleyblank 1983: 411–66, esp. 416–23. For a discussion of the conceptual problem in treating all the "Qiang" as one ethnic group, see Wang Mingke.1994: 98–102. Zhao Lin 1983.

56. Numerous studies on the problem of Chinese-babarian relations have been written by Chinese and Japanese scholars, for example, Zhao Tiehan 1965: 314–47; Meng Wentong 1958; Kodô Kinpei 1962; N. Di Cosmo 1999: 919–51. For a discussion of the use of the term "tribe," see Morton H. Fried 1983. Fried questions the concept of tribe and its applicability in discussing the rise of state in China as well as other places. Since my object here is to discuss the Chinese attitude toward foreigners, whether they should be referred to as "tribes" or "people" is of less immediate concern.

57. See Wang Guowei. 1975: 583–605. Jaroslav Prušek 1971: 18–20; N. Di Cosmo 1999: 919.

58. Jaroslav Prušek 1971: 126–27. The author of this inscription obviously equated Xianyun with Rong.

59. *Zuozhuan* 4/14b, year 9 of Duke Yin.

60. Zhao Tiehan 1965: 315.

61. *Zuozhuan* 32/8b, year 14 of Duke Xiang. Fan Xuanzi addresses the Rong leader as "Qiang-Rong."

62. *Liji* 12/26–27.

63. *Erya* 7/8.

64. Sun Yirang 1974: 86, 112–13; Wang Xianshen 1974: 132.

65. See Wang Guowei 1975.

66. See Chen Suizheng 1993; Wang Ermin 1977: 441–80.

67. Chen Suizheng 1993.

68. Yu Rongchun 1986; see page 76 for documentation.

69. Tang Lan 1934: 6–9.

70. Hu Houxuan 1972: 2–3; Yü Xingwu 1981: 1–10; esp. 2–3; Zheng Jiexiang 1994: 157ff. See also D. N. Keightley 2000; idem, in M. Loewe and E. Shaughnessy eds. 1999: 269.

71. See Wang Zhongfu 1989: 363–76; Ogura Yoshihiko 1967.

72. Zhou Fagao 1975: 3952–54.

73. Su Bingqi 1997: 105.

74. See discussion, Huber 1983: 181–83 in D. Keightley ed. 1983: 181–83.

75. Zhou Fagao 1975: 3624–28.

76. Elena Cassin 1987; Jean Bottéro 1975: 108–9.

77. *ANET*, 75.

78. *ANET*, 77.

79. *ANET*, 77.

80. Cooper 1983b: 31.

81. Cooper 1983b: 31.

82. Cooper 1983b: 31.

83. Cooper 1983b: 32.

84. Cooper 1983b: 32.

85. B. Alster 1975: 67.

86. Joan G. Westenholz 1997: 294.

87. A. L. Oppenheim 1967: 72.

88. Cooper 1983b: 30.

89. Elena Cassin 1987: 42.

90. J. Klein 1993, 1996.

91. H. Vanstiphout 1999.

92. H. Frankfort 1939: 15–29.

93. Frankfort 1939: 22–23. M. Brandes 1979: Tafel 3.

94. Frankfort 1939: pls. V d, e, f, i; VI a.

95. Frankfort 1939: pl. XXII b.

96. Edith Porada 1995: 84, fig. 59.

97. S. Langdon 1924: pl. XXXVI.1; see Postgate 1992: 29, fig. 2:5.

98. W. Helck 1971: 4–12; D. B. Redford 1992: 20–23. For Egypt's relationship with the outside world in general, see Rolf Gundlach 1994; Dominique Valbelle 1990. A general account can be found in D. B. Redford ed. 2001: vol I, 544–48.

99. See a recent discussion, S. Mark 1997: 88–124.

100. See W. Helck 1974: 167–72.

101. For a more reserved view of the Narmer palette, see Whitney Davis 1992: 160–233, in which Davis refrains from making positive identifications of the enemies.

102. E. J. Baumgartel 1960: 92; H. Goedicke 1963; D. B. Redford 1994.

103. A. J. Spencer 1980: no. 576, 79–80; for discussion, Davis 1992: 119–44, where Davis tentatively identifies the lion with the ruler.

104. E. S. Hall 1986 = MÄ 44: figs. 5, 6, 7, 10–20; Davis 1992: 127, 214–5.

105. See Alan Shulman 1988; R. Müller-Wollermann 1988, disagrees with Shulman's interpretation of the execution scenes as "ceremonial executions," since no evidence to such ceremony has been found. Instead she sees the scenes as deriving from three possible sources: copying of royal monumental motive, or the king served as intermediate between the god and the man who possessed the stela, or the scene copies the scene on the pylon before which the stela was brought as votive.

106. Goedicke 1963; G. Posener 1956: 104.

107. R. Schulz and M. Seidel 1997: 40; the inscription accompanying the scene says: "Conquerer of foreign lands."

108. Uphill 1967.

109. T. Säve-Sörderberg 1941; B. Trigger 1976; Karola Zibelius-Chen 1988.

110. Gundlach 1994: 54–57.

111. R. Drenkhahn 1967: 4ff.

112. A. H. Gardiner 1964: pl. XIX; John Baines 1996a.

113. Gundlach 1994: 41–44.

114. Borchardt, 1903, II, pls. 1, 5; broken pieces in Borchardt 1903: 46, fig. 29; 48, fig. 31; pls. 8–11; Pepi II temple, W. Hölscher 1937: 15, fig. 1.

115. Hölscher 1937: 15, n.5.

116. See E. Bresciani 1997; Redford 2001: 544–48.

117. A. Loprieno 1988 .

118. H. Junker 1929–55: vol. II, 194, pl. XVI; vol. III, 166. fig. 27.

119. H. G. Fisher 1961: 44–80.

120. See E. Bresciani 1997.

121. Jessica Rawson ed. 1997: 35, fig. 2. For a definition of the Mongolian type, see G. T. Bowles 1977: 216–32.

122. *Wenwu* 1986, 8, color plate 1.

123. Rawson ed. 1997: 108; Chang Kwangchih 1980: 89, fig. F; Deng Shuping 1995: 148, fig. 37 shows a late Shang or early Zhou kneeling jade person, which resembles early Zhou jade figure found at Gansu. See Gansusheng bowuguan wenwudui 1977, 2:120, fig. 19:1.

124. For reference, see Chang Kwangchih 1983a: 361–63; idem, 1983b: 61–80; S. Allan 1992. On the other hand, Hayashi Minao 1986: 161ff., considers all the human figures on Shang bronzes as "deities." This, nevertheless, dose not explain why the facial features of one such deity, fig. 11–18, are so prominently "foreign."

125. For discussions of this view, see the above note.

126. For discussion, see Poo 1998b: 23–29; D. N. Keightley 1999: 262.

127. Rawson ed. 1997: 104.

128. For infromation on oracle bone inscriptions concerning the sacrifice of Qiang prisoners, see Hu Houxuan 1974, 8.

129. For archaeological testimony of human sacrifice in the Shang period, see Huang Zhanyue 1990.

130. Chang Kwangchih 1980: 117–24.

131. Chang Kwangchih 1980: 329–35; Han Kangxin and Pan Qifeng 1985.

132. Rawson ed. 1997: 61, fig. 22; 64, fig. 23; see Steven F. Sage 1992: 14–28, for the historical background of this site.

133. Rawson ed. 1997: 167, fig. 78.

134. Qu Xiaoqiang et al. eds. 1993: 85–90.

135. Rawson ed. 1997: 142, fig. 2.

136. Lu Liancheng and Hu Zhisheng 1988: vol. 1, 315, 375.

137. Rawson ed. 1997: 133 fig. 2; 157.

138. Rawson ed. 1997: 151–53.

139. Yin Shengping 1986. Another small bronze statue of a Scythian was found in Xinjiang, dated eighth to third century BCE, but one could argue that Xinjiang was not yet part of "China" at this early stage. The statue was certainly not made in the Central Plain.

140. For a discussion of pre-Qin Chinese artistic representations of human figures, see Mary Fong 1988; Dietrich Seckel 1993; Guolong Lai 1999. There is almost certainly more evidence to be discovered. A group of small bronze figurines, now on display at the British Museum and dated to the early Western Zhou period show considerable non-Mongolian facial features. Their small size, i.e., no more than 20 cm high, indicates that they were ornamental objects and not used in any formal way to make any monumental suggestions. More has to be learned before we can make further comments.

141. For a few statues that may represent foreigners, see Hayashi Minao 1985: fig. 31, 32, 36, 37, 38, 39, 42. For representations of foreigners after the Han Dynasty, see Jane. G. Mahler 1959; E. Schloss 1969.

142. *Zuozhuan* 29/22a, year 4 of Duke Xiang; Legge 1985: vol. V, 424.

143. *Zuozhuan* 15/21, year 24 of Duke Xi; Legge 1985: vol. V, 192.

144. In fact, the reality of musical performances and theory in the Eastern Zhou period is much more complex than what "five sounds" could represent. See Lothar von Falkenhausen 1993: 199ff.

145. *Zuozhuan* 11/1b, year 1 of Duke Min; Legge 1985: vol. V, 124. Similar expressions are found elsewhere, for example, in *Guoyu* 2/3a, the official Fu Chen says: "The nature of the Di is that of the wolfs."

146. For this point, see Di Cosmo 2002: 7.

147. Study of the way people dressed shows that not all the Chinese folded the front lappet from the right and that not all the barbarians folded their lappet from the left. See Hayashi Minao 1985.

148. *Mengzi* 12b/7b; Legge 1985: vol. II, 442.

149. *Liji* 12/26–27; Legge 1976: 229.

150. *Lüshi chunqiu*, 20/2 "Shi-jun," translation follows John Knoblock and Jeffrey Riegel 2000: 512.

151. *Mengzi* 6b/4; Legge 1985: vol. II, 442.

152. For example, Wu Hung 1995: 74, fig. 1.79 (b).

153. M. Liverani 1990: 36–37.

Chapter 4. Relations and Attitudes

1. D. and J. Oates 1976: 102.

2. D. Potts 1982: 36–39; John Curtis ed. 1993.

3. *ANET*, 265.

4. A. Kuhrt 1995: 26.

5. See a synopsis of Sumerian and Elamite political relations during the third millennium in Potts 1982. In Hans-J. Nissen and Johannes Renger ed. 1982.

6. Jacobsen 1966: 95, iv 5–6.

7. Michalowski 1989: 47.

8. *ANET*, 455–463.

9. *ANET*, 613.

10. See Adele Berlin 1984: 17–24.

11. As discussed in Heda Jason 1977.

12. See Adele Berlin 1984: 18.

13. Lambert 1996: 113.

14. For a discussion of the foreign threat during the late Old Babylonian period, see R. Pientka 1998: 257–72.

15. E. A. Speiser 1955: 35–76, esp. 56.

16. The attitude toward the Babylonians, however, is more of that between equals. See recent publications of the correspondence of Sargon II, which, nonetheless, confirm that conflicts between Assyria and Babylonia were quite intense during the late eighth and early seventh century BCE. See S. Parpola and A. Fuchs 2001, part III: xiii–xxiii.

17. C. Zaccagnini 1978.

18. F. M. Fales 1978.

19. E. S. Hall 1986: figs. 5, 6, 7, 10–20; Alan Shulman 1988; R. Müller-Wollermann 1988: 69–76, disagrees with Shulman's interpretation of the execution scenes as "ceremonial executions," since no evidence to such ceremony has been found. Instead she sees the scenes as deriving from three possible sources: copying of royal monumental motives, that the king served as intermediate between the god and the man who possessed the stela, or that the scene copies the scene on the pylon before which the stela was brought as votive.

20. J. H. Breasted 1906: vol. I, 59, 66.

21. *Urkunden* I, 102–5. Lichtheim 1973–80: vol. I, 20. For the land of the sand dwellers as denoting the Eastern Delta, see Goedicke 1963.

22. *Urkunden* I, 125–27. Lichtheim 1973–80: vol. I, 26.

23. Lichtheim 1973–80: vol. I, 25.

24. J. H. Breasted 1906 I: 1, 163; *Urkunden* I, 133, 12–15.

25. J. Osing 1976:133–85; W. Helck and E.Otto eds.1975–89: vol. I: 67–69.

26. G. Posener 1940; *ANET*, 328–29.

27. Lichtheim 1973–80: vol. I, 98–200.

28. Lichtheim 1973–80: vol. I, 119.

29. Lichtheim 1973–80: vol. I, 137.

30. Lichtheim 1973–80: vol. I, 188.

31. Lichtheim 1973–80: vol. I, 152.

32. See discussion in M. Lichtheim 1973–80: vol. I, 149–50. For an interpretation of this text in the context of the Near Eastern literary tradition of the destruction of cities, see J. F. Quack 1997: 345–54. In B. Pongratz-Leisten et al. eds. 1997.

33. Lichtheim 1973–80: vol. I, 141.

34. D. Lorton 1973: 65–70.

35. Gay Robins 1997: 160, fig. 189; Frank. M. Snowden Jr. 1983: fig. 35.

36. For an example of Amenhotep III, represented in the tomb of Anen in Thebes, with figures of Nubian and Asiatic on the footrest, and various bound foreigners painted on the side of the base of the pavilon, see G. Robins 1997: 137. For general discussion, see Jean Vercoutter et al. 1976: 64–88.

37. Chang Kwang-chih 1986: 214ff.

38. Chen Mengjia 1956: 270–76.

39. Yao Xiaosui 1979: 337–91.

40. Li Xueqin 1959: 94.

41. Yao Xiaosui 1979: 362.

42. For information concerning the sacrifice of Qiang prisoners on oracle bone inscriptions, see Hu Houxuan 1974: 8.

43. Yao Xiaosui 1979: 368–82.

44. Yao Xiaosui 1979: 386.

45. For archaeological testimony of human sacrifice in the Shang period, see Huang Zhanyue 1990: 41–68. Cf. Chang Kwang-chih 1980: 121–24; D. N. Keightley 1983: 266–67.

46. Yao Xiaosui 1979: 382–85.

47. Hsu Choyun and K. M. Linduff 1988: 68ff.; M. Loewe and E. Shaughnessy 1999: 320–23.

48. *Shiji* 4/112 (Gong Liu); 4/118 (Gu Gong Tan Fu).

49. *Shiji* 33/1517, 1524; *Hou-Han shu* 85/2808.

50. Hsu and Linduff 1988: 186ff.

51. Ma Chengyuan ed. 1988; translation: M. Loewe and E. Shaughnessy 1999: 321–22. Translation follows Shaughnessy, except for the number of captured chiefs and sheep, which Shaughnessy gives as two and thirty eight respectively.

52. Ma Chengyuan ed. 1988: no. 437; translation E. Shaughnessy 1999: 346.

53. Shaughnessy 1999: 346.

54. Shaughnessy 1999: 346–47.

55. *Shijing* 10b/2–3; James Legge 1985: vol. IV, 281.

56. *Shijing* 9c/12; James Legge 1985: vol. IV, 258.

57. *Shangshu* 3/14; Legge 1985: vol. III, 39–40.

58. *Zuozhuan* 20/19b, year 18 of Duke Wen; Legge 1985: vol. V, 283.

59. See Qu Wanli 1975: 3; M. Loewe 1993: 377–78.

60. See discussion in M. Loewe ed. 1993: 67–76; Yuri Pines 1997: 100–16.

61. Yang Lien-sheng 1968: 20–33.

62. *Zuozhuan* 11/1b, year 1 of Duke Min; Legge 1985 vol. V, 124.

63. *Mengzi* 12b/13, Legge 1985: vol. II, 447–48.

64. Volkert Haas 1980: 37–44.

65. J. Van Dijk 1978: 97–110. In Hans-J. Nissen and J. Renger eds. 1978.

66. Haas 1980: 39.

67. Guillermo Algaze 1993: 1–6

68. J. Curtis ed. 1993.

69. Y. Koenig 1987:105–10.

70. G. Pinch 1995: 45.

71. Papyrus Anastasi I, see E. Wente 1990: 108.

72. T. G. Allen 1974: 20 (*Book of the Dead* 15 A5 S4).

73. A. Erman 1901: 50–51; translation from J. P. Sørensen 1992: 164–81, esp. 173. In P. Bilde, T. Engberg-Pedersen, L. Hannestad and J. Zahle eds. 1992.

74. H. Goedicke 1984; cf. G. Pinch 1995: 141.

75. A. H. Gardiner 1935: 18.

76. T. G. Allen 1974.

77. Yüan Ke 1981: 378; Cheng Hsiao-chieh et al. tr. 1985: 226.

78. Yüan Ke 1981: 413; Cheng Hsiao-chieh et al. tr. 1985: 237.

79. Yüan Ke 1981: 434; Cheng Hsiao-chieh et al. tr. 1985: 248.

80. Yüan Ke 1981: 436–437; Cheng Hsiao-chieh et al. tr. 1985: 249.

81. Poo 1998b, chapter 4.

82. F. Dikötter 1992: 10–17.

83. G. Buccellati 1966: 338.

84. G. Buccellati 1966: 338–39.

85. M. Lichtheim 1973–80: vol. I, 19.

86. M. Bietak 1988: 35–40.

87. P. E. Newberry 1893: pls. 28, 30, 31.

88. See N. Grimal 1992: 218–19.

89. See in general A. Shulman 1979: 177–93; G. Robins 1993: 30–36.

90. W. L. Moran 1992: 8–9.

91. W. L. Moran 1992: 93.

92. W. L. Moran 1992: 1.

93. W. L. Moran 1992: 93.

94. D. B. Redford 1984: 37.

95. S. A. Meier 2000: 165–73. In R. Cohen and R. Westbrook eds. 2000: 165–73.

96. W. L. Moran 1992: 8–9.

97. *ANET*, 202.

98. *ANET*, 199. See S. Langdon and A. H. Gardiner 1920: 179–205, 185. See also Mario Liverani 1990, for a general treatment of international relations in the ancient Near East in the second millennium BCE.

99. Hsu and Linduff 1988: 267.

100. *Shiji* 4/ 135–36.

101. *Zuozhuan* 2/29b, year 2 of Duke Yin.

102. *Zuozhuan* 32/10b, year 14 of Duke Xiang.

103. For the entire episode, see *Zuozhuan* 32/10, year 14 of Duke Xiang. For translation, cf. Legge 1985: vol. V, 463–64.

104. See chapter 3 above.

105. Legge 1985: vol. V, 463–64.

106. *Zuozhuan* 4/4b, 13/15a, 24/1b; Legge 1985: vol. V, 23, 156, 322, where Legge translates the character *fa* as "to attack," which does not entirely capture the full meaning of the word.

107. See J. Prušek 1971: 227–28. Prušek emphasizes (p. 227) that there was no sharp awareness of contrast between Chinese and barbarian as was found in the Greek conception of the barbarians. I agree partially with this statement; in practice the interrelations between Chinese and the barbarians might have been simply a problem of power relations. Yet this does not mean that, to the intellectual elites, "barbarian culture" was conceptually compatible with the Chinese *li* (propriety) and *i* (righteousness).

108. *Zuozhuan* 15/21–2, year 24 of Duke Xi; Legge 1985 vol. V, 192; *Shiji* 110/2881.

109. *Zuozhuan* 24/9b, year 15 of Duke Xuan.

110. See the legends about the ancestors of the Wu and Chu, *Shiji* 40/1690–92. For discussion of the Wu, see Wang Mingke 1997: 255–88.

111. Wang 1997: 255–88. A recent study suggests that the Rong people in early Spring and Autumn period, as recorded in the *Zuozhuan*, were probably the descendents of the Shang people who fled into the mountains after the Zhou take over. If this suggestion is further substantiated, it could have a fundamental effect on our understanding of the Rong-Chinese relations. See Zhang Huaitong 2001: 21–27.

112. Adams 1975: 12.

113. Zaccagnini 1978: 416–17

114. Zaccagnini 1978: 413.

115. Zaccagnini 1978: 414.

116. Zaccagnini 1978: 416.

117. "Mehrsprachigkeit," in W. Helck and E.Otto eds. 1975–89: vol. III, 7.

118. H. G. Fisher 1961: 44–80.

119. M. Lichtheim 1973–80: vol. I, 103–4. A similar attitude can be found later in the New Kingdom school texts such as Papyrus Anastasi I. See Antonio Loprieno 1988: 22–23.

120. Lichtheim 1973–80: vol. I, 226.

121. See H. Brunner et al. 1952: 131–33.

122. Lichtheim 1973–80: vol. I, 213.

123. E. Wente 1990: 127.

124. Lichtheim 1973–80: vol. I, 231–32.

125. Lichtheim 1973–80: vol. I, 233.

126. Lichtheim 1973–80: vol. I, 141.

127. Lichtheim 1973–80: vol. I, 152.

128. See W. Helck 1964: 103 ff.; Loprieno 1988: 22 ff.

129. Valbelle 1990: 135–95. See next chapter.

130. Lichtheim 1973–80: vol. II, 98.

131. See Erik Hornung 1999.

132. *ANET*, 257–58.

133. *ANET*, 255–56; 262–63.

134. Zibelius–Chen 1988: 223.

135. H. Goedicke: 1975.

136. See Lichtheim 1973–80: vol. II, 226; H. Goedicke 1975.

137. K. A. Kitchen 1986: 255–71.

138. *Zhanguoce* 19/9ff.; *Shiji* 43/1806ff.

139. Sun Yirang 1974: 115–16; see Poo 1990: 25–62.

140. For an explanation of this process, see Wang Mingke 1997: 119–50.

141. For further discussion, see J. K. Fairbank ed. 1968; M. Rossabi 1983; Sechin Jagchid and Van J. Symons 1989; Thomas J. Barfield 1989; N. Di Cosmo 1999: 964–66; idem 2002: 161–252.

142. For the eastern Zhou period, I make a distinction between the political elite and the intellectual and cultural elite, as the political elites were the holders of political power, while the intellectual elites were experts in the ritual and historical knowledge that emerged during this time. Their different outlook in matters of religion has been discussed in Poo 1998b, chapter 3.

Chapter 5. Foreigners Within

1. G. Cardascia 1958.

2. I. J. Gelb 1973.

3. J. N. Postgate 1992: 254–55.

4. I. J. Gelb 1973.

5. R. Harris 1975: 338–41. Finkelstein 1955. For Subartu, see Michalowski 1999.

6. G. Buccellati 1966: 337.

7. G. Buccellati 1966: 340–42.

8. G. Buccellati 1966: 356–57.

9. H. Limet 1972.

10. A. Kuhrt 1995: vol. I, 338–39.

11. B. Oded 1979.

12. H. D.Galter 1988: 280–81.

13. H. Tadmor 1982: 449–70, esp. 451.

14. *CAH* III, pt. 2, 209.

15. S. C. Layton 1988: 172–89; quoted in Kuhrt 1995: vol. II, 397.

16. H. Tadmor 1982: 450–51.

17. H. Tadmor 1982: 455–58.

18. *CAH* III, pt. 2, 208.

19. N. Postgate 1989: 1–10, esp. 10.

20. B. N. Porter 1993: 119–54.

21. See, for example, J. E. Curtis and J. E. Reade eds. 1995: 72–73; R. D. Barnett 1958: figs. 39–46; 130–31; 138.

22. J. A. Brinkman 1984:11.

23. G. Frame 1992: 32–51.

24. N. Grimal 1992: 67.

25. B. Vachala 1991: 94–101. In E. Endesfelder ed. 1991.

26. *Urkunden* I, 217.3–5; 77.4. Quoted in Loprieno 1997: 194.

27. See M. Bakir 1952; W. Helck 1971: 982–87.

28. A. Loprieno 1997: 197–98.

29. W. C. Hayes 1955: 89–90; Pritchard 1969: 553–54.

30. This is the basic legal meaning of "slavery," although, needless to say, there are many different degrees of existence from totally "unfree, chattle-like" slaves to the "totally free" citizens. In fact, as M. I. Finley once emphasized, there has never existed a state where there are "totally free" or "totally unslaved" people. See M. I. Finley 1973: 67: "Absolute freedom is an idle dream."

31. BM stela 1628, 13–15, quoted in A. Loprieno 1997: 196.

32. El-Lahun Papyri, table 12.6–11, quoted in A. Loprieno 1997: 199.

33. W. Helck and E. Otto eds., 1975–89 vol. 5: 982–87, "Sklaven"; A. Loprieno 1997: 201–8.

34. A. Loprieno 1997: 209.

35. H. G. Fisher 1963.

36. Lichtheim 1973–80: vol. I, 19–20.

37. H. Goedicke 1967: 62–63.

38. H. G. Fisher 1961.

39. Fisher 1961: 48; Lichtheim 1973–80: vol. I, 90.

40. E. Wente 1990: 35.

41. E. Wente 1990: 39.

42. E. Wente 1990: 53.

43. E. Wente 1990: 106.

44. J. M. A. Janssen 1951: 50–62; W. Helck 1971: 342–69, 442–73; E. Bresciani 1997.

45. W. A. Ward 1994.

46. K. A. Kitchen 1991.

47. Ward 1994: 68.

48. E. Bresciani 1997: 241.

49. T. E. Peet 1930; A. H. Gardiner 1941–52.

50. *Urkunden* IV, 1344; E. Wente 1990: 27.

51. J. B. Pritchard 1969: 246.

52. Wente 1990: 36.

53. C. Alderd 1949: 30; J. Vercoutter et al. 1976: 38, 41, fig.7.

54. Baines 1996: 378–79.

55. F. Gomaà 1974.

56. K. A. Kitchen 1986: 85ff.

57. Vercoutter et al. 1976: 96–97, fig. 80.

58. E. Feucht 1990a; 1990b; 1995: 300–4.

59. Lichtheim 1973–80: vol. II, 44.

60. See discussions in chapter 4.

61. Li Xueqin 1959: 80–81.

62. *Shangshu* 6/30–33; translation, Legge 1985 vol. III, 147, with minor change. For the possible date of this passage, contained in the chapter "Yu Gong," see M. Loewe 1993: 377–78.

63. *Liji* 12/26–27; translation see James Legge 1976: 229.

64. *Zhouli* 38/14.

65. Richard Adams 1975: 12.

66. D. T. Potts 1997: 100–2.

67. P. R. S. Moorey 1994: 5–6; 85–86; 97.

68. P. R. S. Moorey 1994: 217–20; 234–35; Potts 1997: 177–79; 174–75.

69. *ANET*, 268.

70. *ANET*, 268–69.

71. S. Cohen 1973: 59–1; Th. Jacobsen 1987: 275–319.

72. See W. Moran 1992: 27–34.

73. W. Moran 1992: 36.

74. B. I. Faist 2001: 239–43.

75. A. Kuhrt 1995: 669–70

76. G. Cardascia 1958: 115.

77. H. Kees 1961: 135–43.

78. For a recent study, see W. A. Griswold 1992.

79. P. Peregrine 1991: 1–10; Griswold 1992: 222–24.

80. For example, the Parlemo Stone mentions the importation of myrrh and elec-trum from Punt, see Breasted 1906: vol. I, 70. See further discussion, S. Ratié 1979: 146–47.

81. E. Wente 1990: 15–16.

82. Lichtheim 1973–80: vol. I, 214.

83. See Vabelle 1990: 154–64.

84. See J. Vercoutter 1976: 47ff.

85. S. Ratié 1979: 139–45.

86. *Urkunden* IV 1708: 7–9.

87. *Urkunden* IV 2029: 1–2.

88. See W. Helck 1974: 505–75.

89. Daniel Sivan and Zipora Cochavi-Rainey 1992.

90. J. E. Hoch 1994: 462–71.

91. J. E. Hoch 1994: 470.

92. J. E. Hoch 1994: 474–77.

93. See Helck 1974: 505ff, see nos. 38, 60, 69, 137, 203, 231, 266, 287.

94. For example, Helck 1974: 495–504.

95. M. Loehr 1949: 128; Emma C. Bunker, C. Bruce Chatwin, Ann R. Frakas 1970: 80–83; W. Watson 1971: 52–63; Lin Yun 1986; Chen Fangmei 1992; Du Zhengsheng 1993.

96. Yin Weizhang and Cao Shuqin 1990; Du Zhengsheng 1993:300–1.

97. *Zhanguoce*, 3/10b; cf. N. Di Cosmo 1999: 963.

98. For the particular passage, see *Mutianzi zhuan* 2:1–3. Translation in French, R. Mathieu 1978; idem 1993.

99. Yü Ying-shih 1967: 133ff.

100. Xiao Tong 1982: 115.

101. An Zuozhang 1979; L. Boulnois 1966; Liu Xinru 1994.

102. B. Trigger 1997: 137–43; the quotation is on page 140.

Chapter 6. The Transformation of the Barbarians

1. *Mengzi* 5b/5a; Legge 1985: vol. II, 253. For the whole story, see 246–57.

2. *Lunyu* 14/9b; Legge 1985: vol. I, 282. For an example of the "barbarian" way of having lappets on the left side, see Hayashi Minao 1985: fig. 36. However, it seems that not all the examples of the "barbarians" cited in this article have their lappets on the left side, see figs. 32, 37.

3. *Lunyu* 9/6b; Legge 1985: vol. I, 221.

4. *Lunyu* 3/3b; Legge 1985: vol. I, 156.

5. This is examplified by a recently published eighteen volume-series on Chu culture. See Zhang Zhengming ed. 1995; T. Lawton ed. 1991; Constance A. Cook and John S. Major eds. 1999. Also see Lothar von Falkenhausen 1999: 450–544, esp. 514–25

6. *Mengzi* 6a/10; Legge 1985: vol. II, 273.

7. *Shangshu* 13/1–2; Legge 1985: vol. III, 345–49.

8. *Lunyu* 16/2a; Legge 1985: vol. I, 309.

9. *Lüshi Chunqiu* 2/10b. Cf. J. Knoblock and J. Riegel 2000: 91.

10. Song Zhimin 1993: 221–24. For a study of the material remains of the northern barbarians during this period, see Sophia-Karin Psarras 1994: 1–125.

11. Song Zhimin 1993: 223.

12. Charles D. Weber 1968.

13. Alain Thote 1999: 10–41.

14. Wu Hong 1985; Pulleyblank 1983.

15. Robert W. Bagley 1988: 78ff.; idem, in Michael Loewe and Edward L. Shaughnessy eds. 1999: 124–231. See Qu Xiaoqiang, et al. eds. 1993: for a general account. Also see a recent review of the problems involved with this find, Lothar von Falkenhausen 2002.

16. Ma Changshou 1962: 6–18; Li Xueqin 1991: 75–85; Nicola Di Cosmo 1999: 949–50.

17. Gilbert L. Mattos 1997:104–11.

18. It was not until the Tang dynasty that the Chinese developed a more confident attitude with regard to accepting foreign culture, as symbolized by the acceptance of the title "Heavenly Khan" offered by the Turks to the Tang emperor Taizong. Even then, material novelty was still a major theme connected with foreign lands, see H. Schafer 1963. Buddhist monks, however, were exceptions, since from the beginning they considered the Indian monastic way of life superior.

19. See Sechin Jagchid and Van J. Symons 1989; A. Waldron 1990: 13–29, offers the

view that "the Great Wall" never existed as one continuous wall to begin with, although defensive walls and fortresses were certainly built along the northern borders, and were rebuilt from time to time throughout Chinese history. His view is quite convincing, although, without further archaeological investigation, it will remain speculative.

20. Lattimore 1951: 441.

21. *Shiji* 110/ 2902; *Hanshu* 94B/3810; translation B. Watson 1961: II, 173.

22. See Postgate 1992: 43.

23. *Shiji* 5/192–93; except minor changes, translation follows W. H. Nienhauser Jr. ed. 1994: vol. I, 100–1.

24. The story appears in *Hanfeizi* 48–50; *Lüshi chunqiu* 24/1; *Shuoyuan* 20/463.

25. *Hanshu* 68/2959–67.

26. See, for example, H. J. Wiens 1967: which shows the very complex process of cultural encounter and assimilation.

27. See Wang Mingke 1997.

28. See William G. Boltz 1993: 25–29.

29. *Zhouli* 38/14.

30. For examples, *Shiji* 120 Xiongnu liezhuan; *Hanshu* 94 Xiongnuzhuan.

31. *Zhouli* 33/9.

32. T. Barfield 1989: 32–59.

33. Jia Yi, *Xinshu*: 4/2a.

34. Huan Kuan, *Yantie lun*: 2/13a.

35. Wang Fu, *Qianfu lun*: 5/21–22.

36. Yan Zhitui, *Yanshi jiaxun*: 1/6.

37. E. Zürcher 1990 charaterizes the general picture of Buddhism in the western region of Han when it began to be transmitted into China: extreme hybridization, the diffuse incorporation of disparate elements, no coherent complexes of doctrines or scripture, but rather a random collection of single translated texts.

38. See E. Zürcher 1959: 254–85.

39. Zibelius-Chen 1988: 224–25.

40. Lichtheim 1973–80: vol. II, 144.

41. Lichtheim 1973–80: vol. II, 98.

42. K. A. Kitchen 1979: II, 206, 15–16. For discussion, see Kitchen 1990.

43. K. A. Kitchen 1979: V, 91, 5–7.

44. Hans-Werner Fischer-Elfert 1986: 158–93.

45. Harold Haarmaan 1986: 209ff.

46. K. Kitchen 1986: 282. Redford, however, has some reservations on the truth of this marriage, see Redford 1992: 309–11. But even if the marriage was not true, other incidents that show the fact that Pharaohs' daughters could be married to commoners indicates the declining prestige of the Egyptian king. See Kitchen 1986: 276, 282.

47. For example, Masahert the Lybian was acting no differently from his Egyptian conterparts. See E. Wente 1990: 208.

48. H. Jacquet-Gordon 1960.

49. A. Kamal, 1906; H. Gauthier 1919.

50. For discussion, see A. Leahy 1985: 51–65; R. Ritner 1990:101–8; Karl Jansen-Winkeln 2000.

51. Karl Jansen-Winkeln 2000.

52. L. Török 1997:189ff.

53. Kitchen 1986: 399–410; B. G. Trigger et al. 1983: 288–99; N. Grimal 1992: 354–59.

54. John Ray 1994: 51–66.

55. Trigger 1983: 316.

56. Trigger 1983: 281. For Greek mercenaries in Egypt, see M. M. Austin 1970: 15–22; for other foreigners such as Phoenicians, Jews, Syrians, etc., see F. K. Kienitz 1953: 39f.

57. Herodotus, *Book* II, 36–42.

58. Herodotus, *Book* II, 41.

59. John Ray 1994. The quotations are from pages 57 and 65.

60. G. Posener 1936: 1–29; Lichtheim 1973–80: vol. III, 36–41; John Baines 1996: 83–92. For a discussion of the political implications in the biographies of the late period, see E. Otto 1954: 102–18.

61. Lichtheim 1973–80: vol. III, 39.

62. A. B. Lloyd 1982: 166–80; esp. 180.

63. Lichtheim 1973–80: vol. III, 41–44.

64. Lichtheim 1973–80: vol. III, 45–58.

65. Lichtheim 1973–80: vol. III, 48.

66. G. Lefebvre 1923–24.

67. Lichtheim 1973–80: vol. III, 6. For a similar epitaph for a small child by the name of Isenkhebe, see Lichtheim 1973–80: vol. III, 58–59.

68. See P. Bilde et al. eds. 1992; J. H. Johnson ed. 1994.

69. See Paul Garelli 1997: vol. I, 69–70.

70. D. Frayne 1993: 220–23.

71. D. Frayne 1993: 220.

72. Limet 1995.

73. Sophie Lafont 1998: 161–81, esp. 92.

74. J. A. Brinkman 1976: 383–84, text no. 9.

75. See A. Kuhrt 1995: 333–48. See L. Sassmannshausen 1999.

76. A. Kuhrt 1995: 398.

77. N. Postgate 1989.

78. Irene J. Winter 1980: 355–82, esp. 356–57.

79. Irene J. Winter 1980: 357.

80. Irene J. Winter 1980: 364.

81. Oppenheim 1967: 27–28.

82. G. Frame 1992: 57.

83. See a general study of the Chinese-Nomad relations, Thomas J. Barfield 1989.

Chapter 7. Conclusion

1. I. J. Gelb 1968.

2. Valbelle 1990: 189–92.

3. See Loprieno 1988, passim.

4. Loprieno 1988: 73–83; H. te Velde 1977.

5. *Urkunden* VI, 17.22ff.; quoted in Bresciani 1997: 249.

6. E. G. Pulleyblank 1983: 421, 460.

7. Owen Lattimore 1951: 345.

8. *Shangshu* 11/15.

9. Wang Mingke 1997. This does not mean that only the people in the central plain area were agricultural. It is a common knowledge that vast areas in the prehistorical East Asian continent already practiced agriculture. See Chang Tetzu 1983: 65–94; Chang Kwangchih 1986: 71ff.

10. *Liji* 12/26–27; Legge 1976: 229.

11. *Zhouli* 38/14.

12. *Yizhoushu* 7/6–7.

13. Norbert Elias and John Scotson 1994: xv–lii.

14. E. Hornung 1982: 213–16.

15. Clifford Geertz has the following to comment on the Chinese attitude and policy of acculturation imposed on the minority people in western China during the past several hundred years: "In China, as elsewhere, it is not licentiousness (referring to the sexual custom of the Na minority people of Western China) that powers most fear. Nor was immorality. It is difference." See *The New York Review of Books,* XLVIII, no. 16, Oct. 18, 2001: 30.

16. I leave out India, as we have not dealt with it in this study.

17. E. Hall 1989; F. Hartog 1988; P. Georges 1994; J. E. Coleman and C. A.Walz 1997.

18. See, for example, Prasenjit Duara 1995.

19. Here we should forego the usual reiteration of the definition of "civilization, " that it has to do with "civic," with the development of cities, writing, complex social hierarchy, etc. For discussion, see N. Elias 1982.

20. Norbert Elias 1987: xi–xiii.

21. See Frank Dikötter 1992; Frank Dikötter ed. 1997: 12–33; 34–52; Shen 1997.

22. Qian Mu 1970: 20.

23. Qian Mu 1970: 1.

24. E. H. Schafer 1963; John Kieschnick 2002.

25. For a latest study, see David E. Mungello 1999.

26. See a recent exposition of this issue, Pamela K. Crossley 1999.

27. J. K. Whitemore 1969; A. B. Woodside 1971: 18–22, 60–111; C. Y. Lee 2003.

28. Wu Shilian 1984: vol. 1, 67–68; vol. 2, 515, 550; C. Y. Lee 2003:465–68.

29. Barry Kemp 1991: 31–35.

Bibliography

Adams, Richard N. 1975. *Energy and Structure: A Theory of Social Power*. Austin and London: University of Texas Press.

Adams, Robert McC. 1981. *Heartland of Cities, Surveys of Ancient Settlement and Land Use on the Central Floodplain of the Euphrates*. Chicago: University of Chicago Press.

Adams, W. Y. 1997. "Anthropology and Egyptology: Divorce and Remarriage?" In *Anthropology and Egyptology: A Developing Dialogue*, ed. Judith Lustig, 25–32. Sheffield: Sheffield Academic Press.

Alderd, C. 1949. *Old Kingdom Art in Ancient Egypt*. London: A. Tiranti.

Algaze, Guillermo. 1993. *The Uruk World System*. Chicago: University of Chicago Press.

Allan, Sarah. 1992. "Art and Meaning." In *The Problem of Meaning in Early Chinese Ritual Bronzes*, ed. R. Whitfield, 23–25. London: Percival David Foundation of Chinese Art.

Allen, T. G. 1974. *The Book of the Dead, or Going Forth by Day*. Chicago: University of Chicago Press.

Alster, B. 1975. *Studies in Sumerian Proverbs*. Copenhagen: Akademisk Forlag.

An, Zuozhang 安作璋. 1979. *Liang Han yu Xiyu guanxi shi* 兩漢與西域關係史. Shandong: Qilu Shushe.

Anderson, B. 1991. *Imagined Communities*. London: Verso.

Austin, M. M. 1970. *Greece and Egypt in the Archaic Age*. Proceedings of the Cambridge Philological Society, Supplement no. 2. Cambridge: Cambridge Philological Society.

Bagley, Robert W. 1988. "Sacrificial Pits of the Shang Period at Sanxingdui in Guanghan County, Sichuan Province." *Arts Asiatiques* 43:78–86.

Bagnall, R. S. 1993. *Egypt in Late Antiquity*. Princeton: Princeton University Press.

Baines, John. 1996. "On the Composition and Inscriptions of the Vatican Statue of Udjahorresne." In *Studies in Honor of William Kelly Simpson*, vol. I. ed. P. Der Manuelian, 83–92. Boston: Museum of Fine Arts.

———. 1996a. "Contextualizing Egyptian Representations of Society and Ethnicity." In *The Study of the Ancient Near East in the Twenty-First Century*, ed. J. S. Cooper and G. Swartz, 339–84. Winona Lake: Eisenbraun.

———, ed. 1988. *Pyramid Studies and Other Essays Presented to I. E. S. Edwards*. London: Egypt Exploration Society.

———, and Norman Yoffee. 1998. "Order, Legitimacy, and Wealth in Ancient Egypt and Mesopotamia." In *Archaic States*, ed. Gary M. Feinman and Joyce Marcus, 199–260. Sante Fe: School of American Research Press.

Bakir, M. 1952. *Slavery in Pharaonic Egypt*. Cairo: Institut francais d'archéologie.

Bamshad, Michael J., and Steve E. Olsen. 2003. "Does Race Exist?" *Scientific American* vol. 289, no. 6: 50–57.

Banton, M. 1987. *Racial Theories*. Cambridge: Cambridge University Press.

Barfield, Thomas J. 1989. *The Perilous Frontier: Nomadic Empires and China*. Cambridge: Basil Blackwell.

Barnett, R. D. 1958. *Assyrian Palace Reliefs*. London: Batchworth Press.

Barth, F., ed. 1969. *Ethnic groups and Boundaries*. Boston: Little, Brown.

Baumgartel, E. J. 1960. *The Cultures of Prehistoric Egypt*. Oxford: Greenwood Publishing Group.

Baxter, W. H. 1995. "A Stronger Affinity . . . Than Could Have Been Produced by Accident: A Probabilistic Comparison of Old Chinese and Tibeto-Burman." In *The Ancestry of the Chinese Language*, ed. W. S.-Y. Wang, 1–39. Journal of Chinese Linguistics Monograph Series no. 8.

Berlin, Adele. 1984. "Ethnopoetry and the Enmerkar Epics." In *Studies in Literature from the Ancient Near East dedicated to Samuel Noah Kramer*, ed. Jack M. Sasson, 17–24. New Haven: American Oriental Society.

Bietak, M. 1988. "Zur Marine des Alten Reiches." In *Pyramid Studies and Other Essays Presented to I. E. S. Edwards*, ed. John Baines, 35–40. London: Egypt Exploration Society.

Bilde, P., T. Engberg-Pedersen, L. Hannestad, and J. Zahle, eds. 1992. *Ethnicity in Hellenistic Egypt*. Aarhus : Aarhus University Press.

Blackburn, J. 1979. *The White Man: The First Response of Aboriginal Peoples to the White Man*. London: Orbis.

Boltz, William G. 1993. "Chou li." In *Early Chinese Texts: A Bibliographical Guide*, ed. M. Loewe, 24–32. Berkeley: Society for the Study of Early China and Institute of East Asian Studies, University of California.

———. 1994. *The Origin and Early Development of the Chinese Writing System*. New Haven: American Oriental Society.

———. 1999. "Language and Writing." In *The Cambridge History of Ancient China*, ed. M. Loewe and E. Shaughnessy, 74–123. Cambridge: Cambridge University Press.

Borchardt, L. 1903. *Das Grabdenkmal des Königs Neuserre*. Leipzig: J.C. Hinrich.

Bottéro, Jean. 1975. "L'homme et l'autre dans la pensée babylonienne et la pensée israélite." In *Hommes et Bêtes: Entretiens sur le Racisme*, ed. L. Poliakov, 103–13. Paris: Mouton.

———. 1995. *Mesopotamia: Writing, Reasoning, and the Gods*. Chicago: University of Chicago Press.

Boulnois, L. 1966. *The Silk Road*. London: Geroge Allen and Unwin.

Bowles, G. T. 1977. *The People of Asia*. New York: Scribner.

Bowman, A. K. 1986. *Egypt after the Pharaohs*. Berkeley: University of California Press.

———, and G. Woolf, eds. 1994. *Literacy and Power in the Ancient World*. Cambridge: Cambridge University Press.

Brandes, M. A. 1979. *Siegelabrollungen aus den archaischen Bauschichten in Uruk-Warka*. (Freiburger Altorientalische Studien 3). Wiesbaden: Steiner.

Breasted, J. H. 1906. *Ancient Records of Egypt, 5 vols.*. Chicago: University of Chicago Press.

Bresciani, E. 1997. "Foreigners." In *The Egyptians*, ed. Sergio Donadoni, 221–53. Chicago: University of Chicago Press.

Brinkman, J. A. 1976. *Materials and Studies for Kassite History Vol. I: A Catalogue of Cuneiform Sources Pertaining to Specific Monarchs of the Kassite Dynasty*. Chicago: University of Chicago Press.

———. 1984. *Prelude to Empire*. Philadelphia: Occasional Publications of the Babylonian Fund.

Broze, M., and Ph. Talon, eds. 1992. *L'Atelier de L'orfèvre, Mélanges offerts à Ph. Derchain*. Leuven: Peeters.

Brunner, H., et al. 1952. *Literatur: Handbuch der Orientalistik*, I. Bd., II Abs.. Leiden: Brill.

Bryan, B. M., and D. Lorton, eds. 1994. *Essays in Egyptology in Honor of Hans Goedicke*. San Antonio: Van Siclen.

Buccellati, G. 1966. *The Amorites of the Ur III Period*. Naples: Istituto Orientale di Napoli.

Bunker, Emma C., and C. Bruce Chatwin, and Ann R. Frakas. 1970. *"Animal Style" Art from East to West*. New York: The Asia Society.

Butzer, Karl. 1976. *Early Hydraulic Civilization in Egypt*. Chicago: University of Chicago Press.

Cardascia, G. 1958. "Le statut de l'étranger dans la Mesopotamie ancienne." In *L'Étranger (Recueils de la Societé Jean Bodin pour l'histoire comparative des institutions* IX), 105–17. Bruxelles: De Boeck Université

Cassin, Elena. 1987. "Le semblable et le different: Babylone et Israel." In *Le semblable et le different*. ed. E. Cassin, 36–49. Paris: Découverte.

———, ed. 1987. *Le semblable et le different: Symbolismes du pouvoir dans le Proche-Orient ancient*. Paris: Découverte.

Cawgill, G., and N. Yoffee, eds. 1986. *The Collapse of Ancient Civilizations*. Albuquerque: University of New Mexico Press.

Celenko, T., ed. 1996. *Egypt in Africa*. Indianapolis: Indianapolis Museum of Art.

Chang, Kwang-chih. 1980. *Shang Civilization*. New Haven: Yale University Press.

———. 1983a. "Shang-Zhou Qingtongqi shang de dongwu wenyang 商周青銅器上的動物紋樣." In *Zhongguo Qingtong shidai* 中國青銅時代, 361–63. Taipei: Lianjing.

———. 1983b. *Art, Myth and Ritual*. Cambridge: Harvard University Press.

———. 1986. *The Archaeology of Ancient China*, 4th ed. New Haven: Yale University Press.

———. 1999. "China on the Eve of the Historical Period." In *The Cambridge History of Ancient China*, ed. Michael Loewe and Edward Shaughnessy, 37–73. Cambridge: Cambridge University Press.

Chang, Te-tzu. 1983. "The Origins and Early Cultures of the Cereal Grains and Food Legumes." In *The Origins of Chinese Culture*, ed. D. N. Keightley, 65–94. Berkeley: University of California Press.

Chapman, Malcolm, Maryon McDonald, and Elizabeth Tonkin, 1989. "Introduction." In *History and Ethnicity*, ed. E. Tonkin, M. McDonald, and M. Chapman, 1–21. London: Routledge.

Chen, Fangmei 陳芳妹. 1992. "Gugong suocang Yin zhi Zhouchu de yixing bingqi jiqi suo fanying de wenhua guanxi wenti 故宮所藏殷至周初的異形兵器及其所反映的文化關係問題." *Zhongguo yishu wenwu taolunhui lunwenji* 中國藝術文物討論會論文集, 257–307. Taipei: National Palace Museum.

Chen, Suizheng 陳穗錚. 1993. "Zhongguo cicheng de qiyuan yu yuanyi 中國詞稱的起源與原義." *Shi Yuan* 史原 19: 1–38.

Chen, Mengjia 陳夢家. 1956. *Yinxu buci zongshu* 殷墟卜辭綜述. Beijing: Kexue chubanshe.

Cheng, Hsiao-chieh, et al., tr. 1985. *Shan Hai Ching, Legendary Geography and Wonders of Ancient China.* Taipei: National Institute for Compilation and Translation.

Cohen, R., and R. Westbrook, eds. 2000. *Amarna Diplomacy: The Beginnings of International Relations.* Baltimore: Johns Hopkins University Press.

Cohen, S. 1973. *Enmerkar and the Lord of Aratta.* Dissertation: University of Pennsylvania.

Coleman, J. E., and C. A. Walz, 1997. *Greeks and Barbarians.* Bethesda: CDL Press.

Cook, Constance A., and John S. Major, eds. 1999. *Defining Chu.* Honolulu: University of Hawaii Press.

Cooper, Jerrold S. 1973. "Sumerian and Akkadian in Sumer and Akkad." *Orientalia* 42 (1973): 239–46.

———. 1983a. *Reconstructing History from Ancient Inscriptions: The Lagash-Umma Border Conflict.* Malibu: Undena.

———. 1983b. *The Curse of Agade.* Baltimore: Johns Hopkins University Press.

———. 1999. "Sumerian and Semitic Writing in Ancient Syro-Mesopotamia." In *Languages and Cultures in Contact at the Crossroads of Civilizations in the Syro-Mesopotamian Realm,* ed. K. van Lerberghe and G. Voet, 61–77. Leuven: Peeters.

———, and Glen Swartz, eds. 1996. *The Study of the Ancient Near East in the Twenty-First Century.* Winona Lake: Eisenbraun.

Cooper, Richard. S. and Jay S. Kaufman, and Ryk Ward. 2003. "Race and Genomics." *New England Journal of Medicine* vol. 349, no. 12: 1166–70.

Crossley, Pamela K. 1999. *A Translucent Mirror: History and Identity in Qing Imperial Ideology.* Berkeley: University of California Press.

Curtis, John E., ed. 1993. *Early Mesopotamia and Iran: Contact and Conflict, 3500–1600 BC.* London: British Museum.

Curtis, John E., and J. E. Reade, eds. 1995. *Art and Empire: Treasures from Assyria in the British Museum.* New York: Metropolitan Museum of Art.

Davis, Whitney. 1992. *Masking the Blow: The Scene of Representation in Late Prehistoric Egyptian Art.* Berkeley: University of California Press.

de Graef, Katrien. 1999a&b. "Les étrangers dans les textes paléobabyloniens tardifs de Sippar. Abi-ešuh—Samsuditana." *Akkadica* 111 (1999):1–48; 112 (1999)1–17.

Deng, Shuping 鄧淑蘋. 1995. *Lantian shanfang cang baiyu xuan* 藍田山房藏百玉選. Taipei: Nianxi wenjiao jijinhui.

Dentan, R. C., ed. 1955. *The Idea of History in the Ancient Near East.* New Haven: Yale University Press.

Der Manuelian, P., ed. 1996. *Studies in Honor of William Kelly Simpson,* 2 vols. Boston: Museum of Fine Arts.

Derchain-Urtel, M-Th. 1992. "T3-mrj—Terre d'héritage." In *L'Atelier de L'orfèvre,*

Mélanges offerts à Ph. Derchain, ed. M. Broze and Ph. Talon, 55–61. Leuven: Peeters.

Despres, L. A., ed. 1975. *Ethnicity and Resource Competition in Plural Societies*. The Hague: Mouton.

Desroches-Noblecourt, Ch. 1963. *Tutankhamen, Life and Death of a Pharaoh*. London: Penguin Books.

Di Cosmo, Nicola. 1999. "The Northern Frontier in Pre-Imperial China." In *The Cambridge History of Ancient China*, ed. M. Loewe and E. Shaughnessy, 885–966. Cambridge: Cambridge University Press.

———. 2002. *Ancient China and Its Enemies*. Cambridge: Cambridge University Press.

Dikötter, Frank. 1992. *The Discourse of Race in Modern China*. Stanford: Stanford University Press.

———, ed. 1997. *The Construction of Racial Identities in China and Japan*. Honolulu: University of Hawaii Press.

Donadoni, Sergio, ed. 1997. *The Egyptians*. Chicago: University of Chicago Press.

Drenkhahn, R. 1967. *Darstellungen von Negern in Aegypten*. Hamburg: Hamburg University dissertation.

Du, Zhengsheng 杜正勝. 1993. "Ouya caoyuan dongwu wenshi yu Zhongguo gudai beifang minzu zhi kaocha 歐亞草原動物文飾與中國古代北方民族之考察." *Bulletin of the Institute of History and Philology* 64, 2: 231–408.

Duara, Prasenjit. 1995. *Rescuing History from the Nation: Questioning Narratives of Modern China*. Chicago: University of Chicago Press.

Edzard, D. O., ed. 1972. *Gesellschaften im alten Zweistromland und in den angrenzenden Gebieten*: XVIII Rencontre assyriologique internationale, München, 29. Juni bis 3. Juli 1970. München: Verlag der Bayerischen Akademie der Wissenschaften : In Kommission bei C.H. Beck.

Eickberg, Edgar, ed. 1969. *Historical Interaction of China and Vietnam: Institutional and Cultural Themes*. Kansas: University of Kansas.

Eisenstadt, S. N., ed. 1986. *The Origins and Diversities of Axial Age Civilizations*. Albany: State University of New York Press.

Elias, Norbert. 1982. *The Civilizing Process*. Oxford: Blackwell.

———. 1987. *Involvement and Detachment*. Oxford: Blackwell.

———, and John L. Scotson. 1994. *The Established and Outsiders*. London: Sage.

Endesfelder, E., ed. 1991. *Probleme der Frühen Gesellschaftsentwicklung im alten Ägypten*. Berlin: Humboldt-universität.

Eriksen, T. H. 1993. *Ethnicity and Nationalism: Anthropological Perspectives*. London: Pluto.

Erman, Adolf. 1901. "Zaubersprüche für Mutter und Kind." In *Abhandlungen der Berliner Akkademie der Wissenschaften*, 50–51. Berlin: Akkademie der Wissenschaften.

———. 1966. *The Ancient Egyptians: A Sourcebook of Their Writings*. New York: Harper Torchbooks.

Erya 爾雅 (Shisanjing zhushu 十三經注疏 edition). Taipei: Yiwen yinshuguan reprint, 1976.

Fairbank, J. K., ed. 1968. *The Chinese World Order: Traditional China's Foreign Relations*. Cambridge: Harvard University Press.

Faist, B. I. 2001. *Der Fernhandel des Assyrischen Reiches zwischen dem 14. und 11. Jh. v. Chr.*. Münster: Ugarit Verlag.

Fales, F. M. 1978. "The Enemy in Assyrian Royal Inscriptions: 'The Moral Judgment.'" In *Mesopotamien und Seine Nachbarn* Teil 2, ed. Hans-J. Nissen and J. Renger, 425–35. Berlin: Dietrich Reimer Verlag.

Falkenhausen, Lothar von. 1993. *Suspended Music*. Berkeley: University of California Press.

———. 1999. "The Waning of the Bronze Age: Material Culture and Social Developments, 770–481 BC" In *The Cambridge History of Ancient China*, ed. M. Loewe and E. Shaughnessy, 450–544. Cambridge: Cambridge University Press.

———. 2002. "Some Reflections on Sanxingdui." In *Regional Culture, Religion, and Arts before the Seventh Century*, ed. I-tien Hsing, 59–98. Taipei: Academia Sinica.

Faulkner, R. A. 1969. *Ancient Egyptian Pyramid Texts*. Oxford: Clarendon Press.

Feinman, Gary M., and Joyce Marcus, eds. 1998. *Archaic States*. Sante Fe: School of American Research Press.

Feldman, Louis H. 1993. *Jew and Gentile in the Ancient World*. Princeton: Princeton University Press.

Feucht, E. 1990a. "Kinder Fremder Völker in Ägypten I." *HÄB* 30: 29–48.

———. 1990b. "Kinder Fremder Völker in Ägypten.II." *SAK* 17:177–204.

———. 1995. *Das Kind im Alten Ägypten: die Stellung des Kindes in Familie und Gesellschaft nach altägyptischen Texten und Darstellungen*. Frankfurt: Campus.

Finkelstein, J. J. 1955. "Subartu and Subarians in Old Babylonian Sources." *JCS* 9: 1–7.

Finley, M. I. 1973. *The Ancient Economy*. Berkeley: University of California Press.

Fischer-Elfert, and Hans-Werner. 1986. *Die Satirische Streitschrift des Papyrus Anastasi I: Übersetzung und Kommentar*. Wiesbaden: Otto Harrassowitz.

Fisher, H. G. 1961. "The Nubian Mercenaries of Gebelein during the First Intermediate Period." *Kush* 9: 44–80.

———. 1963. "Varia Aegyptiaca." *JARCE* 2: 34–39.

Fletcher, R. 1997. *The Barbarian Conversion, from Paganism to Christianity*. Berkeley: University of California Press.

Fong, Mary. 1988. "The Origin of Chinese Pictorial Representation of the Human Figure." *Artibus Asiae* 49: 5–38.

Frame, G. 1992. *Babylonia 689–627 BC: A Political History*. Istanbul: Nederlands Historisch-Archaeologisch Institute.

Frankfort, Henri. 1939. *Cylinder Seals*. London: Macmillan.

Frayne, Douglas. 1993. *Sargonic and Gutian Periods, 2334–2133 BC: The Royal Inscriptions of Mesopotamia, Early Periods*, volume 2. Toronto: University of Toronto Press.

Fredrickson, George M. 1997. *The Comparative Imagination: On the History of Racism, Nationalism, and Social Movements*. Berkeley: University of California Press.

Fried, Morton H. 1983. "Tribe to State or State to Tribe in Ancient China?" In *The Origins of Chinese Civilization*, ed. David N. Keightley, 467–93. Berkeley: University of California Press.

Friedman, John B. 1981. *The Monstrous Races in Medieval Art and Thought*. Cambridge: Harvard University Press.

Galter, H. D. 1988. "Zwischen Isolation und Integration: Die soziale Stellung des

Fremden in Mesopotamien im 3. und 2. Jahrtausend v. Chr. " In *Soziale Randgruppen und Aussenseiter im Altertum,* ed. I. Weiler, 280–281. Graz: Leykam.

Gansusheng bowuguan wenwudui 甘肅省博物館文物隊. 1977. "Gansu lingtai baicaopo xizhoumu 甘肅靈台白草坡西周墓." *Kaogu xuebao* 考古學報 1977, 2: 99–130.

Gardiner, A. H. 1935. *Hieratic Papyri in the British Museum,* third series, vol. I. London: British Museum.

———. 1941–52. *The Wilbour Papyrus,* 4 vols.. Oxford: Oxford University Press.

———. 1961. *Egypt of the Pharaohs.* Oxford: Oxford University Press.

Gardiner-Garden, John R. 1987. "Greek Conceptions on Inner Asian Geography and Ethnography from Ephoros to Eratosthenes." *Papers on Inner Asia* no. 9. Bloomington: Indiana University.

Garelli, Paul. 1997. *Le Proche-Orient Asiatique,* 2 vols. Paris: Presses Universitaires de France.

Gauthier, H. 1919. "Variétés historiques: V. Les "Fils royaux" de Ramsès." *ASAE* 18: 254–64.

Gelb, I. J. 1960. "Sumerians and Akkadians in their Ethno-Linguistic Relationship." *Geneva* 8: 258–71.

———. 1961. "The Early History of the West Semitic Peoples." *JCS* 15: 29–47.

———. 1968. "An Old Babylonian List of Amorites." *Journal of the American Oriental Society* 88: 39–44.

———. 1973. "Prisoners of War in Early Mesopotamia." *JNES* 32: 70–98.

Gelb, Ignace J. et al., eds. 1956. *The Assyrian Dictionary of the Oriental Institute of the University of Chicago.* Chicago: University of Chicago Press.

Georges, Pericles. 1994. *Barbarian Asia and the Greek Experience.* Baltimore: Johns Hopkins University Press.

Givens, R. D., and M. A. Nettleship, eds. 1976. *Discussions on War and Human Aggression.* The Hague: Mouton.

Giveon, R. 1971. *Les Bédouin Shasou des documents égyptiens.* Leiden: Brill.

Goedicke, Hans. 1960. "The Title *imy-rᶜ ᶜ3m* in the Old Kingdom." *JEA* 46: 60–64.

———. 1963. "The Alleged Military Campaign in Southern Palestine in the Reign of Pepi I." *Revista degli Studi Orientali* 38: 187–97.

———. 1966. "Brief Communications." *JEA* 52: 72–174.

———. 1967. *Königlisch Dokumente aus dem alten Reich.* Wiesbaden: Otto Harrassowitz.

———. 1975. *The Report of Wenamon.* Baltimore: Johns Hopkins University Press.

———. 1979. "'IRSU, THE KHARU' in Papyrus Harris." *WZKM* 71: 1–17.

———. 1984. "The Cannanite Illness." *SAK* 11:91–105.

Gomaà, F. 1974. *Die Fürstentümer des Deltas vom Tod Osorkons II bis zur Wiedervereinigung Ägyptens durch Psametik II.* Wiesbaden: Ludwig Reichert.

Grimal, Nicolas. 1992. *A History of Ancient Egypt.* Oxford: Blackwell.

Griswold, W. A. 1992. "Imports and Social Status: The Role of Long-Distance Trade in Predynastic Egyptian State Formation." Cambridge: Harvard University Dissertation.

Gu, Jiegang 顧頡剛. 1980. "Cong guji zhong tansuo woguo de xibu minzu—Qiangzu 從古籍中探索我國的西部民族——羌族." *Shehui kexue zhanxian* 社會科學戰線 1: 117–52.

Gudykunst, W. B., ed. 1988. *Language and Ethnic Identity*. Philadelphia: Multilingual Matters.

Gundlach, Rolf. 1994. *Die Zwangsumsiedlung auswärtiger Bevölkerung als Mittel Ägyptischer Politik bis zum Ende des Mittleren Reiches*. Stuttgart: Franz Steiner Verlag.

Gunn, B. 1927. "Quelques Ostraca Hiératiques inédits de Thèbes au Musée du Caire. " *ASAE* 27:183–210.

Guoyu 國語 (Sibu beiyao edition). Taipei: Zhonghua shuju reprint, 1970

Hölscher, W. 1937. *Libyer und Aegypter*. Glückstadt: J. J. Augustin.

Haarmann, Harold. 1986. *Language in Ethnicity: A View of Basic Ecological Relations*. Berlin: Walter de Gruyter.

Haas, Volkert. 1980. "Die Dämonisierung des Fremden und des Feindes im Alten Orient." *Rocznik Orientalistyczny*, XLI, 2: 37–44.

Hall, E. S. 1986. *The Pharaoh Smites His Enemies: A Comparative Study*. München: Deutscher Kunstverlag.

Hall, Edith. 1989. *Inventing the Barbarian: Greek Self-definition through Tragedy*. Oxford: Oxford University Press.

Hall, Jonathan M. 1997. *Ethnic Identity in Greek Antiquity*. Cambridge: Cambridge University Press.

Han, Kangxin 韓康信, and Pan Qifeng 潘其風. 1985. "Yinxu jisikeng rentougu de zhongxi 殷墟祭祀坑人頭骨的種系." In *Anyang Yinxu tougu yanjiu* 安陽殷墟頭骨研究, ed. Zhongguo shehui kexueyuan lishi yanjiusuo and Zhongguo shehui kexueyuan kaogu yanjiusuo, 82–108. Beijing: Wenwu chubanshe.

Hanfeizi 韓非子. 1974. Taipei: Shijie shuju.

Hanshu 漢書. Beijing: Zhonghua shuju, 1960 punctuated edition.

Harris, R. 1975. *Ancient Sippar*. Istanbul: Nederlands Historisch-Archaeologisch Instituut.

Harrison, Thomas, ed. 2002. *Greeks and Barbarians*. Edinburgh: Edinburgh University Press.

Hartog, F. 1988. *The Mirror of Herodotus*. Berkeley: University of California Press.

Hayashi Minao 林巳奈夫. 1985. "Shūnjū Sengoku jidai no jinnin to gyonin 春秋戰國時代の金人と玉人." *Sengoku jidai shutsudo no bunbu no kenkyū* 戰國時代出土文物の研究. Kyoto: Kyoto University.

———. 1986. *In Shū seidōki monyō no kenkyū—In Shū seidōki sōran Pt. 2* 殷周青銅器紋樣の研究——殷周青銅器綜覽二. Tokyo:Yoshikawa Kobunkan.

Hayes, W. C. 1955. *A Papyrus of the Late Middle Kingdom in the Brooklyn Museum*. New York: Brooklyn Museum.

Helck, Wolfgang, 1964. "Die Aegypter und die Fremden." *Saeculum* 15.2: 103–114.

———. 1971. *Die Beziehungen Aegyptens zu Vorderasien im 3. und 2. Jahrtausand v. Chr.* 2d ed. Wiesbaden: Otto Harrassowitz.

———. 1974. *Die altägyptischen Gaue*. Wiesbaden: Ludwig Reichert Verlag.

———, and E. Otto, eds. 1975–89. *Lexikon der Aegyptologie* 7 vols. Wiesbaden: Otto Harrassowitz.

Herodotus, *The Histories*. (Trans. A. de Sélincourt) Harmodsworth: Penguin Books. 1974.

Hobsbawn, Eric, and T. Ranger, eds. 1983. *The Invention of Tradition*. Cambridge: Cambridge University Press.

Hoch, James. E. 1994. *Semitic Words in Egyptian Texts of the New Kingdom and Third Intermediate Period*. Princeton: Princeton University Press.

Hodder, Ian. 1991. *Reading the Past*. Cambridge: Cambridge University Press.

Hodgson, Marshall G. S. 1993. *Rethinking World History: Essays on Europe, Islam, and World History*. Cambridge: Cambridge University Press.

Holloman, R. E., and S. A. Arutiunov, eds. 1978. *Perspectives on Ethnicity*. The Hague: Mouton.

Hornung, Erik. 1982. *The Conceptions of God in Ancient Egypt*. Ithaca: Cornell University Press.

———. 1990. *The Valley of the Kings: Horizon of Eternity*. New York: Timken.

———. 1991. *Das Grab Sethos' I.* Zurich and Munich: Artemis Verlag.

———. 1999. *Akhenaten and the Religion of Light*. Ithaca: Cornell University Press.

Horowitz, W. 1998. *Mesopotamian Cosmic Geography*. Winona Lake: Eisenbrauns.

Hou-Han shu 後漢書. Beijing: Zhounghua shuju, punctuated edition 1960.

Hölscher, W. 1937. *Libyer und Aegypter*. Glückstadt: Verlag Augustin.

Hsu, Cho-yun, and K. M. Linduff. 1988. *Western Zhou Civilization*. New Haven: Yale University Press.

Hu, Houxuan 胡厚宣. 1972. "Lun wufang guanian ji Zhongguo chengwei zhi qiyuan 論五方觀念及中國稱謂之起源." In *Jiaguxue Shangshi luncong chuji* 甲骨學商史論叢初集. Taipei: Datong.

———. 胡厚宣. 1974. "Zhongguo nuli shehui de renxun he rensheng 中國奴隸社會的人殉和人牲." *Wenwu* 8: 56–67, 72.

Huan, Kuan 桓寬. *Yantie lun* 鹽鐵論 (Sibu beiyao edition). Taipei: Zhonghua shuju reprint, 1976.

Huang, Zhanyue 黃展岳. 1990. *Zhongguo gudai de rensheng renxun* 中國古代的人牲人殉. Beijing: Wenwu chubanshe.

Huber, P. 1983. "The Relationship of the Painted Pottery and Lung-shan Cultures." In *The Origins of Chinese Civilization*, ed. D. Keightley, 181–83. Berkeley: University of California Press.

Idema, W. I., and E. Zürcher, eds. 1990. *Thought and Law in Qin and Han China*. Leiden: Brill.

Jacobsen, Thorkild. 1960. *The Harp That Once...* New Haven: Yale University Press.

———. 1966. *The Sumerian King List*. Chicago: University of Chicago Press.

Jacquet-Gordon, H. 1960. "The Inscriptions on the Philadelphia-Cairo Statue of Osorkon II." *JEA* 46:12–23.

Jagchid, Sechin, and Van J. Symons. 1989. *Peace, War, and Trade along the Great Wall: Nomadic-Chinese Interaction through Two Millennia*. Bloomington: Indiana University Press.

Jahoda, G. 1961. *White Man: A Study of the Attitudes of Africans to Europeans in Ghnan before Independence*. London: Oxford University Press.

Jansen-Winkeln, Karl. 2000. "Die Fremdherrschaften in Aegypten im 1. Jahrtausend v. Chr." *Orientalia* 69:1–20.

Janssen, J. M. A. 1951. " Fonctionnaires sémites au service de l' Égypte." *Chronique d'Égypte* 26:50–62.

Jason, Heda. 1977. *Ethnopoetry: Form, Content, Function*. Bonn: Linguistica Biblica.

Jia, Yi 賈誼. *Xinshu* 新書 (Sibu beiyao edition). Taipei: Zhonghua shuju reprint, 1971.

Johnson, Janet H., ed. 1994. *Life in a Multicultural Society: Egypt from Cambyses to Constantine and Beyond*. Chicago: University of Chicago Press.

Junker, Hermann. 1929–55. *Giza*. (Denkschriften der Kaiserlichen Akademie der Wissenschaften in Wien, Phil.-hist. Kl.).Wien: Kaiserlichen Akademie der Wissenschaften.

Kamal, A. 1906. "Rapport sur quelques localités de la Basse-Égypte." *ASAE* 7: 232–47.

Kamp, K. A., and N. Yoffee. 1980. "Ethnicity in Ancient Western Asia during the Early Second Millennium BC: Archaeological Assessments and Ethnoarchaeological Perspectives." *Bulletin of American School of Oreintal Research* 237: 85–104.

Katz, V. 1993. *Gilgamesh and Akka*. Groningen: STYX.

Kees, H. 1961. *Ancient Egypt*. Chicago: University of Chicago Press.

Keightley, David N. 1983a. "The Late Shang State: When? What? Where?" In *The Origins of Chinese Civilization*, ed. D. Keightley, 523–64. Berkeley: University of California Press.

———, ed. 1983b. *The Origins of Chinese Civilization*. Berkeley: University of California Pres.

———. 1999. "The Shang: China's First Historical Dynasty." In *The Cambridge History of Ancient China*, ed. M. Loewe and E. Shaughnessy, 232–91. Cambridge: Cambridge University Press.

———. 2000. *The Ancestral Landscape: Time, Space, and Community in Late Shang China. ca. 1200–1045 B.C.* Berkeley: University of California Press.

Kemp, Barry J. 1991. *Ancient Egypt: Anatomy of a Civilization*. London: Routledge, 29–31.

Keyes, C. F. 1976. "Towards a New Formulation of the Concept of Ethnic Group." *Ethnicity* 3: 202–13.

Kienitz, F. K. 1953. *Die Politische Geschichte Ägyptens vom 7. bis zum 4. Jahrhundert vor der Zeitwende*. Berlin: Akademie-Verlag.

Kieschnick, John. 2002. *The Impact of Buddhism on Chinese Material Culture*. Princeton: Princeton University Press.

Kitchen, K. A. 1975–89. *Ramesside Inscriptions*, 8 vols. Oxford: Blackwell.

———. 1986. *The Third Intermediate Period in Egypt*, 2d. ed. Warminster: Aris and Phillips.

———. 1990. "The Arrival of the Libyans in Late New Kingdom Egypt." In *Libya and Egypt c. 1300–750 BC*, ed. A. Leahy, 15–113. London: SOAS.

———. 1991. "Non-Egyptians Recorded on Middle Kingdom Stelae in Rio de Janeiro." In *Middle Kingdom Studies*, ed. S. Quirke, 87–90. New Malden: SIA Publishing.

Klein, J. 1993. "Additional Notes to 'The Marriage of Martu.'" In *Kinattūtu ša dārâti: Raphael Kutscher Memorial Volume*, ed. A. F. Rainey, 3–106. Tel Aviv: Institute of Archaeology.

———. 1996. "The Marriage of Martu: The Urbanizaiton of 'Barbarian Nomads.'" In *Mutual Influences of Peoples in the Ancient Near East*, ed. M. Malul, 83–96. *Michmanim* 9. Haifa: University of Haifa.

Knoblock, John, and Jeffrey Riegel. 2000. *The Annals of Lü Buwei*. Stanford: Stanford University Press.

Kodō Kinpei後藤均平. 1962. "Shunjū jidai no Shū to Ron 春秋時代の周と戎." In *Chūgoku kodai shi kenkyū* 中國古代史研究, ed. Chūgoku kodai shi kenkyūkai 中國古代史研究會, 71–102. Tokyo: Yoshikawa ,

Koenig, Y. 1987. "La Nubie dans les textes magiques." *Revue d'Égyptologie* 38: 105–10.

Kraus, F. R. 1970. *Sumerer und Akkader: Ein Problem der altmesopotamischen Geschichte.* Amsterdam: North-Holland Publishing.

Kroeber, Alfred. 1944. *Configurations of Culture Growth.* Berkeley: University of California Press.

Kuhrt, Amelie. 1995. *The Ancient Near East, c. 3000–330 BC.*, 2 vols. London: Routledge.

Kupper, J. R. 1957. *Les nomades en mésopotamie au temps des rois de Mari.* Paris: Bibliothèque de la faculté de philosophie et lettres de l'université de Liège.

Lafont, Sophie. 1998. "Le roi, le juge et l'étranger a Mari et dans la Bible." *Revue d'assyriologie et d'archéologie orientale* 92: 161–81.

Lai, Guolong. 1999. "Uses of the Human Figure in Early Chinese Art." *Orientations.* 6: 49–55.

Lambert, Wilfred G. 1996. *Babylonian Wisdom Literature.* Winona Lake: Eisenbraun.

Langdon, S. 1924. *Excavations at Kish* I. Paris: P. Geuthner.

———, and A. H. Gardiner. 1920. "The Treaty of Alliance between Hattušili, King of the Hittites, and the Pharaoh Ramesses II of Egypt." *JEA* 6: 179–205; 185.

Lattimore, Owen. 1951. *Inner Asian Frontiers of China.* New York: American Geographical Society.

Lawton, T., ed. 1991. *New Perspectives on Chu Culture.* Washington DC: Smithsonian Institution.

Layton, S. C. 1988. "Old Aramaic Inscription." *Biblical Archaeologist* 51: 172–89.

Leahy, A. 1985. "The Libyan Period in Egypt: An Essay in Interpretation." *Libyan Studies* 16: 51–65.

Lee, Cheuk Yin 李焯然. 2003. "Zhuzi sixiang yu yuenan ruxue 朱子思想與越南儒學." *Zhongguo wenhua yanjiuso xuebao* 中國文化研究所學報 12: 453–71.

Lefebvre, G. 1923–24. *Le tombeau de Petosiris,* 3 vols. Cairo: Institut francais d'archeologie orientale.

Legge, James. 1976. *The Li Ki.* In *The Sacred Books of the East,* vol. 27., ed. Max Mueller. Oxford University Press, 1885; reprint 1976 by Motilal Banarsidass.

———. 1985. *The Chinese Classics,* 5 vols. Taipei: Southern Materials Center, rpt of 1885 edition.

Lerberghe, K. van, and G. Voet, eds. 1999. *Languages and Cultures in Contact at the Crossroads of Civilizations in the Syro-Mesopotamian Realm.* Leuven: Peeters.

Li, Xiaoding 李孝定. 1982. *Jiagu wenzi jishi 甲骨文字集釋.* Taipei: Academia Sinica, Institute of History and Philology.

Li, Xueqin 李學勤. 1959. *Yindai dili jianlun 殷代地理簡論.* Beijing: Kexue chubanshe.

———. 1985. *Eastern Zhou and Qin Civilizations.* New Haven: Yale University Press.

———. 1991. *Dongzhou yu Qindai wenming 東周與秦代文明.* Beijing: Wenwu chubanshe.

Lichtheim, Miriam. 1973–80. *Ancient Egyptian Literature,* 3 vols. Berkeley: University of California Press.

———. 1983. *Late Egyptian Wisdom Literature in the International Context.* Orbis Biblicus et Orientalis 52. Freiburg: Universitätsverlag.

Liji 禮記 (Shisanjing zhushu edition). Taipei: Yiwen yinshuguan reprint, 1976.

Limet, Henri. 1972. "L'Étranger dans la societé Sumerienne." In *Gesellschaften im alten Zweistromland und in den angrenzenden Gebieten,* ed. D. O. Edzard, 123–38. RAI XVIII, München: Verlag der Bayerischen Akademie der Wissenschaften : In Kommission bei C.H. Beck.

———. 1978. "Étude sémantique de ma.da kur, kalam." *Revue d'Assyriologie* 72, 1: 1–12.

———. 1995. "L'émigre dans la societé Mesopotamienne." In *Immigration and Emigration within the Ancient Near East,* ed. K. van Lerberghe and A. Schoors, 165–179. Uitgeverij Peeters, Leuven.

Lin, Yun 林澐, 1986. "Shang wenhua qingtongqi yu beifang tiqu qingtongqi guanxi zhi zaiyanjiu 商文化青銅器與北方地區青銅器關系之再研究." In *Kaoguxue wenhua lunji* (1) 考古學文化論集 (一), 129–155. Beijing: Wenwu chubanshe.

Liu, Xinru, 1994. *Ancient India and Ancient China, Trade and Religious Exchanges, AD 1–60.* Dehli: Oxford University Press.

Liverani, Mario. 1990. *Prestige and Interest: International Relations in the Near East ca. 1600–1100 BC.* Padova: Sargon Srl.

Lloyd, A. B. 1982. "The Inscription of Udjahorresnet, a Collaborator's Testament." *JEA* 68: 166–80.

———. 1988. "Herodotus on Egyptians and Libyans." In *Hérodote et les peuples non Grecs. Entretiens sur l'antiquité classique* XXXV, ed. Oliverier Reverdin and Bernard Grange, 215–253. Vandoeuvres-Genève: Fondation Hardt.

———. 1993. *Herodotus, Book II.* Leiden: Brill.

Lloyd, G. E. R. 1996. *Adversaries and Authorities: Investigations into Ancient Greek and Chinese Science.* Cambridge: Cambridge University Press.

———. 2002. *The Ambitions of Curiosity: Understanding the World in Ancient Greece and China.* Cambridge: Cambridge University Press.

———, and Nathan Sivin. 2002. *The Way and the Word: Science and Medicine in Early China and Greece.* New Haven: Yale University Press.

Loehr, Max. 1949. "Weapons and Tools from Anyang, and Siberian Analogies." *American Journal of Archaeology* LIII, no. 2: 126–144.

Loewe, Michael, ed. 1993. *Early Chinese Texts: A Bibliographical Guide.* Berkeley: Society for the Study of Early China and Institute of East Asian Studies, University of California.

———, and Edward Shaughnessy. eds. 1999. *The Cambridge History of Ancient China.* Cambridge: Cambridge University Press.

Loprieno, Antonio. 1988. *Topos und Mimesis: Zum Ausländer in der ägyptischen Literatur.* Ägyptologische Abhandlungenm, 48. Wiesbaden: Otto Harrassowitz.

———. 1995. *Ancient Egyptian: A Linguistic Introduction.* Cambridge: Cambridge University Press.

———. 1997. "Slaves." In *The Egyptians,* ed. S. Donadoni, 185–220. Chicago: University of Chicago Press.

Lorton, David. 1973. "The So-called Vile Enemies of the King of Egypt in the Middle Kingdom and Dyn. XVIII." *JARCE* 10: 65–70.

Lu, Liancheng 盧連成, Hu Zhisheng 胡智生. 1988. *Baoji Yuguo mudi* 寶雞强國墓地, 2 vols. Beijing: Wenwu chubanshe.

Lunyu 論語 (Shisanjing zhushu edition). Taipei: Yiwen yinshuguan reprint, 1976.

Lüshi chunqiu 呂氏春秋 (Sibu beiyao edition). Taipei: Zhonghua Shuju reprint, 1972.

Lustig, Judith, ed. 1997. *Anthropology and Egyptology: A Developing Dialogue*. Sheffield: Sheffield Academic Press.

Ma, Changshou 馬長壽. 1962. *Beidi yu Xiongnu* 北狄與匈奴. Beijing: Sanlian.

Ma, Chengyuan 馬承源, ed. 1988. *Shang-Zhou qingtongqi mingwen xuan* 商周青銅器銘文選. Beijing: Wenwu chubanshe.

MacMullen, Ramsay. 1984. *Christianizing the Roman Empire, AD 100–400*. New Haven: Yale University Press.

Mahler, Jane. G. 1959. *The Westerners among the Figurines of the T'ang Dynasty of China*. Rome: Instituto Italiano per il Medio ed Estremo Oriente.

Mark, S. 1997. *From Egypt to Mesopotamia: A Study of Predynastic Trade Routes*. London: Chatham.

Mathieu, R. 1978. *Le Mu Tianzi zhuan: Traduction annotée-Étude critique*. Paris: College de France Institut des Hautes Études Chinoises.

———. 1983. *Étude sur la Mythologie et l'Ethnologie de la Chine Ancienne: Trad. annotée du Shanhaijing*. Paris: College de France—Institut des Hautes Études Chinoise, Mem. de Inst. des Hautes Études Chinoise, XXII, tome 2.

———. 1993. "Mu t'ien tzu chuan." In *Early Chinese Texts: A Bibliographical Guide*, ed. M. Loewe, 342–46. Berkeley: Society for the Study of Early China and Institute of East Asian Studies, University of California.

Mattos, Gilbert L. 1997. "Eastern Zhou Bronze Inscriptions." In *New Sources of Early Chinese History: An Introduction to the Reading of Inscriptions and Manuscripts*, ed. Edward. L. Shaughnessy, 104–11. Society for the Study of Early China and Institute of East Asian Studies, University of California, Berkeley.

Mcfie, A. L. 2000. *Orientalism: A Reader*. Edinburgh: Edinburgh University Press.

Mei, Tsu-lin, and Jerry Norman. 1976. "The Austroasatics in Ancient South China: Some Lexical Evidence." *Monumenta Serica* 32: 274–301.

Meier, S. A. 2000. "Diplomacy and International Marriages." In *Amarna Diplomacy: The Beginnings of International Relations*. ed. R. Cohen and R. Westbrook, 165–73. Baltimore: Johns Hopkins University Press.

Meng, Wentong 蒙文通. 1958. *Zhou-Qin shaoshu minzu yanjiu* 周秦少數民族研究. Shanghai: Longmen lianhe shuju.

Mengzi 孟子 (Shisanjing zhushu edition). Taipei: Yiwen yinshuguan reprint, 1976.

Michalowski, Piotr. 1989. *The Lamentation over the Destruction of Sumer and Ur*. Winona Lake: Eisenbrauns.

———. 1999. "Sumer Dreams of Subartu: Politics and the Geographical Imagination." In *Languages and Cultures in Contact at the Crossroads of Civilizations in the Syro-Mesopotamian Realm*, ed. K. van Lerberghe and G. Voet, 305–15. Leuven: Peeters.

Momingliano, A. 1990. *Alien Wisdom: The Limit of Hellenization*. Cambridge: Cambridge University Press.

Moorey, P. R. S. 1994. *Ancient Mesopotamian Materials and Industries: The Archaeological Evidence*. Oxford: Clarendon.

Moran, W. L. 1992. *The Amarna Letters*. Baltimore: Johns Hopkins University Press.

Mu Tianzi zhuan 穆天子傳. Yingyin wenyuange siku quanshu 影印文淵閣四庫全書, vol. 1042. Taipei: Shangwu, reprint, 1983.

Müller-Wollermann, R. 1988. "Der Mythos vom Ritus 'Erschlagen der Feinde.'" *Göttinger Miszellen* 105: 69–76.

Mungello, David E. 1999. *The Great Encounter of China and the West, 1500–1800*. Lanham: Rowman and Littlefield.

Newberry, P. E. 1893. *Beni Hasan*, vol. I. London: K. Paul, Trench, Trübner.

Nibbi, A. 1981. *Ancient Egypt and Some Eastern Neighbors*. Park Ridge, N.J.: Noyes.

Nienhauser, W. H. Jr., ed. 1994. *The Grand Scribe's Records*, vol. I. Bloomington: Indiana University Press.

Nippel, Wilfried. 2002. "The Construction of the 'Other.'" In *Greeks and Barbarians*, ed. Thomas Harrison, 278–310. Edinburgh: Edinburgh University Press.

Nissen, Hans-J. and Johannes Renger, eds. 1982. *Mesopotamien und Seine Nachbarn: Politische und Kulturelle Wechselbeziehungen im Alten Vorderasien vom 4. bis 1. Jahrtausend v. Chr.*. XXV Rencontre Assyriologique Internationale Berlin. Berlin: Dietrich Reimer Verlag.

O'Connor, David. 1997. "Ancient Egypt: Egyptological and Anthropological Perspectives." In *Anthropology and Egyptology: A Developing Dialogue*, ed. Judith Lustig, 13–24. Sheffield: Sheffield Academic Press.

Oates, David, and Joan Oates. 1976. *The Rise of Civilization*. New York: Elsevier-Phaidon.

Oates, J. 1986. *Babylon*. London: Thames and Hudson.

Oberhuber, K. 1990. *Sumerisches Lexikon*. Innsbruck: Institut für Sprachwissenschaft der Universität Innsbruck.

Oded, B. 1979. *Mass Deportations and Deportees in the Neo-Assyrian Empire*. Wiesdaben: Reichert.

Ogura Yoshihiko 小倉芳彦. 1967. "I i no toriko: Saden no Ka I kannen 裔夷の俘——左傳の華夷觀念." In *Chūgoku kodai shi kenkyū* 2, 中國古代史研究 (第二), ed. Chūgoku kodai shi kenkyūkai 中國古代史研究會, 153–87. Tokyo:Yoshikawa.

Oppenheim, A. Leo. 1967. *Letters from Mesopotamia*. Chicago and London: University of Chicago Press.

Osing, J. 1976. "Ächtungstexte aus dem Alten Reich." *MDAIK* 32: 133–85.

Otto, Eberhard. 1954. *Die Biographischen Inschriften der Aegyptischen Spätzeit*. Leiden: Brill.

Parpola S. and A. Fuchs. 2001. *The Correspondence of Sargon II*, part III. Helsinki, Finland: Helsinki University Press.

Peden, A. J. 1994. *Egyptian Historical Inscriptions of the Twentieth Dynasty*. Sweden: Paul Astroms Forlag.

Peet, T. E. 1930. *The Great Tomb-Robberies of the Twentieth Egyptian Dynasty*. Oxford: Oxford University Press.

Peregrine, P. 1991. "Some Political Aspects of Craft Specialization." *World Archaeology* 23: 1–10.

Petrie, W. F. 1953. *Ceremonial Slate Palettes*. London: British School of Egyptian Archaeology.

Piankoff, Alexander. 1964. *The Litany of Re*. New York: Bollingen.

Pientka, R. 1998. *Die Spätaltbabylonische Zeit, Teil I*. Münster: Rhema.

Pinch, G. 1995. *Magic in Ancient Egypt*. Austin: University of Texas Press.

Pines, Yuri. 1997. "Intellectual Change in the Chunqiu Period: The Reliability of the Speeches in the *Zuo Zhuan* as Sources of Chunqiu Intellectual History." *Early China* 22: 100–16.

Poliakov, L., ed. 1975. *Hommes et Bêtes: Entretiens sur le Racisme*. Paris: Mouton.

Pongratz-Leisten, B., et al., eds. 1997. *Ana šadī Labnāni lū allik, Beiträge zu altorientalischen und mettelmeerischen Kulturen*. Neukirchen-Vluyn: Neukirchener Verlag.

Poo, Mu-chou. 1990. "Ideas Concerning Death and Burial in Pre-Han and Han China." *Asia Major* 3rd series, 3.2: 25–62.

———. 1994. "The Emergence of Cultural Consciousness in Ancient Egypt and China: A Comparative Perspective." In *Essays in Egyptology in Honor of Hans Goedicke*, ed. Betsy M. Bryan and David Lorton, 191–200. San Antonio, Tex.: Van Siclen Books.

———. 1998a. "Encountering the Strangers: A Comparative Study of Cultural Consciousness in Ancient Egypt, Mesopotamia, and China." *Proceedings of the Seventh International Congress of Egyptologists*, 885–92. Louven: Peters.

———. 1998b. *In Search of Personal Welfare: A View of Ancient Chinese Religion*. Albany: State University of New York Press.

———. 1999. "Gudai Zhongguo, Aiji yu Lianghe liuyu dui yizu taidu zhi bijiao yanjiu 古代中國、埃及與兩河流域對異族態度之比較研究." *Hanxue yanjiu* 漢學研究 17:2: 137–68.

Porada, Edith. 1995. *Man and Images in the Ancient Near East*. Wakefield, R.I.: Moyer Bell.

Porter, B. N. 1993. *Images, Power, and Politics: Figurative Aspects of Esarhaddon's Babylonian Policy*. Philadelphia: American Philosophical Society.

Posener, G. 1936. *La premiere domination perse en Égypte*. Cairo: Institut Français d'Archéologie Orientale.

———. 1940. *Princes et Pays d'Asie et de Nubie*. Bruxells: Fondation égyptologique reine Elisabeth.

———. 1956. *Littérature et politique dans l'Égypte de la XIIᵉ dynastie*. Paris: H. Champion.

Postgate, N. J. 1989. "Ancient Assyria—A Multiracial State." *ARAM* 1: 1–10.

———. 1992. *Early Mesopotamia: Society and Economy at the Dawn of History*. London and New York: Routledge.

Potts, D. T. 1982. "The Zagros Frontier and the Problem of Relations between the Iranian Plateau and Southern Mesopotamia in the Third Millennium B.C." In *Mesopotamien und Seine Nachbarn* Teil 1, ed. Hans-J. Nissen and J. Renger, 33–56. Berlin: Dietrich Reimer Verlag.

———. 1997. *Mesopotamian Civilization: The Material Foundations*. London: Athlone.

Pritchard, J. B. 1954. *The Ancient Near East in Pictures Relating to the Old Testament*. Princeton: Princeton University Press.

———. 1969. *Ancient Near Eastern Texts Relating to the Old Testament*. Princeton: Princeton University Press.

Prušek, Jaroslav. 1971. *Chinese Statelets and the Northern Barbarians, 1400–300 BC*. Dordrecht, Holland: Riedel.

Psarras, Sophia-Karin. 1994. "Exploring the North: Non-Chinese Cultures of the Late Warring States and Han." *Monumenta Serica* 42: 1–125.

Pulleyblank, E. G. 1983. "The Chinese and Their Neighbors in Prehistoric and Early Historic Times." In *The Origins of Chinese Civilization*, ed. D. Keightley, 411–66. Berkeley: University of California Press.

Qian Mu 錢穆. 1970. *Guoshi Dagang* 國史大綱. Taipei: Shangwu.

Qiu Xigui 裘錫圭. 1978. "Hanzi xingcheng wenti de chubu tansuo 漢字形成問題的
    初步探索." *Zhongguo Yuwen* 中國語文 3: 162–71.
Qu Wanli 屈萬里. 1975. *Shangshu jinzhu jinyi* 尚書今註今譯. Taipei: Shangwu.
Qu Xiaoqiang 屈小強, et al., eds. 1993. *Sanxingdui wenhua* 三星堆文化. Chengdu:
    Sichuan renmin chubanshe.
Quack, J. F. 1997. "Die Klage über die Zerstörung Ägyptens, Versuch einer Neudeutung
    der ‚Admonitions' im Vergleich zu den altorientalischen Städteklagen." In *Ana šadī
    Labnāni lū allik, Beiträge zu altorientalischen und mettelmeerischen Kulturen*, ed.
    B. Pongratz-Leisten et al., 345–54. Neukirchen-Vluyn: Neukirchener Verlag.
Quirke, S., ed. 1991. *Middle Kingdom Studies*. New Malden: SIA Publishing.
Raphals, Lisa. 1992. *Knowing Words: Wisdom and Cunning in the Classical Traditions
    of China and Greece*. Ithaca: Cornell University Press.
Ratié, S. 1979. *La Reine Hatchepsout, Sources et Problèmes*. Leiden: Brill.
Rawson, Jessica, ed. 1997. *Mysteries of Ancient China, New Discoveries from the Early
    Dynasties*. New York: George Braziller.
Ray, John. 1994. "Literacy and Language in Egypt in the Late and Persian Periods." In
    Literacy and Power in the Ancient World, ed. A. K. Bowman and G. Woolf, 51–66.
    Cambridge: Cambridge University Press.
Redford, Donald. B. 1984. *Akhenaten, the Heretic King*. Princeton: Princeton Uni-
    versity Press.
———. 1992. *Egypt, Canaan and Israel in Ancient Times*. Princeton: Princeton Uni-
    versity Press.
———. 1994. "Some Observations on the Northern and North-Eastern Delta in the Late
    Predynastic Period." In *Essays in Egyptology: Studies in Honor of Hans Goedicke*,
    ed. B. M. Bryan and D. Lorton. San Antonio, Tex.: Van Siclen Books.
———, ed. 2001. *The Oxford Encyclopedia of Ancient Egypt*. Oxford: Oxford University
    Press.
Richards, Janet, and Mary Van Buren, eds. 2000. *Order, Legitimacy, and Wealth in
    Ancient States*. Cambridge: Cambridge University Press.
Riches, D., ed. 1986. *The Anthropology of Violence*. London: Basil Blackwell.
Ritner, R. 1990. "The End of the Libyan Anarchy in Egypt: P. Rylands IX, cols. 11–12."
    Enchoria 17: 101–8.
Robins, Gay. 1993. *Women in Ancient Egypt*. Cambridge: Harvard University Press.
———. 1997. *The Art of Ancient Egypt*. Cambridge: Harvard University Press.
Romm, James S. 1992. *The Edges of the Earth in Ancient Thought: Geography, Explora-
    tion, and Fiction*. Princeton: Princeton University Press.
Rossabi, M. 1983. *China among the Equals : The Middle Kingdom and Its Neighbors,
    Tenth to Fourteenth Centuries*. Berkeley: University of California Press.
Rowton, M. B. 1973. "Autonomy and Nomadism in Western Asia." *Orientalia* 42:
    247–58.
Sage, Steven F. 1992. *Ancient Sichuan and the Unification of China*. Albany: State
    University of New York Press.
Said, Edward. 1979. *Orientalism*. New York: Random House.
Saretta, Phyliis. 1997. "Egyptian Perceptions of West Semites in Art and Literature
    During the Middle Kingdom." New York: New York University Dissertation.
Sassmannshausen, L. 1999. "The Adaptation of the Kassites to the Babylonian Civi-
    lization." In *Languages and Cultures in Contact at the Crossroads of Civilizations*

in the Syro-Mesopotamian Realm, ed. K. van Lerberghe and G. Voet, 409–22. Leuven: Peeters.

Sasson, J. M., ed. 1984. *Studies in Literature from the Ancient Near East Dedicated to Samuel Noah Kramer*. New Haven: American Oriental Society.

———. ed. 1995. *Civilizations of the Ancient Near East*, 4 vols.. New York: Scribners'.

Säve-Söderberg, T. 1941. *Aegypten und Nubien: Ein Beitrag zur Geschichte altägyptischer Aussenpolitik*. Lund: Hakan Ohlssons Boktryckeri.

Schafer, E. H. 1963. *The Golden Peaches of Samarkan: A Study of T'ang Exotics*. Berkeley: University of California Press.

Schloss, E. 1969. *Foreigners in Ancient Chinese Art*. New York: China Institute in America.

Schulz, R., and M. Seidel. 1997. *Ägypten, Die Welt der Pharaonen*. Köln: Könemann.

Schwartz, Benjamin I., ed. 1975. *Wisdom, Revelation, and Doubt, Perspective on the First Millennium BC*. (*Daedalus* Spring 1975). Boston: American Academy of Arts and Sciences.

Seckel, Dietrich. 1993. "The Rise of Portraiture in Chinese Art." *Artibus Asiae* 53: 7–26.

Shang-shu 尚書 (Shisanjing zhushu edition). Taipei: Yiwen yinshuguan reprint, 1976.

Shankman, Steven, and Stephen W. Durrant, eds. 2002. *Early China/Ancient Greece: Thinking through Comparisons*. Albany: State University of New York Press.

Shaughnessy, Edward. L., ed. 1997. *New Sources of Early Chinese History: An Introduction to the Reading of Inscriptions and Manuscripts*. Berkeley: Society for the Study of Early China and Institute of East Asian Studies, University of California.

Shaw, Ian, ed. 2000. *The Oxford History of Ancient Egypt*. Oxford: Oxford University Press.

Shen, Songqiao 沈松喬. 1997. "Wo yi woxie jian xuanyuan: Huangdi shenhua yu wanqing de guozu jiangou 我以我血薦軒轅──黃帝神話與晚清的國族建構." *Taiwan shehui yanjiu jikan* 台灣社會研究季刊 28: 1–77.

Shennan, S. J., ed. 1989. *Archaeological Approaches to Cultural Identity*. London: Unwin Hyman.

Shibutani, T., and K. K. Kwan. 1965. *Ethnic Stratification*. New York: Macmillan.

Shiji 史記. Beijing: Zhonghua Shuju, 1960 punctuated edition..

Shijing 詩經. (Shisanjing zhushu edition). Taipei: Yiwen yinshuguan reprint, 1976.

Shulman, Alan. 1979. "Diplomatic Marriage in the Egyptian New Kingdom." *JNES* 38: 177–93.

———. 1988. *Ceremonial Execution and Public Rewards: some Historical Scense on New Kingdom Private*. Freiburg: Vandenhoeck and Ruprecht.

Shuoyuan 説苑. In *Hanwei chungshu* 漢魏叢書. Changchun: Jilin daxue reprint, 1992.

Simpson, William K. 1977. *The Literature of Ancient Egypt*. New Haven: Yale University Press.

Sivan, Daniel, and Zipora Cochavi-Rainey. 1992. *West Semitic Vocabulary in Egyptian Script of the Fourteenth to the Tenth Centuries BCE*. Negev: Ben-Gurion University of the Negev Press.

Sjöberg, A. W., and E. Bergman. 1969. *The Collection of the Sumerian Temple Hymns*. New York: Texts from Cuneiform Sources 3. Locust Valley, N.Y.: J. J. Augustin.

Smith, William. S. 1965. *Interconnections in the Ancient Near East; A Study of the Relationships between the Arts of Egypt, the Aegean, and Western Asia.* New Haven: Yale University Press.

Snowden, Frank. M. Jr. 1983. *Color before Prejudice.* Cambridge: Harvard University Press,.

Song, Zhimin 宋治民. 1993. *Zhanguo Qin-Han kaogu* 戰國秦漢考古. Chengdu: Sichuan University.

Sørensen, J. P. 1992. "Native Reactions to Foreign Rule and Culture in Religious Literature." In *Ethnicity in Hellenistic Egypt*, ed. P. Bilde et al., 164–81. Aarhus: Aarhus University Press.

Speiser, E. A. 1955. "Ancient Mesopotamia." In *The Idea of History in the Ancient Near East*, ed. R. C. Dentan, 35–76. New Haven: Yale University Press.

Spencer, A. J. 1980. *Catalogue of Egyptian Antiquities in the British Museum, V: Early Dynastic Objects.* London: British Museum.

Spiegelberg, W. 1927. *The Credibility of Herodotus's Account of Egypt in the Light of the Egyptian Monuments.* Oxford: Blackwell.

Steiner, G. 1978. "Der Gegensatz ‚eignes Land': ‚Ausland, Fremdland, Feindland' in den Vorstellungen des Alten Orients." In *Mesopotamien und Seine Nachbarn*, ed. Hans-J. Nissen and J. Renger, 633–64. Berlin: Dietrich Reimer Verlag.

Steinkeller, Piotr. 1980. "The Old Akkadian Term for Easterner." *Revue d'Assyriologie* 74, 1:1–9.

Strassberg, R. E. 2002. *A Chinese Bestiary: Strange Creature from the Guideways through Mountains and Seas.* Berkeley: University of California Press.

Su, Bingqi 蘇秉琦. 1997. *Zhongguo wenming qiyuan xintan* 中國文明起源新探. Hong Kong: Shang-wu.

Sun, Yirang 孫貽讓. 1974. *Mozi Xiangu* 墨子閒詁. Taipei: Shijie shuju.

Tadmor, H. 1982. "The Aramaization of Assyria: Aspects of Western Impact." In *Mesopotamien und Seine Nachbarn*, Teil 2, ed. Hans-J. Nissen and J. Renger, 449–70. Berlin: Dietrich Reimer Verlag.

Tang, Lan 唐蘭. 1934. "Siguo jie 四國解." *Yugong* 禹貢 1, 10: 6–9.

te Velde, H. 1977. *Seth, God of Confusion: A Study of His Role in Egyptian Mythology and Religion.* Leiden: Brill.

Teng, Rensheng 滕壬生. 1996. *Chuxi Jianbo Wenzibian* 楚系簡帛文字編. Hankou: Hubei jiaoyu chubanshe.

Thapar, Romila. 1971. "The Image of the Barbarian in Early India." *Comparative Studies in Society and History* 13: 408–36.

Thote, Alain. 1999. "Intercultural Relations as Seen from Chinese Pictorial Bronzes of the Fifth Century BCE." *Res* 35 (Spring): 10–41.

Tian, Qianjun 田倩君. 1965. "Zhongguo yu Huaxia chengwei zhi xunyuan 中國與華夏稱謂之尋原." *Dalu zazhi* 大陸雜誌 31.1: 17–24, 35.

Tonkin, E., Maryon McDonald, and Malcolm Chapman, eds. 1989. *History and Ethnicity.* London: Routledge.

Török, L. 1997. *The Kingdom of Kush: Handbook of the Napatan-Meroitic Civilization.* Leiden: Brill.

Toynbee, Arnold J. 1957. *A Study of History.* Abridgment by D. C. Somervell, vol. II. Oxford: Oxford University Press.

Trigger, Bruce G. 1976. *Nubia under the Pharaohs.* Boulder, Colo.: Westview Press.

———. 1993. *Early Civilizations: Ancient Egypt in Context.* Cairo: American University in Cairo Press.

———. 1997. "Ancient Egypt in Cross-cultural Perspective." In *Anthropology and Egyptology: A Developing Dialogue*, ed. Judith Lustig, 137–43. Sheffield: Sheffield Academic Press.

———, B. J. Kemp, D. O'Connor, and A. B. Lloyd. 1983. *Ancient Egypt, A Social History.* Cambridge: Cambridge University Press.

Tsien, Tsuen-hsuin. 1962. *Written on Bamboo and Silk.* Chicago: University of Chicago Press.

Uphill, E. 1967. "The Nine Bows." *Jaarbericht Ex Oriente Lux* 19: 393–420.

Vachala, B. 1991. "Zur Frage der Kriegsgefangenen in Aegypten. Überlegungen anhand der schriftlichen Quellen des Alten Reiches." In *Probleme der Frühen Gesellschafts-entwicklung im alten Ägypten*, ed. E. Endesfelder. Berlin: Humboldt-Universität.

Valbelle, Dominique. 1990. *Les Neuf Arcs: L'Égyptien et les Étrangers de la Prehistoire à la Conquête d'Alexandre.* Paris: Armand Colin.

Van de Mieroop, Marc. 1997. *The Ancient Mesopotamian City.* Oxford: Oxford University Press.

Van Dijk, J. 1978. "Fremdsprachige beschwörungstexts in der Südmesopotamischen Literarischen Überlieferung." In *Mesopotamien und Seine Nachbarn* Teil 1, ed. Hans-J. Nissen and J. Renger, 97–110. Berlin: Dietrich Reimer Verlag.

Van Paassen, Ch. 1957. *The Classical Tradition of Geography.* Groningen: Wolters.

Vanstiphout, H. 1999a. "A Meeting of Cultures? Rethinking the Marriage of Martu." In *Languages and Cultures in Contact at the Crossroads of Civilizations in the Syro-Mesopotamian Realm*, ed. K. van Lerberghe and G. Voet, 461–74. Leuven: Peeters.

———. 1999b. "The Twin Tongues: Theory, Technique, and Practice of Bilingualism in Ancient Mesopotamia." In *All Those Nations ... Cultural Encounters within and with the Near East*, ed. H. Vanstiphout, 141–59. Groningen: STYX.

———, ed. 1999. *All Those Nations ... Cultural Encounters within and with the Near East.* Groningen: STYX.

Vercoutter, Jean, et al. 1976. *The Image of the Black in Western Art I: From the Pharaohs to the Fall of the Roman Empire.* New York: William Morrow.

Waldron, Arthur. 1990. *The Great Wall of China: From History to Myth.* Cambridge: Cambridge University Press.

Wang, Ermin 王爾敏. 1977. "Zhongguo mingcheng jiqi jindai quanshi 中國名稱及其近代詮譯." In Wang Ermin, *Zhongguo jindai sixiang shilun* 中國近代思想史論. Taipei: Huashi chubanshe.

Wang, Fu 王符. *Qianfu lun* 潛夫論 (Sibu beiyao edition). Taipei: Zhonghua Shuju, 1971.

Wang, Guanying 王冠英. 1984. "Yin-Zhou de waifu ji chi yanbian 殷周的外服及其演變." *Lishi yanjiu* 歷史研究 5: 80–99.

Wang, Guowei 王國維. 1975. "Gueifang Kunyi Xianyun kao 鬼方昆夷玁狁考." *Guantang jilin* 觀堂集林, 583–605. Taipei: Heluo reprint.

Wang, Mingke 王明珂. 1994. "Shenmo shi minzu: Yi Qiangzu weili tantao yige minzuzhi yu minzushi yanjiu shangde guanjian wenti 什麼是民族: 以羌族為例探討一個民族誌與民族史研究上的關鍵問題." *Bulletin of the Institute of History and Philology* 65, 4: 989–1027.

———. 1997. *Huaxia bianyuan: Lishi jiyi yu zuqun rentong* 華夏邊緣: 歷史記憶與族群認同. Taipei: Yunchen.

Wang, W. S.-Y., ed. 1995. *The Ancestry of the Chinese Language.* Journal of Chinese Linguistics Monography Series no. 8.

Wang, Xianshen 王先慎. 1974. *Han Feizi jijie* 韓非子集解. Taipei: Shijie shuju.

Wang, Zhongfu 王仲孚. 1989. "Shilun chunqiu shidai de zhuxia yishi 試論春秋時代的諸夏意識." *Dierjie guoji Hanxue huiyi lunwenji* 第二屆國際漢學會議論文集 vol.1, 363–76. Taipei: Academia Sinica.

Ward, W. A. 1994. "Foreigners Living in the Village." In *Pharaoh's Workers,* ed. L. H. Lesko, 61–85. Ithaca: Cornell University Press.

Watson, Burton. 1961. *Records of the Grand Historian of China,* vol. II. New York: Columbia University Press.

Watson, W. 1971. *The Cultural Frontier of Ancient China.* Edinburgh: Edinburgh University Press.

Weber, Charles D. 1968. *Chinese Pictorial Bronze Vessels of the Late Chou Period.* Ascona: Artibus Asiae.

Weiler, I., ed. 1988. *Soziale Randgruppen und Aussenseiter im Altertum.* Graz: Leykam.

Wente, E. 1990. *Letters from Ancient Egypt.* Atlanta: Scholar Press.

Westenholz, Joan G. 1997. *Legends of the Kings of Akkade.* Winona Lake: Eisenbrauns.

Whitfield, R. 1992. *The Problem of Meaning in Early Chinese Ritual Bronzes.* London: Percival David Foundation of Chinese Art.

Whiting, R. M. 1995. "Amorite Tribes and Nations of Second-Millennium Western Asia." In *Civilizations of the Ancient Near East,* vol. II, ed. J. M. Sasson, 1231–41. New York: Scribners'.

Whitmore, J. K. 1969. "Vietnamese Adaptations of Chinese Government Sturcture in the Fifteenth Century." In *Historical Interaction of China and Vietnam: Institutional and Cultural Themes,* ed. Edgar Eickberg, 1–10. Kansas: University of Kansas.

Wiens, H. J. 1967. *Han Chinese Expansion in South China.* North Haven: Shoe String Press.

Winter, Irene J. 1980. "Art as Evidence for Interaction: Relations between the Assyrian Empire and North Syria." In *Mesopotamien und Seine Nachbarn,* Teil 2, ed. Hans-J. Nissen and J. Renger, 355–82. Berlin: Dietrich Reimer Verlag.

Woodside, A. B. 1971. *Vietnam and the Chinese Model: A Comparative Study of Vietnamese and Chinese Government in the First Half of the Nineteenth Century.* Cambridge: Harvard University Press.

Wu, Hung. 1985. "Bird Motifs in Eastern Yi Art." *Orientations* 16.10: 30–41.

———. 1995. *Monumentality in Early Chinese Art and Architecture.* Stanford: Stanford University Press.

Wu, Shilian 吳士連. 1984. *Dayue shiji quanshu* 大越史記全書 3 vols. Tokyo: Tōyōbunka kenkyūjo reprint.

Xiao, Tong, 1982. *Wen Xuan,* vol. 1., tr. D. R. Knechtges. Princeton: Princeton University Press.

Xin, Jianfei 忻劍飛. 1991. *Shijie de Zhongguo guan* 世界的中國觀. Hong Kong: San Lien.

Yamauchi, E. M. 1997. "Herodotus—Historian or Liar?" In *Crossing Boundaries and Linking Horizons*, ed. G. D. Young et al., 599–614. Bethesda: CDL Press.

Yan, Zhitui 顏之推. *Yanshi jiaxun* 顏氏家訓 (Sibu beiyao edition). Taipei: Zhonghua, 1979.

Yang, Lien-sheng. 1968. "Historical Notes on the Chinese World Order." In *The Chinese World Order: Traditional China's Foreign Relations*, ed. John K. Fairbank, 20–33. Cambridge: Harvard University Press.

Yao, Xiaosui 姚孝遂. 1979. "Shangdai de fulu 商代的俘虜." *Guwenzi yanjiu* 古文字研究, vol. 1: 337–91.

———, and Xiao Ding 蕭丁. 1985. *Xiaotun nandi jiagu kaoshi* 小屯南地甲骨考釋. Beijing: Zhonghua.

Yin, Shengping 尹盛平. 1986. "Xi Zhou bangdiao rentouxiang zhongzu tansuo 西周蚌雕人頭像種族探索." *Wenwu* 1: 46–49.

Yin, Weizhang 殷瑋璋, and Cao Shuqin 曹淑琴. 1990. "Lingshi Shangmu yu Bingguo tongqi 靈石商墓與丙國銅器." *Kaogu* 7:621–37.

Yinger, J. M. 1994. *Ethnicity*. Albany: State University of New York Press.

Yizhoushu 逸周書 (Sibu beiyao edition). Taipei: Zhonghua shuju reprint, 1972.

Yü, Rongchun 1986. 于溶春. "Zhongguo yizi de youlai yanbian jiqi yu minzu de guanxi 中國一詞的由來演變及其與民族的關係." *Neimenggu shehui kexue* 內蒙古社會科學 2: 75–80.

Yü, Xingwu 于省吾. 1981. "Shi Zhongguo 釋中國." *Zhonghua xueshu lunwenji* 中華學術論文集. ed. Zhonghua shuju, 1–10. Beijing: Zhonghua shuju.

Yü, Ying-shih. 1967. *Trade and Expansion in Han China*. Berkeley: University of California Press.

Yüan, Ke 袁珂. 1981. *Shanghaijing jiaozhu* 山海經校注. Taipei: Hungshih.

Yurco, F. J. 1996. "Two Tomb Wall Painted Reliefs of Ramesses III and Sety I and Ancient Nile Valley Population Diversity." In *Egypt in Africa*, ed. T. Celenko, 109–11. Indianapolis: Indianapolis Museum of Art.

Zaccagnini, C. 1978. "The Enemy in the Neo-Assyrian Royal Inscriptions: The 'Ethnographic' Description." in *Mesopotamien und Seine Nachbarn* Teil 2, ed. Hans-J. Nissen and J. Renger, 409–24. Berlin: Dietrich Reimer Verlag.

Zhang, Chunshu 張春樹. 1976. *Handai bianjiangshi lunji* 漢代邊疆史論集. Taipei: Shihuo.

Zhang, Huaitung 張懷通. 2001. "Chunqiu Zhuanggong sanshier nian faxing zhi 'di' kao 春秋莊公三十二年伐邢之 '狄' 考." *Zhongyuan wenwu* 中原文物 3: 21–27.

Zhang, Zhengming 張正明, ed. 1995. *Chuxue wenku* 楚學文庫. Wuhan: Hubei jiaoyu chubanshe.

Zhanguoce 戰國策 (Sibu beiyao edition). Taipei: Zhonghua shuju reprint, 1972.

Zhao, Lin 趙林. 1983. "Shangdai de Qiangren 商代的羌人." *Bianzheng yanjiusuo nianbao* 邊政研究所年報 14 :31–68.

Zhao, Tiehan 趙鐵寒. 1965. "Chunqiu shiqi de Rong-Di dili fenbu jiqi yuanliu 春秋時期的戎狄地理分布及其源流." In *Gushi kaoshu* 古史考述, 314–47. Taipei: Zhengzhong shuju.

Zheng, Jiexiang 鄭杰祥. 1994. *Shangdai dili gailun* 商代地理概論. Zhengzhou: Zhongzhou guji.

Zhongguo shehui kexueyuan kaogu yanjiusuo 中國社會科學院考古研究所 ed. *Baoji Beishouling* 寶雞北首嶺. Beijing: Wenwu chubanshe.

Zhongguo shehui kexueyuan lishi yanjiusuo 中國社會科學院歷史研究所 and Zhongguo shehui kexueyuan kaogu yanjiusuo 中國社會科學院考古研究所, eds. 1985. *Anyang Yinxu tougu yanjiu* 安陽殷墟頭骨研究. Beijing: Wenwu chubanshe.

Zhou, Fagao 周法高. 1975. *Jinwen gulin* 金文詁林. Hong Kong: Chinese University.

Zhouli 周禮 (Shisanjing zhushu edition). Yiwen yinshuguan reprint, 1976.

Zibelius-Chen, Karola. 1988. *Die Aegyptische Expansion nach Nubien, Eine Darlegung der Grundfaktorn.* Wiesbaden: Ludwig Reichert Verlag.

Zou, Heng 鄒衡. 1980. "Lun xianzhou wenhua." In *Xia-Shang-Zhou kaoguxue lunwenji* 夏商周考古學論文集, 297–356. Beijing: Wenwu chubanshe.

Zuozhuan 左傳 (Shisanjing zhushu edition). Taipei: Yiwen yinshuguan reprint, 1976.

Zürcher, Eric. 1959. *The Buddhist Conquest of China*, 2 vols. Leiden: Brill.

———. 1990. "Han Buddhism and the Western Region." In *Thought and Law in Qin and Han China*, ed. W. I. Idema and E. Zürcher, 158–82. Leiden: Brill.

Index